The
BORDER
in BLOOM

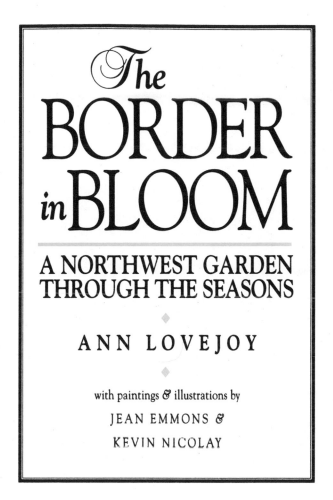

The BORDER *in* BLOOM

A NORTHWEST GARDEN THROUGH THE SEASONS

◆

ANN LOVEJOY

◆

with paintings & illustrations by

JEAN EMMONS &

KEVIN NICOLAY

SASQUATCH BOOKS

Seattle, Washington

Lovejoy, Ann, 1951–
    The border in bloom: a Northwest garden through the seasons / by Ann Lovejoy; with
paintings and illustrations by Jean Emmons and Kevin Nicolay.
        p.   cm.
    ISBN 0-912365-26-9 : $14.95
    1. Garden borders—Northwest. Pacific.   I. Title.
SB424.L68   1990
635.9'63—dc20   90-32901
                                                                     CIP

Design by Elizabeth Watson and Jane Jeszeck
Cover Illustration and Color Insert by Jean Emmons
Interior Illustrations by Kevin Nicolay
Typeset by Scribe Typography

"Ornamental Edibles: Vegetables to Grow for Show," "Tulips That Triumph: Species Tulips
Thrive Where Others Fail," "Passive Composting: A Low-Tech Guide for Bemused Gardeners," and "Ornamental Herbs to Savor" appear courtesy of *Horticulture.*

"Beyond Petunias: Self-Perpetuating Annuals for the Harried Gardener" appears courtesy of
Harrowsmith.

"Major Impact from Minor Bulbs" appears courtesy of *National Gardening.*

Published by Sasquatch Books
1931 Second Avenue
Seattle, WA 98101
(206) 441-5555

Other books by Ann Lovejoy

> *The Year in Bloom*
> *Three Years in Bloom*
> *Eight Items or Less*

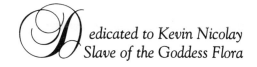 edicated to Kevin Nicolay
Slave of the Goddess Flora

CONTENTS

The BORDER in HIGH SUMMER 135

The BORDER in AUTUMN 183

The BORDER in EARLY WINTER 223

INTRODUCTION

GARDENING WHERE YOU LIVE

The Gardening Year

The garden's seasons are sixfold. Spring melts into early summer, high summer precedes autumn. Early winter slides into late winter, which blossoms again into spring. Each of these small seasons has distinguishing qualities and characteristics which set it apart from the others, yet each laps quietly over the next, so that all are bound in a flowing, unified whole. Though these are not traditional divisions, they are no more artificial than any other, and better reflect the actual conditions and changes within the garden than do the usual four seasons. (Bound by solstice and equinox, winter is supposed to begin in late December, and the high point of summer is supposed to be the end of June.)

This book begins in January, at the turning of the year, when each day sees the sun rise a bit sooner and shine a little longer. Plants respond to the changing light pattern almost at once; by midmonth, the ground is thick with emerging shoots. In late winter—January and February—rosettes thicken, roots begin to grow and buds to swell. The end of this period, late February, sees the emergence of the gardener, who, trug and tools in hand, begins to clear away winter damage and prepare the garden for the visitation of spring. "Spring" in this book indicates March and April, while "early summer" means May and June. The (sometimes) hotter months of July and August are called "high summer," which mellows into "autumn" during September and October. The garden year slows to a slumbrous halt in "early winter," November and December, yet shows definite signs of renewal in the earliest weeks of the new year.

The Garden

If these are the garden's seasons, what is the garden itself? Though most of us know a garden when we see it—even if it does not look like our kind of garden—I suppose few of us could actually agree upon a definition. To the visitor, a garden may be no more than the sum of its contents. Others may forever see it as it appeared during a memorable June, or they may think of it as a changing tapestry they pass by on the way to work. For the gardener, the process—the art and effort of gardenmaking—offers the most direct experience of the garden. For us, a garden is an engaging place to live and work and dream. For us a garden lies more in the making than in any mere collection of plants or formal ordering of brick and trelliswork. Our gardens may or may not look like picturebook gardens, but they always have a distinct identity, the true children of our vision and experience.

What Is a Border?

While we may recognize a garden instantly, we aren't always so sure about its various components. There exists a certain confusion about the terms "border" and "bed," particularly when they are supplemented by the word "island." Though often used interchangeably, each does have its own meaning: properly speaking, a border *borders* something, while a bed is freestanding, surrounded by grass, gravel, or paths. Borders are backed by hedges or walls and are generally longer than they are wide. A border may run along the property line, in front of a fence, or up the driveway. It may be sedately oblong or it might describe swooping curves as it snakes around to encompass trees and shrubs or encircle the house. An island border is like a bed in that it is surrounded by grass or paths on all sides; but it is different from a bed in that it has a spine of taller, usually woody and often evergreen plants that fills the center so that one side is invisible from the other side. In effect, an island border is a doublesided border. (These are quite difficult to make well, and seldom worth the effort.)

Further, beds are most often filled with a changing array of annuals— the "bedding-out material" of the nursery trade. Borders, on the other hand, might be filled with practically anything; there are shrub borders, herbaceous borders (in which perennials play the leading role), herb borders, and theme borders, often restricted to plants with flowers or foliage of one or two colors. There are seasonal borders, perhaps designed for winter beauty or intended to shine both spring and fall and then lie fallow during the summer when the family is away on holiday. Specialty borders are devoted to plants of a certain category—one might be entirely filled with gladiolas, another with plants from South America, or even an assortment of plants which were all named for the same person. The most lastingly interesting are mixed borders, in which shrubs and small trees form a backdrop for plants of all categories. Perennials mingle with vines, biennials blend with subshrubs, while annuals and bulbs punctuate running ground covers.

Why a Border?

Since most of us garden in relatively small spaces, borders are preferable to beds for several reasons. Small lawns look restless when cluttered up with little flowerbeds, and mowing and trimming such chopped-up lawns is a loathsome chore. When the grass is left in (or restored to) clean sweeps, it sets off the garden serenely. It is also far easier to deal with, which increases its likelihood of getting regular care. The effect is like replacing a distracting flurry of scatter rugs with a wall-to-wall carpet.

Perimeter borders remove plants from the house walls and place them where they can be appreciated from indoors as well as outside. Beds or borders set under the house eaves are often invisible from inside, and foundation plants may soon rob downstairs rooms of light and air. When we clear most of the plants away from the house, we can then deliberately create garden views for each window. The evergreen and shrubby plants which form the backdrop for a mixed border can transform our yards into havens of peace and privacy when they are ranged about the property line rather than set smack against the house. Plants block street noise more effectively and screen out unsightly views more attractively than do fences. (Fences are a useful adjunct, however, for they can simplify and accelerate the process of gardenmaking. Most of us will be making our border backdrop with young, small evergreens and shrubs, plants that will take a few years to weave into a significant barrier. Fences, however homely, stand ready at once to carry a thick veil of gold-splashed ivy, climbing roses, and scrambling honeysuckle and clematis vines. Fences or walls will clearly delineate the youthful garden, protecting it from harsh winds and marauding pets.)

Borders simplify things for the gardener in terms of design and maintenance. A continuous border looks more purposeful than a yard dotted with small beds. In a small space, one or two broad, natural curves look nicer than a series of fussy little meanderings. A design that is too elaborate for its setting results in visual chaos; when the overall plan is simple, thoughtful plantings will make it fascinating. A permanent backbone of evergreens establishes the garden's form and makes the placement of ephemerals—annuals, perennials, and so forth—a delightfully straightforward matter of developing personally pleasing combinations.

Gardening Where We Live

Gardens everywhere begin in dreams. Practical or romantic, urban or rural, each gardener has a vision for each plot, whatever the scale. As seasons pass and gardens grow, few of our schemes fulfill the goals which gave them birth. Though most gardeners get as much pleasure from the process of gardenmaking as from the results, some are discouraged when their efforts don't match their enticing inner vision. Often the problem is simply one of impatience; a new garden won't feel substantial and settled for perhaps 5 years, and needs 8 or 10 years of steady growth to look mature. More serious troubles arise when gardeners with tiny lots centered by a split-level ranch house want to replicate Sissinghurst. Here the difficulty is twofold. First, no copy or emulation ever has the flavor or impact of the original. Second, America is not England. Before you can make wonderful gardens, you've got to know your territory.

Say "English garden" and images of billowing borders fill the inner eye. Say "American garden" and the picture becomes jumbled, confused. Just what is an American garden? In truth, we might well exercise our imaginations more freely than we generally do; American gardening could be as varied as America itself. Limiting our palettes to English border plants is as myopic and arbitrary as deciding to grow only prairie grass and rudbeckias. Horticulturally we Americans are in our teens, still discovering and defining ourselves. This can be a delightful experience, especially when it leads us to relish our national diversity. America is a big and complex country; rather than seeking to codify a single American school of gardenmaking, we can rejoice in the many American styles and celebrate the emerging strengths and character of each region in turn.

Here in the Pacific Northwest we have far more options than do gardeners in Florida, Minnesota, or Arkansas. Here, if anywhere, one might indeed attempt to recreate Sissinghurst, or Great Dixter, or Hidcote—but why should we? Our goal ought rather to be the creation of a distinctive, flexible school of gardening which combines American practicality and flair with the English love of plants. In the end, the greatest legacy we receive from the English will prove not to be garden designs or border plans but the concept of learning one's plants thoroughly and using them with sensitive affection. Only when we know our plants experientially and specifically can we embark on the process that is gardenmaking, the fruit of which is the garden of our dream.

Since successful gardenmaking is most likely to occur if the dream garden is within the realm of possibility, regional garden books are a necessity. Only gardeners who know the territory can offer sound ideas and conjure up images to replace the improbable. This does not mean that we can't draw inspiration from anywhere but our own back yard, but it does require that we learn more about our particular territory. Gardening wakes us up in all sorts of ways, making us aware of seasonal changes, of weather patterns and microclimates, of differences in soils and water. Knowing the territory also means recognizing the bounty of the local flora. No matter what *won't* grow where you live, there is plenty that *will* grow. Even our weeds can give us clues; where knotweeds thrive, so may more gardenworthy polygonums. If our lawns are choked with moss, we might as well remove the grass entirely, or relegate it to a more promising site. In its place, thick carpets of moss, now encouraged, may be woven with hostas and hellebores, ferns and ivies, rhododendrons and Carolina allspice (*Calycanthus floridus*). Should the grass wither when summer bakes the ground dry, yuccas and rockroses (*Cistus* species), California fuchsia (*Zauschneria* species), poppies, and many herbs will thrive. Nicola Ferguson's wonderful book *Right Plant, Right Place* offers excellent help for gardeners faced with difficult or varying conditions; though English in origin, many of the suggested plants are American natives or have hardy, attractive counterparts among our native flora.

Walking though local woods and meadows and observing natural plant relationships and combinations can be as instructive as visiting gardens and arboretums. Visits over the year will reveal early-rising perennials that could mask fading bulb foliage, sturdy late-summer bloomers that are sure sources of splendid fall color, and plants with winter beauties of berry and bark. Throughout the country, indigenous plants have been joined by enterprising newcomers that naturalize with ease. Sometimes this entrepreneurial spirit can be harmful, as when imported lythrums crowd out less invasive native species. More often the interlopers are innocuous and their milder success indicates plant families that might be introduced safely. In the woods of the maritime Northwest, one often finds the expatriate European spurge laurel (*Daphne laureola*), tall foxgloves, and the giant bell-flowered knotweed (*Polygonum campanulatum*). These and other members of their respective clans can all be welcomed into our gardens without serious repercussions.

There are multiple options to pursue in our search for specific regional information. Though private gardens are seldom publicly accessible in this country, membership in a garden club or plant society often grants entree to numerous gardens. Arboretums, parks departments, and water companies are all promoting the benefits of gardening with native plants, through instructional classes and demonstration gardens. The USDA Cooperative

Extension Service master gardener programs are often excellent places to find out about local plants and conditions. Lots of community colleges offer courses in native plant identification and often include field trips. Native plant societies abound, a terrific resource in regions where conventional border plants can't handle local conditions.

Any such investigation has several rewards: it is tremendous fun in itself, it gives us the company of like-minded people, and it can enrich our gardens enormously. Those who fear that native plants will make the garden dull and frumpy will be reassured almost at once; some American natives are spectacular, and many others which appear drab when starved are transformed by decent garden conditions. America is rich in wonderful plants; literally hundreds of English border plants are expatriates from these shores. Continental finishing school left some of them too delicate to return to their native soil, but quite often their heartier country cousins will fill their garden niches with aplomb. Salvias and solidagos, asters and artemisias, all boast native species and garden varieties which will thrive anywhere in the United States. At first we may regard these plants as substitutes for their more tender counterparts, but as we gain confidence and understanding we value them for their own qualities.

Once our plant palette is expanded to include the local flora, we can begin to play with variations on regional themes. In one spot we may choose to mirror a combination frequently found in field or wood—perhaps wild cherry, native willow, and Indian plum (*Osmaronia cerasiformis*), or the spumy cream bush (*Holodiscus discolor*) and the handsome russet-leafed buffaloberry (*Shepherdia canadensis*), knit together with a native honeysuckle (*Lonicera ciliosa*). In another place we may alter the original group by exchanging the species plant for hybrids, supplementing it with imported cousins, or reflecting it obliquely by using completely different plants that share the same colors. As repeated patterns build throughout the garden, colors and relationships echo and shift into new pictures which refer to each other even as they change through the seasons.

When we seek out our native plants in their natural habitats, we can observe firsthand how plants grow together in nature—trees and large shrubs sheltering smaller shrubs and perennials, the whole laced together by creeping ground covers punctuated with bulbs and low-growing annuals. When employed in our borders, these lessons from the wild help to unite unruly collections of plants. Arrayed in naturalistic patterns, the plants happily mimic the healthy, harmonious relationships found in nature.

Well-placed plants form floral communities that work together, living gardens kept in bounds as much by natural laws as by the busy hand of man.

Gardening with native plants means that we take advantage of what nature offers us, though slavish imitations of nature will be no more successful than those pseudo-Sissinghursts. For one thing, gardening is by definition interference with nature, and despite the flagrant untruths of the poets, nature unassisted rarely achieves what most of us would consider to be a garden. We *can* draw inspiration and concepts from a model, however—transposing plants and architectural elements freely to suit our personal aesthetic, giving preference to local materials. In the Pacific Northwest this may mean fences of raw timber, arches of whole, crotched trees, treillage of bark-covered branches (a rough-hewn style which, if well conceived and carried out, results in elegant funk). In New Mexico it might translate into walls of adobe and patios of glazed tile, while in New Hampshire flat flagstones cut from native granite and fences made from fieldstone would be appropriate. Again, one need not be limited to a strict palette; in gardening, as in architecture, an individual example that is free of trendiness and is well related to its regional setting will age better than a garden that is made to fit into the inappropriate environment of an immediate neighborhood.

The design stage is where too many of us falter. Here we are often hampered more by our fear of transgressing the mysterious laws of Good Taste than by our inexperience. Take courage, inform yourself thoroughly and well, and dare to try. Over time, and through trial and error, the garden of your inner eye will form itself under your hands. As your taste changes and experience clarifies your desires, the garden will follow your lead. Never let a lack of formal training keep you from arranging your garden according to your individual light. Garden mistakes are easily rectified, and plants are by and large willing workers, both flexible and forgiving. Gardeners grow farsighted, planting trees for a future they may never see. Time is the gardener's friend; there is no hurry about making a garden, for the process, rather than the product, is the point.

Gardening where you live means more than using native plants and materials, more than echoing regional landscape elements; it means making a garden which changes with your life and taste, showcasing your current fancies and interests. Professionally designed gardens may be pleasing, yet they are almost never personal; the very best gardens in the world are all the children of a personal dream. Your ideal garden may overflow with blossoms, a floral extravaganza for half the year, restful and quiet the other half. I may prefer a cool, sheltered retreat filled with a tapestry of foliage, vines trailing from every tree, exotic perfumes heavy on the air. Someone else may long for lilacs and daylilies, rambling roses on arching white arbors, red peonies nodding in a trim, grassy yard enclosed by a white picket fence. No matter what is trendy, our individual taste and personal plant loves should influence the shape of our own gardens more than pressures of fashion or the dreary dictates of "good design." And any original, however eclectic, has more life and character than the most tasteful copy.

When we garden boldly, trusting our instincts, our gardens become distinct and individual in the process, faithful representations of our thoughts and loves. When our gardens suit our needs, offering us places to work and to rest, to play and to dream, we enjoy them to the fullest through every season. As we grow secure in our knowledge of plants, sure of the rightness of our personal choices, we will be making new and lasting contributions to the regional schools of American gardening, united with gardeners all across the country in making gardens where we can live.

Bainbridge Island
January, 1990

The BORDER in LATE WINTER

JANUARY ■ FEBRUARY

LATE WINTER

In January the garden door begins to open. At first it is just a crack; we find a snowdrop in a pool of sun, a golden aconite gleaming through the broken leaves. One night the chinook blows in, leaving the garden filled with a clinging, warm mist that smells unmistakably of spring. When we walk the garden paths the following morning, the leaves no longer crunch underfoot and their tracery of frost rime has disappeared. The robins busy themselves at ground level again—worms are emerging from their frozen sleep. The garden door opens wider and things begin to happen fast. Bulbs quicken, pushing their hard, glossy snouts through the chilly soil, and green shoots appear everywhere. Twigs show definite thickenings at every node—the leaves are waking up. The alders blush red, the willows are hazed with green and gold. Catkins begin to swell, pink and rippled silver on the willows, a bright, mahogany red on the alders.

By the end of the month the winter-blooming plants are all in full fig. The whippy arms of winter jasmine are studded with fat golden buds and dozens of its small trumpets are blowing down the wind. *Prunus mume* opens tender, cupped flowers filled with drops of dew that sprinkle the earth with each small breeze, libations to spring. Snow crocus burst through a carpet of blue-eyed vinca. The green blossoms of *Helleborus fœtidus* stand up in icy bunches, surrounded by ruffled collars of dark, slim-fingered new leaves. Primroses spill from every bed, rose and cream, apricot and peach, sapphire and garnet. Some are oxblood red, each petal neatly banded in gold; others are cheerful runs of lavender and pink, their edges trimmed with silver. A few great clumps are packed with oversized Barnhaven primroses, their velveteen petals lustrous and tinted like dark jewels. Banks of candytuft (*Iberis*) are whitening under a snow of flowers, and the indefatigable feverfew opens a tentative spray of little daisies, pure and pale. It is impossible to work in the beds without harming something, for the entire ground is pricked with minuscule shoots. They are almost invisible when viewed from above; they are only seen from ground level, where the gardener stoops to pull a weed or wonder at a silken, diaphanous crocus, its overlapping petals a shimmering series of transparencies. From near the earth, the ground looks furred with faint green as the skin of the earth is rejuvenated.

In January fruit trees may be shorn of water shoots, and crowded ornamental maples judiciously thinned, twig by twig. Paths can be weeded, their underlying barriers of newspaper or burlap renewed, their top-dressing of wood shavings, shredded bark, or pine needles restored. Edging stones and bricks are reset. Mulch may be replenished where bulbs will soon bloom. These are not bustling chores, but thoughtful, contemplative ones. While we work we review the garden's design, considering anew each curve and each angle, every bed and every bush, evaluating the patterns both of plants and hardscape.

Inspiration often comes during this reflective season, poised between stolid winter and hasty spring. The garden no longer feels empty; it is gathering strength for the heedless, headlong rush into summer. Our ideas and energies have been accumulating all winter, and now they unite in horticultural renewal. We see and sense how a more generous curve would bring a feeling of peace and plenty to a cramped and awkward border, where a broad and unifying path would define an unfocused side yard, where a large and imposing shrub would soothe a restless, fragmented planting. The possibility of change is in the very air, warm and smelling of wet earth, rising sap and new beginnings. Capture them on paper, for they are fleeting as swallows, these inspirations. Visions fly too fast to hold with memory alone when the air and the gardener alike are saturated with spring. The sun gathers in south-facing hollows, making tea breaks irresistible. Benches are hard and cold, the yielding ground is sodden, but a tattered piece of old oilcloth keeps out the damp sufficiently and brings one in satisfying contact with the earth. Leaning against a bank of sun-warmed thyme, the sharp, clean scents of rosemary and lavender mingling with the brisk citrus smell of lemon thyme and the acrid, cloudy fragrance of Lapsang, one can scarcely wish the season otherwise. June will come, sure as the days roll along, but this, too, is a time to savor.

Plants: Bernhaven primroses
winterjasmine

Gardening by Design

s the empty garden stands stark, its shape laid bare for all to see, the gardener quite naturally begins to think about gardening by design. It is not flowers that fill our imaginations at this still season, but colder thoughts of bones, garden bones, of paths unmade and lines undrawn. Out comes the graph paper, and many a paper garden blooms and fades on the kitchen table before the exigent gardener is satisfied. A plan, a master plan, is born; a plan that unites the house, the garage, the alley, and the dog yard with garlands of borders and beds. This is all very good, but paperwork doesn't get any paths laid. The sad truth is that few of us ever achieve even a satisfactory paper plan, and fewer still transfer that plan to earth and stone. Some know this well in advance, and regard the New Year's paper garden as the latest in a series of quiet dreams, never meant to be realized. Others turn in frustration to professional help, and sometimes this is not a bad idea.

What can you expect from a professional designer? Much depends on what you want from your garden, on your budget and time schedule, and how well you communicate with your professional, but perhaps the single most crucial factor is whether you choose the services of a landscape architect (an "L.A." to the knowing) or a garden designer (not "G.D," except in extremis). There is a world of difference between the two schools, and unless the would-be improver is aware of these differences, disappointment and confusion are bound to follow.

Landscape architects are certified; they come armed with degrees and are generally credited with greater skills and expertise than are garden designers, who may or may not have formal training in their craft. L.A.'s are certainly much better paid, and many have names that demand recognition in monied circles. Indeed, while it might be too tacky to say outright just how many thousands one paid for a garden job, merely to say *who* did it can speak volumes—with each volume clearly priced—to the proper audience. L.A.'s rarely concern themselves with residential design, but when they do, the result is nearly always a formal green space. Now, a formal green space is exactly what many people want; it's suitable for entertaining in, and just right for gracing the cover of a glossy magazine, they should be so lucky. Strongly architectural in form and design, such a garden requires less (though often more costly) maintenance than a more floral planting might, but the real payoff is that year-in, year-out, it looks exactly the same, changing neither more nor less than one's designer living room (flowers may appear seasonally in each place, to perform precisely the same role).

Flower and plant lovers will seldom find themselves in sympathy with these lean green spaces, yet there are sites for which no other sort of garden is appropriate. Certain very modern houses do not marry well with plants —or other living things—and many public spaces are too harsh an environment to allow for much more. For the plant-minded, however, an arrangement of woody plants and paths—however softened by English benches, patterned brickwork, and trellising—is simply not a garden. For such as these, the services of a garden designer will bring far greater satisfaction than will those of even the trendiest L.A.

Good garden designers know and use plants of all kinds—woody, perennial, and bulbous—to make a garden, whereas the L.A. leans heavily toward the structural. This is not to say that an L.A. garden won't have plants; trees and shrubs, most of them evergreen, make up the typical L.A. palette, which varies surprisingly little from garden to garden. Some favor yew, photinia, and rhododendron; others prefer azalea, thuja, and laurel; but the net result is quite similar. Again, nothing is wrong with this approach, and for the impatient, it is almost perfect, because only in this genre is the Instant English Clone Garden a real possibility.

(This is not unripe grapes talking; a nurseryman friend once enrolled at a prestigious L.A. school, where he announced that he was interested in learning a lot about plants. This innocent remark was met with mild surprise, and he was told that if he indeed learned about plants, he would be an asset to any firm he joined, for horticulture was not necessary knowledge in their degree program. Come to find out, very few L.A. programs require more than a minimal class or two of horticulture. The overall thrust is on city planning and large-scale public works rather than on residential gardens. This general nonemphasis on plants persists, too; at a recent meeting of the American Society of Landscape Architects, of some 60 lectures, not one was about plants.)

Perhaps the happiest compromises are achieved when landscape architects work with garden designers who are fine horticulturists. Some marvelous true gardens arise in this way, where the clean architectural lines of an overall design are brought to life by thoughtfully planted borders and beds that enrich without overwhelming, to make a satisfying whole. Then, too, there are a few hybrid landscape designers who know and value perennials, vines, and bulbs, as well as woody plants. One such is Dan Borroff, who had traveled further up the woody path than most L.A.'s ever venture, before discovering perennials. "I knew the familiar charges against them," he says cheerfully. "High maintenance, need a lot of fussing, hard to establish quickly...Still, I began noticing marvelous plants like (*Thalictrum aquilegifolium,*) the columbine-leafed meadow rue. Here was a plant with superb foliage that stood on tall, strong stems without support. It had great flowers, no diseases, it suppressed weeds and blended well with shrubs. There had to be more plants like this, and I determined to find them."

Borroff is comfortable working on large-scale designs, where he and his crew prepare the soil and install the plants, contracting out the carpentry and stonework to qualified specialists. Some of his projects have been very grand indeed, involving hundreds of thousands of dollars, but he finds as much pleasure in making modest gardens that are successful in meeting both the challenges of the site and the needs of the clients. He sees his role as part facilitator, part magician, helping clients define their needs and showing them a new vision for their property. "Of course one uses the givens of the place, but there must also be fantasy, magic, surprises," he points out. "Bringing a garden out of nothing is a sort of magic; the Taj Mahal didn't occur because it was just the spot for a great mausoleum." The designer's vision should translate well, Borroff insists; each garden must respond to the site, but should not be beholden to it. "Every garden needs something that delights, that captures the imagination," he explains; most L.A.'s do this with structure rather than with plants, but Borroff likes to use both to mutual advantage. This fusion, rather than any signature plant or combination, is the motif that unites all his gardens.

Though he uses exceptional plants, often nursing them through the shock of intercontinental travel and federal quarantine regulations in order to grow things commercially unobtainable in the U.S., Borroff is emphatically appreciative of the importance of structural elements in any garden. "I wish more people valued craft skills and recognized their place even in small gardens," he says. It's hard to see a fine design distorted or ruined because a client balks at the cost of the best work. This attitude is shortsighted, for garden bones give definition and character, and poor-quality work is not a good investment. The most exciting jobs, for Borroff, are those for clients with a sense of the future, people who want to plan and plant for generations yet unborn, as well as for their own present pleasures. The great gardens of Europe were such gardens of faith, he points out, many planted in politically troubled times. Slow but long-term plants like oaks, magnolias that might take 20 years to blossom, and the dawn redwood will, like well-made stonework, last many lifetimes and become important parts of the greater communal landscape.

Not all gardens can or should be made with an eye to the future, and Borroff is quick to add: "It is always possible to make a true, growing garden that looks attractive right away." Amateurs don't always do this gracefully, but sometimes the missing ingredient is patience. Remember the ugly duck-ling, Borroff counsels, for in maturity, that awkward homemade garden might well be a silver swan.

Apricot Blossoms in the Snow

February

The occasional bitter frosts of February may nip many a bud before its time, but happily those of *Prunus mume*, the Japanese apricot, usually escape unscathed. Despite the squalling, wet winds and bursts of hail that often punctuate this month of sudden weather, each interlude of sunshine coaxes forth a tentative scattering of small flowers from the swelling buds that line the twiggy stems like little pink marbles. The finely textured petals are as insubstantial as a tissue, and the most common forms open blossoms of muted, coppery reds or warm pinks that pale to cream at the throat. By month's end, each bare, twiggy stem is smothered under a flurry of soft, perfumed flowers as delicate as moth wings.

Not a true apricot, mumes may also be labeled 'Japanese plum'. It isn't a true plum either, and its hard little fruits are bitterly sour, yet under any name at all, it is a true beauty. In a mild year, the flowers will open in sporadic bursts as early as January. A warm, sunny spell in any winter month can cause a sprinkling of buds to pop, releasing their heady fragrance through the garden, carried on the least breath of wind. March is their month of triumph, when the blossoms open thick and fast. The common species carries single pink flowers, of which the quality and color can vary a good deal, though all are delightful. Those who prefer double flowers and stronger color must seek out named forms, of which there are many. White-flowered mumes are somewhat less fragrant than the colored forms, but bear the most beautiful flowers of all. 'Viridicalyx', an old-fashioned double, has clean white blossoms, each clasped in a showy green cup (the calyx). 'Rosemary Clarke' is another double-white in which the prominent calyx is a deep, glowing red.

Grown as a standard, *Prunus mume* becomes in time a small tree with a good deal of character. As such, it stands up to the considerable challenge of being a focal point of the garden in winter, and thoughtful underplanting with glossy little sarcococcas, evergreen daphnes, and hardy cyclamen will assist the picture a good deal. In small gardens, this prunus may easily be kept to shrubby dimensions by an initial hard pruning, followed by the annual removal (down to stubs) of perhaps a quarter to a third of all the oldest branches. However, if you intend to do this, it is crucial to start either with stock on its own roots (quite rare) or with what is known as a "bottom graft," in which the mume stem stock is grafted onto the host stock just above the host's roots. A quick check of the trunk will reveal the graft, which is slightly lumpy, and has rougher bark than the rest of the trunk. It is not uncommon for standard grafts to be placed at anything over two feet above ground level, in which case low, hard pruning would leave you with a good thicket of the host (usually a sturdy but undistinguished plum) and no mume.

One excellent way to ensure that you have a low graft is to seek out plants prepared for bonsai enthusiasts. Although the plants will be small, they will be nicely shaped, often with the multiple trunks that make for especially interesting mature plants. Grown this way, mumes look wonderful in large containers or half barrels. Buying bonsai stock is a sound, economical proposition, for *Prunus mume* is a very quick grower. The little seedling you pick up for five dollars this year will grow into a thirty-dollar plant next year. Furthermore, it blooms well at a tender age, satisfying the most impatient with its precocity.

Though quite common in California, *P. mume* is seldom seen in the Northwest, where the cool, damp climate can promote peach leaf curl, a disease to which mumes are regrettably prone. The plants in the Seattle Arboretum are not usually afflicted, however, and my own plants have never had this problem, which is more disfiguring than harmful. It is a perfectly simple matter to place a mume behind other deciduous shrubs that will mask it in summer, when its charms are not in evidence. Those who favor such things will find that dormant sprays of Bordeaux or other oil mixtures will prevent or at least reduce leaf curl. A calcium polysulphide blend (Lilly-Miller's "Polysul"), a spray of mixed lime and sulphur, is considered the most ecologically acceptable of these. It is highly toxic, however, and merits the same cautious handling called for with all "skin toxic" chemicals, even when they are considered environmentally safe. Wear protective clothing, sturdy gloves, and a face mask with goggles when using this stuff at home. It is used in varying proportions at different stages of growth, with the strongest concentration going on dormant plants. Where plants have been badly affected, or where you know the disease is prevalent, you may feel the need to take prophylactic measures, and excellent directions for use at three stages—

dormant, bud crack, then when leaves are out in full—accompany the product (which I have never had cause to use).

Perhaps some readers will wonder why a plant with problems is recommended in these pages. In truth, most plants have a fault or two which an honest, unbiased appraisal will reveal, though it is not usually the business of garden writers to mention them. *P. mume* is a plant that is loaded with redeeming virtues, one that more than earns its keep during the dullest months of the gardening year. It may well look sorry in midsummer, but then, so does the grass. So do the forsythia, the lilac, and the callicarpa. When desirable plants have an obvious shortcoming, it becomes a challenge to the gardener to place them to fullest advantage, using plants with other, complementary strengths to minimize or disguise the embarrassing moments of its life. Wouldn't it be nice if somebody did as much for the rest of us? (Mail-order mumes, bonsai or unpruned, are available from Maple Leaf Nursery, Placerville, California.)

Daffodil Soufflé

In late winter, our sunny kitchen window sill is generally glorified by large vases of evergreens and forced flowers, their fresh scent and color all the more welcome for the continuing frosts outside. Glossy-leafed magnolias, the tightly wrapped buds barely open and showing the tiniest hint of color, mingle with bright wands of weeping willow and forsythia. Kerria and quince have their own vases, fronted now by a row of tiny pots. Each is only two or three inches across, and each is sprouting a number of tiny narcissus, some yellow, others white or nearly green. All look much like typical border daffodils, yet none are over six inches in height, and most are smaller.

These are species daffodils, the original progenitors of those taller, chunkier blooms that will crowd the border later in the spring. When the big bulbs are set in the borders, these diminutive ones are potted up tenderly and left in our unheated sun porch until the first buds appear. These are usually hoop petticoats (N. *bulbocodium* varieties), whose first blossoms will open in late January. All the bulbocodiums produce flaring, cone-shaped flowers with narrow, almost threadlike petals, and they look rather like something a very small Cinderella would be proud to wear to the ball. February brings on the tiny white hoops of N. *b. monophyllus* and its varieties, followed quickly by N. *b. tenuifolius* with thin, grassy foliage and sporty little inch-long trumpet flowers stained green at the base. There are quite a few forms of these cheerful little creatures, blooming in cream, moonlight, butter and warmer yellows. After the pans are bloomed indoors, the little bulbs are set out in the garden where they ripen and fade into dormancy. Given an ordinary, well-drained garden soil and a spot under the skirts of deciduous shrubs where they won't be disturbed while sleeping, hoop petticoats proliferate willingly in the Northwest, even to the extent of seeding themselves into the grass. Endangered in the wild, these little bulbs take kindly to cultivation, and are produced in large quantities by several reputable Dutch firms.

The mountains of Spain are home to the delicate *Narcissus asturiensis* (*minimus*), smallest of all, which lifts minute golden trumpets to the spring sky. Its slight scent is highly attractive to the year's first bees, who can scarcely fit their eager snouts into such tiny flowers. This form likes to be in gritty soil with excellent drainage, and dislikes the company of any but the flattest, laciest ground covers. The neat little vinca called 'Miss Jeckyll's White' is just the thing, and *Veronica pectinata* also works well. It has small leaves, woolly and grey, and spreads in open mats which don't seem to distress the bulbs. The winking, blue-eyed flowers which cover this carpeter in summer are a nice bonus.

Having wintered over in the cold but sunny glassed-in porch, the triandrus daffodils are scurrying into bloom by mid-February, well ahead of their normal out-of-doors schedule. As a group, *N. triandrus* seldom exceed five inches in height, and a happy bunch looks like a tiny flock of squid, so reflexed and narrow are the petals above the tubular trumpets. The true species are difficult to keep going in the garden unless planted in almost pure grit or coarse sand, and the blooms are so small that they can easily be overlooked. It's pleasant to grow them in pots, bringing them inside to admire the bloom at close range. Perhaps more people would grow Angel's Tears, the white form, if they knew that the angel in question was the native guide on Peter Barr's plant-hunting expedition into the Asturian mountains of Spain. Early in this century, Barr dragged his weary guide ever further up the unfriendly slopes in search of this and other species. When they finally found the white triandrus Barr sought, the exhausted guide burst into tears —all that work and struggle, for such a measly small flower as that? If you prefer to think that he cried at the incredible purity of form, you are welcome to—and you might be right.

Last fall I planted several dozen bulbs together: the white triandrus (*N. t. albus*) along with some Iberian relatives in palest yellow (*N. t. concolor*), and the softly bicolored *N. t. pulchellus*. They look exceedingly charming foaming out of a white soufflé dish lined first with gravel, then sphagnum moss, then a mixture of sand and compost. I use the dish as a centerpiece, much to my husband's disgust, for it means one of his favorite cooking dishes has been out of service for months and is likely to remain so for some time to come.

This planting of bulbs and plants into cooking utensils is a dreadful habit, and one I learned at my mother's knee. When nobody could find the baking sheets, they would turn up in the studio, daubed with paint, or in the greenhouse, covered with pots. Bulbs might be planted in Lusterware mugs, violets in a pretty teacup, primroses in a cream jug. Knives were invariably discovered on the potting bench, often rather the worse for wear. When I was more of a cook than a gardener, that scandalized me, but I have come to view it as an important form of recycling. When the Teflon coating begins to peel off the baking sheets, they move to the sun porch to hold pots and keep the window sill dry. Those who are fearful of Alzheimer's can use con-demned aluminum pans for mixing small batches of fertilizers, foliar sprays, or for sterilizing soil. Many things have many uses, and linear thinking is one of the most destructive problems of our harried age. How else could we ever taste the joys of daffodil soufflé?

Gardens with Backbone

trolling through our new garden last June, we found plenty to admire: shafts of apricot foxgloves, great trusses of terra-cotta rhododendrons, swags of ancient roses cascading through the old orchard trees, the lustrous pleated leaves of a shrubby purple hazel. Overall, however, these effects, though pleasing in themselves, were spotty and uneven. This is almost inevitable in a new garden, even when it is set into the shell of an old one, as this was. Still, it can be disappointing to the hopeful gardener who expected to see thriving shrubs where only bare sticks appear, and sweeping masses of perennials where there exists only a handful of seedlings. Intellectually, we all know quite well that ready-made mature gardens are to be had only with an enormous application of money, time, and effort. Since we applied only the last two out of the three, the results, as they say, ain't bad, but they ain't great.

After taking six months to assess the light and soil of the place, after giving a great deal of thought to the effects we wanted to create, the plants we wanted to showcase, the level of maintenance we wanted to commit to, we began the new garden. By the time another six months had passed, it was clear that although much was promising, the garden as a whole needed more backbone—more than we had imagined. This is a common deficiency, and a perfectly understandable one; we all tend to use lots of plants we love, and whose first plant love was ever a yew? Indeed, most amateur gardeners underestimate the need for those solid, often unprepossessing background shrubs that make up the skeleton of a satisfying garden. On the other hand, most professional designers err in the other direction, giving so much room to their favorite workhorses that there is precious little space left for anything else.

The ordinary makeshifts—filling the gaps in young gardens with coarse but quick-growing perennials, or packing the beds with flats of eager annuals—make showy, short-term effects that take the eye but cannot keep it. There is nothing to interest us once the primary impression has been absorbed. Furthermore, there is nearly always a restless, uneasy quality to instant gardens of this sort; like guests at a dull party, the plants refuse to mingle. Combining too many plants that have small, similarly shaped leaves yields the same unfortunate effect. Just as a stack of paintings is not an exhibit, a collection of plants is not a garden, and for the same reason; both require an appropriate setting to be fully appreciated. When plants stubbornly remain individuals, refusing to coalesce into a garden, it is nearly always because the border or group lacks permanent structure.

Many famous gardens rely heavily on architectural support. England is rife with gorgeous old walls, castle turrets and church spires, brick and timber pergolas, and the living walls made by antique hedges. Such props are exceedingly useful when defining the garden areas; indeed, the flimsiest border can hardly help but look striking when framed between soldierly ranks of mature yews and low boxwoods clipped to geometric perfection. A small experiment will bear this out: next time you go garden hopping or browse through the glossy pages of those endless cappuccino-table books about dreamy English gardens, cover the top half of the scene—the wall, hedge, or castle part—with the *London Times* or your invitation to the Queen's garden party. You will discover that surprisingly often the apparent majesty and strength of the floral display is diminished, if not completely lost, when the crucial architectural element is removed.

In America we generally lack that kind of backdrop to start with—a fifties ranch house will never have the visual impact of Sissinghurst—yet we are not without options. Lacking a castle, and unwilling to devote serious portions of free time to hedge manicures, we are forced to rely on evergreen plants of various kinds to lend structure and make up the backbone of our gardens. Fortunately, there are literally hundreds of good choices for gardens of any size, many of which lend beauty that comes to the fore in winter, when the dazzle of the border is dimmest.

If your young border is persistently amorphous despite your best intentions, an infusion of backbone might be in order. The fastest way to do this is to center the new around the old, should you be fortunate enough to have any sort of mature plants at all on your property. Small ornamental trees are the ideal starting place, but even a matronly old shrub of spotted aucuba may be transformed from an eyesore into an advantage. Complementary company will give weight and dignity to your group. You may need to transport the whole border across the yard in order to take advantage of an overlooked bit of backbone, but the results will almost certainly justify the work.

If you don't have an established tree, start a new bed around any existing shrub at all, unless it is so far past its prime that the only kind course is to remove the poor thing entirely. Remember, backbone is not meant to be stunning so much as supportive, and unassuming plants are generally to be preferred over flamboyant ones. If your yard is empty, gird yourself up to buy at least three big evergreens. They won't come cheap, but they will anchor your plantings and make any further additions appear to have settled in almost at once. Infant gardens where nothing is mature offer the gardener luxurious freedom of choice, but instant, dramatic results require a dramatic plant budget. Where patience is in greater supply than cash, the gardener can derive great pleasure by exercising his inner eye, in getting to know his shrubs and trees as yearlings, and in watching his dream garden materialize over time.

Cash-poor gardeners can often find a mother lode of maturing plants ready at hand, for though yards with actual gardens are rare, the house that isn't screened from public view by a prim row of foundation plants is rarer still. Transport these to the garden proper and it will be far easier to wash windows and paint trim. The shrubs will now take on the strong, silent, supporting role behind the stars of your border, which will shine brighter for the backup. The American habit of shielding the base of the house as if it were indecent somehow smacks of Victorian prudery. When it's time to mend the plumbing or replace the siding, the reasoning behind such coverup planting seems even more absurd. Foundation plants are widely held to "tie the house to the setting," but no quantity of junipers and rhododendrons could secure a split-level to a bare lot, or make an old farmhouse look anything but self-conscious. How much more sensible to rearrange such plants where they can define the garden, screen views, provide shelter and privacy. The formerly useless evergreens will contribute a defining framework to our borders all through the year, setting off garden scenes to be enjoyed from each window in the house as well as out-of-doors.

In small yards, shrubs and trees can quickly outgrow their positions, overwhelming the garden proper unless they are carefully chosen. When you cruise the nurseries looking for just the right components for your new bed, remember to ask how big each shrub will be in its maturity and how long it will take to get there. It is always worthwhile to opt for slow-growing shrubs and small trees, though you may have to settle for a smaller specimen than you really want. Give your treasures pride of place, but it won't hurt to tuck in some short-term structural companions. Choose faster-growing shrubs, like ceanothus or broom, which are short-lived by nature and won't swamp the main player. You must, however, be firm in your resolve to sacrifice the short-term plants, for it is a sure thing that they will require removal just when they reach their prime.

It is fatally easy to forget that plants of practically any size can be moved, but this is a key part of developing a garden. As the garden matures and the gardener's vision is refined, the trees and shrubs are maturing too. In time, some detail or other of the arrangement of the backbone plants is likely to require significant adjustment, or may simply cease to please. Hire some help if you have to, but don't leave a plant in an unsatisfactory position merely because it is already there. Emerson held that the unexamined life is not worth living, and the garden, too, must be constantly reexamined if the heart is not to go out of it. After all, the essence of the garden is change.

Where Crocuses Blow

n between snowfalls the observant will find that the first crocuses are blooming and the early narcissus are pushing their small, determined snouts through the unnaturally chilly ground. One of the prettiest sights in the garden occurs when valiant little *Crocus tomasinianus*, lavender blue with cold, open their frail cups to the sun through a blanket of new snow. In our island garden, they do this beneath a stand of gnarled old apple trees. In older parts of Seattle's Capitol Hill and Madison Park, species crocus of gold or lavender or soft blue similarly spangle the grass surrounding aging fruit trees that date back to the time when much of the Madison slope running down to the Arboretum held orchards and small farms. These early crocus are tough little creatures that multiply readily and are quite capable of holding their own against mere lawn grass for a hundred years or so. Such insouciance is endearing to the modern gardener, who hesitates before committing to any relationship which requires upkeep.

Bulbs like these, that promise effortless show in return for benign neglect, would seem to be a natural for the low-maintenance school. Not infrequently, however, stands of naturalized crocus that flourish in neglected old yards surrounding older homes are sadly dwindling just a few years after the houses are renovated by well-meaning new owners. The bewildered homeowner may search for reasons; do the crocuses need thinning, or feeding, or resetting? In truth, that bulbous insouciance is not a pose; left alone, many species crocus and other small bulbs can compete successfully with grass. Given enough light early in the year, and reasonable soil, they will often proliferate abundantly, so that where a hundred are planted, a thousand may bloom 10 years down the road. Unfortunately, when these small crocuses meet up with the modern gardener, they often meet their match.

The orchards that were once mown by grazing animals, if at all, have become lawns, and far too many of them are kept immaculate. In the maritime Northwest, grass grows with unmatched vigor in late winter and early spring. In many households the first chore of the season is to rev up the power mower and give the yard a close shave. Well, unfortunately, that close shave is just a little too close for the bulbs, for the one thing they can't tolerate is being mown before their leaves have ripened. To survive over the long term, they must be allowed to stand until the foliage is brown at least halfway down its length. In this climate, that may well translate into a horrifying statement: Don't mow until Mother's Day.

Laissez-faire gardeners may not have a problem with that, but the tidy-minded—who may, however unaccountably, be closely related to the former types by blood and/or marital vows—do. In spades. If your house is divided in this way, a review of some of the alternatives to the Total Lawn look may be helpful. Where Tidy gives no ground, reset the crocuses around deciduous shrubs in borders or beds. Here they will give no trouble to anybody, and if you inadvertently dig up dormant bulbs, you can just shove them back into the earth with a finger. Perhaps the most desirable option is to persuade Tidy to mow much as usual, but with a few minor modifications. A swale of longer grass where the ripening bulbs are thickest might be tolerated, if only in the short term; longer grass has lovely texture, and such a swale can look handsome if it is artistically shaped.

If that won't fly, the crocus area—only a small portion of the total yard, after all—might be renamed "the meadow." This is trendy, and has a certain cachet even among nongardeners. If this gambit succeeds, sprinkle the long grass with meadowy perennials like Queen Anne's lace, ox-eye daisies, and blue chicory, self-sowing annuals such as larkspur and love-in-a-mist, along with all the spring- and fall-blooming bulbs you can muster. Snowdrops will willingly consort with your crocus, spangling the grass at an early date. Certain narcissus will, too, particularly little hoop petticoats, *Narcissus bulbocodium*, the reflexed, startled-looking *cyclamineus*, and late-blooming *N. poeticus*. Checkered lilies, the tweedy European *Fritillaria meleagris*, come in blends of pink and grey, lavender and faded plum, or plain cream. The named sorts like 'Alba', lavender-mauve 'Artemis' or plum dark 'Charon' run a bit larger than the plain species, but the standard commercial mixture looks delightfully natural nodding in young grass. If you go whole hog and introduce fall bloomers—autumn crocus and colchicums—one good mowing in late August will give these a chance to be admired. Meadows that aren't watered or fertilized excessively may need no further attention until spring. Otherwise, another cut in late fall or early winter will keep the grassy carpet tight and low so that your spring bulbs can shine undimmed.

If none of these options prove acceptable, you may want to preserve your heritage crocus in pans—not preserving pans, but the short, wide clay or plastic containers known as bulb pans. It can be hard to find crocuses in long grass once they pass out of bloom, so mark them with plant tags or labels when they bloom. Once the flowers have faded, dig up a chunk of the lawn and remove the bulbs. You can often simply cut a flap in the turf, lift and wiggle it to loosen everything, then slide the bulbs out backwards (bulb end first) from beneath, using gentle but firm pressure. Remember to replace your divots, or face the wrath of Tidy.

Set the bulbs into good soil in their pans, let the foliage ripen off untrimmed, then put them aside in an out-of-the-way corner to enjoy a summer baking without attracting any attention (the pots look totally empty, and well-meaning friends are apt to tip them into the compost heap for you). Those who consider their yards too small to permit indulgence in ephemera might take another look around. A friend who lives on a houseboat keeps his crocus in deep pots which take on summer boarders, often long-blooming geraniums. As the pots become overcrowded (crocuses love close quarters, and his bloom in solid sheets), he repots, dividing the congested clumps and renewing the potting soil. He also has a thriving colony beneath his grapevine, where they get plenty of light early in the year and coexist with summery bedding plants later in the season.

Garden Mystery

THROUGH A VEIL DARKLY

n awful lot of borders, English and otherwise, are loaded with colorful flowers in midsummer. Now that "texture" is a byword, not a few may even display pleasant contrasts of foliage form and tint, yet were we to photograph them using black-and-white film, we would discover that nearly all borders look much the same. Indeed, viewed lengthwise or in profile, most of our pictures would reveal the kind of curve that distinguished the old-fashioned rolltop desk. All the big plants are at the back, the midsize things are snug in the center ranks, and smaller things nestle to the fore. In a word, the average border has the topography of a bread loaf—or rather, half a bread loaf. A loaflike profile is not an unforgivable fault (half a loaf is certainly better than none), yet the occasional reversal of size ordering—putting a tall plant near the front, a cluster of ground huggers surrounding a big-time player at the back—could lend those uniform borders a stimulating air of mystery. Mystery is seldom a desirable quality in bread, but in gardens it is invaluable.

This sort of reversal trick is sometimes known as scrim planting, in reference to the thin gauze curtains used to veil stage sets in certain theater productions. Scrim planting is most often seen in large borders, yet it has applications for nearly everyone. Small gardens, all too quickly explored, can be made to seem much larger by screening off parts of the beds and borders with airy, see-through plants that show enough to allure without revealing all there is to know at a glance. Perhaps the most famous example is Christopher Lloyd's now-classic grouping of alstroemeria with *Verbena bonariensis*, which sends its skinny stems—the bottom foot or so of which are scantily clad with slim, tapered leaves—three to five feet straight up in the air. Each square stem is topped with tightly frizzled bunches of electric purple-blue blossoms. It is definitely an odd plant, and not to every taste, yet when cleverly used it can spark up a nice but rather dull planting no end.

The southwestern American native *Verbena rigida* is another good scrim plant, though on a lesser scale. A pale chalky lavender variety called

'Polaris', some 2½ to 3 feet tall, looks wonderful in front of the low-growing rose 'Lavender Pinocchio', with its curious tea-colored buds and pewtery lavender-pink blossoms. 'Polaris' also is an effective softener of the somewhat harsh mauve and magenta flowers of the dwarf Chinese astilbe, A. chinensis 'Pumilum'. The astilbe is a good foot shorter than the verbena, yet looks all the better when seen through spires of the cooler tones of 'Polaris'; any strident tendencies of the astilbe are mitigated without loss of character.

Meadow rue can work wonders in a small garden, especially the tall, blue-leafed *Thalictrum glaucum* with its spuming billows of tasseled pagoda flowers in Chinese yellow. This can reach seven or eight feet when well situated (it seems equally happy in sun or moderate to light shade, given deep, humusy soil and plenty of water). That may seem rather tall for a small garden, but it is not a dense or massive plant and is only about a yard across at best, despite its dramatic height. When the early summer bloom fades, the silvery brown seedheads which follow are nearly as attractive—at least to those of us who fancy such things—as the flowers in their first freshness. *Thalictrum dipterocarpum* is of similar size, but with lacy, dark green foliage and slender wandlike stems that arch to shower frothy cascades of Wedgwood blue flowers over plants or path. An extremely handsome and free-flowering double form, in which the blue florets are lightened with creamy white petticoats, is called 'Hewitt's Double'; both of these bloom in August, but are a presence in the garden long before they actually flower and for several months after.

A Texan wild flower, *Gaura lindheimeri*, spins out long, spindly arms that break a hundred times into buds of a soft, true pink that quickly fades to clean white. They exactly mimic the coloring and shape of *Rosa moschata* 'Nastarana', a single, small-flowered rose which blooms over an exceptionally long season. Flank the rose with a pair of gauras, set three or four of the fuller artemisias about them—'Powis Castle' or 'Valery Finnis' are great accompanists—and you soon have something pretty indeed. Both the gaura and the rose carry on for months, starting in high summer and trailing off in a prolonged burst through late autumn.

Gaura is a useful veil plant in other situations as well; its lanky arms can rise as much as five feet in the air, though generally developing a few kinks along the way. A tame but pretty grouping of pink and lavender clary sages, blue-flowered 'Six Hills Giant' catmint, hazy blue *Caryopteris* 'Dark Knight' and spiky steel blue oat grass (*Helictotrichon sempervirens*) becomes magical when glimpsed through the gauzy scarf of a well-propped gaura.

Although staking is not my favorite garden activity, gauras truly are fit only to be tied; unrestrained, they flop incorrigibly, groveling useless and unlovely on the mulch. The most effective prop for them is a stout and twiggy piece of a fir tree, say, or a few bits off a birch or alder. The stake needn't be more than a couple of feet tall, but the fuller the better. I often use two or three sticks, cutting the twiggy bits short and arranging them in a circle around the unsuspecting young gaura. The slender shoot that looks so small and meek in June becomes a thrashing multibranched giant by late July. Unless you have done twig duty, the smallest wind will send it tumbling, ruining the intended effect for the rest of the season.

Plants which might be used to alter or disguise an ugly view are generally more solid than the above, but scrim softens rather than conceals, adding the vital element of mystery so often lacking in our small gardens. Many other suitable candidates will come to mind: a kale cousin, *Crambe cordifolia*, sends up sizeable yet insubstantial armloads of delicate florets on wiry, angular stemlets; *Rudbeckia maxima*, a black-eyed Susan relative, has glaucus blue leaf rosettes, smooth and almost matte, but with a hint of shimmer in the leaf. From these emerge willowy stems that drip a profusion of small, drooping, golden blossoms. Zebra grass, *Miscanthus sinensis* 'Zebrinus', a tall, horizontally banded grass in gold and green, shows tantalizing glimpses of whatever lies behind it.

Though the number of plants that readily lend themselves to such practice is clearly limited, once the idea of scrim is introduced it is amazing how quickly inventive gardeners take it up. A scrim plant can pull us around a corner, seem to double the length of a dwarf border, cast a merciful shadow over an unresolved plant relationship or the gawky pains of bioadolescence. Not least, the very concept raises a multiplicity of questions for the thoughtful gardener; anything that causes us to reexamine our gardens and our plants with fresh eyes must always be of value, whether we ultimately embrace it, reject it out of hand, or screen it behind a veil of mystery.

[handwritten margin note: next to roses]

[handwritten note at bottom: Crambe needs lots of grit limy soil or will dye   Full Sun]

Ornamental Edibles

VEGETABLES TO GROW FOR SHOW

*J*ust as one country's weeds must travel to become another land's appreciated ornamentals, so our workaday vegetables deserve thoughtful reappraisal. As the idea of combining ornamental and edible plantings regains favor, we do well to pay careful attention to the looks of our vegetables. Many are undistinguished plants, but most vegetable families boast a variety or two attractive enough to merit garden placement whether you eat them or not. The tremendous kale-cole tribe has gained a certain acceptance in this regard, but this family offers far more scope than the earnest mounds of winter kales might suggest. Red kale itself is a fine foliage plant, and the strains with ruby-toned stems and black-tinged leaves can be planted near purple hazels, smoke bushes (*Cotinus* species), or red barberries to remarkable and mutual advantage. Such horticultural deviation may confound plant snobs, but so what? We might profitably steal a page from Ms. Woodhouse (the dog one, not Emma) and say that there are No Bad Plants, merely poor applications.

Brussels sprouts rarely rate top billing on ornamental/edible plant lists, but the Italian red ones called 'Rubine' merit inclusion in any garden. Young plants are blue with a chalky bloom on leaf and stem alike. The maturing stems darken to midnight purple, while the great leaves expand and turn a murky sea green, richly veined with fuchsia pink and purple. Come fall, dusky red sprouts pack the sturdy stalks, and as winter approaches, the entire plant takes on storm-cloud shades of purple, slate, and black. The plants are very cold-resistant, and if allowed to winter over will flop alarmingly in spring, but further patience rewards the gardener with tall sheaves of small flowers, primrose pale, that will seed true to type. In my garden red Brussels sprouts surround a tree peony with gunmetal foliage and apricot-scented flowers of imperial yellow stained and edged with the same red that tints the sprouts' foliage. Not, perhaps, an orthodox combination, but pleasing all the same. Naturally, one can eat the sprouts; they are not bad at all. However, their strongest suit is certainly their continual loveliness.

Broccoli is seldom considered an ornamental vegetable, but another Italian, 'Romanesco', is equally gardenworthy. This is sometimes sold as a cauliflower, which it most closely resembles. This plant forms unusual, almost bizarre heads packed with creamy curds of lime green. Each head is enfolded in a wide ruff of boldly veined leaves that sets off the whorled florets within. These grow in tight spiraling patterns that gradually loosen, then shoot up into spiky turrets. As the plant matures the turrets bristle with short bloom stalks, their flowers small and of a subdued greenish yellow. Requiring rich soil and an unchecked supply of moisture, 'Romanesco' makes a highly unusual edging for a path or border, or can be remarkably effective when several plants are grown together in an oversized terra-cotta ring pot with trails of golden canary vine (*Tropæolum peregrinum*), vivid nasturtiums, or cool grey lotus vines streaming out between the crowns.

Sea kales are cole cousins that flourish in the sandy soil of European beaches and kitchen gardens. *Crambe maritima* has rippling, wondrous leaves that form flat rosettes two feet wide and only a few inches tall. Hard, glossy purple knobs turn into ice blue leaves a foot in length, ruffled and lacy on silvery purple stems. It blooms in early summer, a crowd of tiny white flowers rising in a frothy mass on short stalks. Like most vegetables, sea kale appreciates a position in full sun, doing best on light, limy soils (as does its better-known ornamental relative, *C. cordifolia*). In sandy soils both crambes will leave scores of rootlets behind when you move or replace the plants, most of which will grow into new plants (nice if you want a nursery or have longing friends). On heavier soils crambes are apt to be slow and sullen, wintering over poorly and often dying out altogether. Adding generous quantities of grit or coarse sand to the root zone when you plant them makes a significant difference, but if you want lots, find a friend with lighter soil to propagate for you, or save seed.

Kale and cabbages have found their niche as ornamentals, but fewer gardeners view lettuce in the same light. 'Ruby', a glossy looseleaf with crinkled bronzed red foliage, makes an unusual ground cover for the smoldering ember red rosettes of *Lobelia fulgens* and its hybrids. As the lobelias gather strength, rising to their full height of a yard or so, the lettuce follows suit on a lesser scale, forming spiky ruffled towers topped with sprays of soft yellow flowers, the seed of which breeds relatively true. Red lettuce also mingles pleasantly with French blue 'Clear Crystals' pansies and upright clumps of scabiosa in purples and mauves.

Common garden parsley has a lovely texture that contrasts effectively with the broad blue blades of iris or strappy green daylily foliage. True rosarians will cringe at the thought, but crimped, cutleaf parsleys look refreshingly healthy and handsome when planted around bedding roses. Allow the plants to set seed and you will generally find plenty of volunteer replacements the following year. Although flat-leaf Italian parsley has the better flavor, it fits uneasily into mixed borders, where it looks distinctly weedy. It makes the most sense to keep this sturdy workhorse in the vegetable patch, and relegate its tasteless but showy sibling to bedding duty.

We do well to reexamine the contents of the vegetable patch with a fresh eye. After all, tomatoes, once known as love apples, were grown strictly as ornamentals until well into the last century, and they are no less lovely now. A glistening, golden-fruited form would strike a new note amid the grass and rudbeckias, and think how an intensely productive cherry type could enliven a cloud of black-leafed dahlias with clear scarlet flowers. A particularly handsome celery might prove just the thing to set between the massive wings of a shrub rose. Twining black beans with glossy dark stems and dusky purple flowers can be every bit as decorative as the gaudiest of ornamental vines. When we plant with freedom and imagination, our gardens can look good enough to eat. Don't worry about what the neighbors will say when the purple basil wreathes round the chalk pink geraniums, for such eclectic, insouciant plantings are definitely in the very best of taste.

Tulips That Triumph

SPECIES TULIPS THRIVE WHERE OTHERS FAIL

box of romance was sitting on the porch steps when we got home—a big, sturdy box, well punctuated with air holes and full of promise. Amid the blowing leaves of fall, the flowers of spring are here. We drag the heavy carton into our farmhouse kitchen and unpack with care. Bag after bag is lifted out, the names on their labels the very stuff of adventure: *Tulipa turkestanica* from the mountains of Turkestan, *T. linifolia* from the wilds of Bukhara, *T. urumiensis* from the northern steppes of Iran. These species of botanical tulips are exotics indeed; small but staunch, they take the scouring wet winds of winter in stride and brighten our worst soil with their blossoms from late February through May.

A surprising number of gardeners assume that tulips are native to Holland; in fact, Europe as a whole is home to only a few species. The daffodil tulip, *Tulipa sylvestris*, blows its bloom like green-gold balloons in marshy English meadows, with related forms found throughout southern Europe. Slim, candy-striped *T. marjolettii* and the red-cupped *T. præcox* still bloom by vineyards and fields in the French and Italian alps; probably not true species, they are classified among the neotulipae by cautious botanists. Most true species tulips originated in the rugged mountains and bleak plains of the southern Mediterranean and Asia Minor. Tulips have been cultivated since the beginning of time, but it wasn't until Clusius came to the Netherlands in the mid-1500s that tulips caught the fancy of Western gardeners. The Dutch were ferociously smitten with the charms of these small flowers, and at once began collecting and hybridizing in a big way. To this day, Holland is the commercial hub of the world's bulb-growing activities.

Big, modern hybrid tulips are as much a symbol of Holland as are windmills or clogs, but species tulips are nurtured there as well, both as commercial crops and as source material for further breeding programs. Even after centuries of hybridizing, many a plump, complacent border beauty shows a touch of wildling blood in her veins. Lily-flowered tulips owe their insouciant curves to *T. acuminata*, the May-flowering horned tulip of the

46

Pyrenees, its weirdly elongated petals of warm yellow flamed with lipstick red. Bouquet or multiflowered tulips can trace their branching habit to *T. præstans*, a very early bloomer that lifts sheaves of blood red tulips on short, wine-dark stems.

Species tulips are often dismissed as of interest only to collectors; they have a reputation for being finicky, expensive, and florally insignificant to boot. In fact, since they bloom so early in the year, when there are no serious competitors, thoughtful plantings of these tulips can stop traffic. Some pack considerable garden wallop, delivering vivid color in pools and patches for weeks, even months at a stretch. Under the right circumstances, botanical tulips have something the later-blooming hybrids don't: staying power. Not plants for the border proper, these little toughs like it hot and dry. Given suitably impoverished conditions, they will return reliably to parts of the garden where most plants would up and die. It takes experimentation to learn which species will thrive in your particular problem area, but such investigative trials are great fun. Twenty dollars of venture capital will get you half a dozen of six or seven types. Make annual trials on the same basis, and as the seasons roll, it becomes clear which are the best investment.

One of the most gratifying qualities of the species tulips is their adaptability to wretched ground. Although there are several areas in our Seattle garden where these bulbs do well, they have performed most consistently on a small hillside. This sloping bed, open to the south and west, was made when Seattle's precipitous streets were regraded many years ago. The soil—subsoil, really—is pure, stolid clay, as heavy and unrelenting as it comes. Some years back, we smothered off a fine crop of Bermuda grass with a foot of bark mulch and planted the hill with Mediterranean subshrubs, all of which take the Spartan conditions in stride. Here among silky *Cistus creticus*, the airy bluebeard, *Caryopteris x cladonensis*, a velvety taco-leafed *Senecio greyi*, and the little grey feathers of *Tanacetum haradjanii*, a number of species tulips have not only persisted but increased. Out of reach of the hose, this area gets no supplementary summer water. Despite the popular misconception, the Pacific Northwest receives little rain through the summer months, so plants on this bank get the same summer baking they would experience in their native homes. True, the heat is not as intense, but it has proved adequate for the following sorts, all of which either self-sow or spread by stolons. Now, as we make our country garden—an open, sunny one encircling an old farmhouse—we are applying the lessons learned on that city slope to good effect.

Shaped like tiny, obese birds, the bulbs of *Tulipa clusiana* have tightly fitting, rough tunics, chestnut-colored with a cinnamon sheen and trimmed with tufts of fur at the neck. Many of the species have these warm coats to protect them from the rigors of their native climates. The varied sizes and shapes of the bulbs fascinate our two small boys, who pull generous handfuls from the mesh bags and arrange them for planting. Young children are ideal assistants at planting time; not only do they take great delight in the process, but unfettered by any latent need to plant in straight lines, they strew bulbs with enviable abandon. These fall in satisfying clusters on the thin, poor soil along the driveway, an unprepossessing area, but we know from experience that species tulips will rise above it undaunted.

Some gardeners flatly dismiss botanical tulips as stumpy and dwarfish. In certain cases, notably the clunky fosteriana hybrids in which enormous blossoms perch upon absurdly short stems, this accusation is well founded. However, such criticism could never apply to the delicate cluster-flowered *T. turkestanica*. Dependable in many gardens, it soon seeds itself about pleasantly, perhaps amid the emerging fluff of Florence fennel, or between trailing branches of needle-leafed *Lithodora rosmarinifolia*. Where winters are mild, its first flowers appear with the golden bunch crocus, *C. ancyrensis*, while the last may not fade till April is well launched; few flowers of any kind can claim a similar season. Each stem carries open sprays of ivory flowers centered with gold; the bristling stamens are tipped with maroon, making a star pattern like that in a cross-cut apple. On rainy days, the long ivory buds shut tightly, showing their bronzy green backs and little else. Even then, they are attractive amid their lax, glaucous foliage, and they reopen most willingly at the first hint of sunshine.

In the coastal gardens of the Pacific Northwest, the waterlily tulip, *T. kaufmanniana*, opens its pale cups in mid-February. Native to the arid steppes of Turkestan, it multiplies only where it is given plenty of light and exceedingly sharp drainage. In our garden, the stodgy clay required a good deal of amendment with fine gravel and coarse builder's sand before we could convince this generous bulb to proliferate. Now, as the stately stalks of *Euphorbia wulfenii* raise their drooping necks to bloom, hundreds of little stars appear about their feet. Creamy blossoms are lit from within by glowing yellow throats, each petal licked with carmine without. A week or two later, its hybrid, 'Ancilla', comes into bloom, the clean white blossoms nestled into rosettes of sea green foliage that is lovely in its own right. The flowers open almost flat to display a golden eye narrowly banded with crimson. *T. kauf-*

manniana 'Stresa' opens at the same time, its tapered buds of deep yellow heavily brushed with red; a highly visible combination that carries remarkably despite its low stature. The mottled burgundy patterning on its leaves proves it a hybrid with the unmistakable greigii tulip.

The full name, *T. greigii Regel*, commemorates an eminent family of horticulturists who botanized the wildest parts of Russia and Asia Minor. The Regels' discoveries enchanted the gardening world, and in the cold Massachusetts garden of my childhood, a lingering clump was persistent proof of the late Victorians' fascination with greigii tulips. *T. greigii* has distinguished foliage, marbled in the Persian patterns of endpapers in fine old books. This striation is generally bequeathed to its offspring, in which it may appear as rich streaks of burgundy or mahogany, often against a subtle background of greyish green. Many of these hybrids are as lovely in leaf as in flower, effective long before the flowers appear. Thickly interplanted with the nonflowering clone of lamb's ears (*Stachys lanata* 'Silver Carpet'), the greigii hybrid 'Sweet Lady' spreads stippled leaves in a much-photographed combination, a crowd pleaser from the time the leaves emerge in January until they fade, tattered and worn, in May. When 'Sweet Lady' opens her salmon pink flowers, the grey background intensifies the sparkling effect of buttery stamens set within the deep-toned petals. The clarion, hot red petals of 'Red Riding Hood' poke perkily above mottled leaves in many gardens. It looks less heavy when paired with its vermilion cousin 'Plaisir', each petal feathered in white and creamy yellow, the inside gaudy with Roman stripes of black and lemon.

A Central Asian, *T. tarda* (*dasystemon*) opens its fat, sunny flowers at ground level. Among the easiest to please, tarda brightens up the tail end of winter in gardens all over the world. The white petals are liberally splashed with buttercup yellow, each bulb offering up a nosegay of blossoms like fried eggs from cheerful chickens. Only slightly taller are the showy, multiflowered *T. præstans* and its several varieties, all early and prolific. Though balanced and shapely, they have strong coloring that makes them a challenge to place well. The orange tint in the flame-colored petals of *T. p.* 'Fusilier' blends well with gingery wallflowers, tawny primroses, and the mustardy florets of an ex-alyssum, *Aurinia saxatilis*. *T. p.* 'Van Tubergen' is a less intense version which combines effectively with apricot-colored 'Clear Crystals' violas.

Many species are brilliantly colored, yet they never really make a big display. These are best planted in intimate areas where their small beauties can be readily appreciated. *T. kolpakowskiana* is such a one, ripe cherry red in the bud, the long, tapered petals of warm yellow elegantly splayed above rippling silver green leaves. The buoyant pink goblets of *T. humilis* (*pulchella*) open widely in the sun, the rosy color distilled to violet in the form *violacea*. *T. saxatilis* offers a gentler pink, its small cups half full of gold. The slender five-inch stems of *T. batalinii* support flashy flowers as fat as goldfish, the amber petals backed with copper in the selected variant 'Bright Gem', with 'Bronze Charm' having a similarly metallic backside. *T. linifolia* is utterly alluring, with sinuous, Chinese red petals elegantly pinched at the tips.

Dozens of equally endearing species await discovery by the venturesome gardener who gives botanical tulips a try. Success is most likely in unlikely spots, open sites where soil is poor and gravelly. Few of the species will tolerate much competition from larger plants, so ground covers must be used with discretion, with preference given to loose, airy ones like *Vinca minor*, or mats and creepers such as prostrate thyme, rosemary, or veronica. Much is made of their need for full sun, but we have found quick, sharp drainage to be of more importance. To promote this, fork up the entire planting area (not just each bulb's hole) and amend generously with fine gravel or builder's sand. I wouldn't plant species tulips in full shade, but as that ultragardener George Schenk has pointed out, anything that grows well in the Pacific Northwest can be classified as shade tolerant. As to the rest, when in doubt, trust in benign neglect. Don't feed, mulch, or water them, and don't worry about dividing them, either. (These bulbs are clearly the busy gardener's friends.) With some experimentation and persistence, your own little desert will be transformed by these exotic adventurers from the wild places of the world.

The BORDER in SPRING

SPRING

 Spring is kind to the new gardener, for she showers her favors liberally, both hands splayed wide. Spring does not measure, she pours and tosses, scatters and sows with carefree generosity. New leaves are as lovely as any flower, glimmering translucencies in a thousand shades of green and gold, red and copper, blue and silver. Shrubs and trees are overwhelmed with blossom, snowed under by a fragrant weight of bloom. Who can count the bulbs of spring? Surely there are thousands, and all of them beauties. The frumps of spring simply do not exist; there may be topheavy hybrid tulips and excessively doubled narcissus here and there, but the grace and abundance of more natural beauties far outweigh these lesser lights. To date, no hybridizer on earth has the skill to mar the face of spring.

Spring spends herself freely, fearlessly, and so ought we; this is no time to be stingy. If there is any lack of color now, mark those spaces well in your garden workbook, along with ideas: "Need a patch of blue beneath the red cutleaf maple—de Caen anemones? Pansies? Scilla?"; "Pool *Tulipa sylvestris* with gold, amber, and peach primroses under the golden elder, or try golden moneywort and 'Hawera' narcissus?" When high summer comes, order reinforcements lavishly. When we plant bulbs, let us plant them in dozens and hundreds, in interlacing clusters and overlapping waves that wash through the garden, scouring away the last traces of winter's reserve. If spring is openhanded, we must be equally prodigal in her service.

One can always find room for more bulbs; they are the most

obliging creatures, sharing space gracefully with all manner of other plants. Bulbs of one kind or another will thrive under deciduous shrubs, around the dry, rooty bases of trees, in rich soil among perennials, in shallow window boxes or deep containers. They can be inserted below or sandwiched between other plants, arranged to bloom companionably or in synchronized sequence. Used in adequate quantities, their effects are potent, heady, yet almost effortless. Well placed, the bulbs will pass unnoticed, their draggled foliage hidden by the green and rising tide of summer abundance.

Spring-blooming shrubs have fewer beauties in other seasons, and their fading is more difficult to disguise, yet it is brief and easy to forgive. A goodly number of spring beauties blaze again in autumn, displaying glories of leaf, berry, and twig. Where space is limited and each plant must earn its position, these are the shrubs and trees of choice. Fothergillas and Japanese azaleas, witch hazels and mountain ashes, crabapples, ornamental cherries, and plums should all be selected as much for their late performance as for their earlier displays. Give preference to plants with interesting leaf shapes and textures; the great, rounded leaves of fothergillas and the lacy, fernlike foliage of mountain ash are good, if quiet, in summer, but nothing is more fierce and splendid in fall than their autumn fire. In summer, they can be given a drape of clematis, a tangled annual vine, or star-spangled potato vine to scramble through their branches and enliven their somber green.

Relatively few perennials are at their floral best in spring, yet in the border the bare earth disappears almost as we watch. Gappy spaces between the plants are filling in and clumpy crowns of phlox and delphinium bristle with promising young shoots. These need to be thinned if the plants are to achieve full strength, but taken with small heels, most of the extraneous shoots will root readily in a sandy compost. Hefty groups of asters and goldenrods, chrysanthemums and late-blooming sages can be lifted, pulled apart, and reset, the extra divisions lined out in the nursery bed to fatten up. (These make wonderful gifts for friends or may be donated to plant sales, if you can't think where to put them.)

Stepping delicately, we weed our way through the border. We greet each emerging plant, note losses and think up their replacements, try to avoid forking up the roots of late risers. Everything in the border will be better off with a tonic feeding mulch, hearty handfuls of compost and aged manure enriched with cottonseed meal and bone meal, kelp and rotted leaves. Every inch of the beds gets a thorough once-over; stronger doses of nutrients mixed in and heaped round the feet of gross feeders, weed-choking mulches renewed everywhere. Fall bloomers are divided and transplanted, volunteer seedlings thinned. Summer annuals and tender bulbs are woven carefully into the tapestry. As the garden begins to overflow, so too does the gardener's heart, filled with unspeakable delight in the unstinting wealth of spring in her first freshness, with summer close on her heels.

Drumsticks and Candelabras

PRIMROSES FOR ALL SEASONS

The sight and scent of thousands of bright-faced primroses flooding into garden center and grocery store prompt most of us to add an armload to the cart, even if our front steps are already crowded with them. These are chiefly juliae hybrids, a happy, hardy seed strain that thrives in the Northwest. In our gentle climate, primroses offer their cheerful color through much of the year—heavily in spring, and sporadically from fall through winter. They are wonderful workhorse plants, and no garden is complete without a few dozen as a bare minimum. However, the primula tribe is both immense and varied, including members which will flower during any given month of the year. Since the maritime Northwest suits this family down to the ground, further exploration will be highly rewarding even for inexperienced gardeners.

Anybody with a poorly drained garden will find the spectacular candelabras (*Primula japonica* and related species) splendid problem solvers, for not only do they relish mucky soil, but they are also perfectly capable of muscling weeds out of their way. Once a few are established, they seed themselves in increasing quantities, taking shade or a good deal of sun in stride as long as their feet remain damp. Where they have been aided and abetted in their good work by rich fall feeding mulches of manure and compost, sheets of these tall, tiered beauties (each bloom stalk can carry between two and six stacked wheels of florets) will whirl their way across bog or border in short order. A seed strain called 'Pagoda' comes in sunset colors, while others may be any shade of pink or lavender, starting with clear red and working through clean white with many stops in between.

The distinctively shaped primulas known as drumsticks (*P. denticulata*) are also fond of damp sites where they will spread their luxuriant leaf rosettes, as showy as many a hosta. The slim scapes rise in late spring, each crowned with fat flowers clustered in loose balls, rose or lavender in the species, but many shades of pink, white, or red in improved varieties. A later-blooming cousin, *P. capitata*, prefers drier, woodsy settings, where it will send up smaller rosettes of handsome, crinkly leaves and similar flower heads of silver blue in midsummer.

Elizabethan variants such as hose-in-hose and Jacks-in-the-green are spring-blooming variations in historical fancy dress. Some primroses are borne on slim, swinging stems, each tipped with two single flowers, one set neatly within the other. An outer blossom replaces the usual green primrose calyx in the hose-in-hose form, which recalls the ruffles tumbling from our ancestors' sleeves. The Jacks are true antiques, relics of the English florists, flower fanciers of centuries past who bred ornate forms of many cottage garden flowers. Jacks have a showy, outsized calyx—usually green, but occasionally colored, and sometimes accompanied by a feathery fluff of surrounding sepals—that dwarfs the actual flowers. Similar Elizabethans have starched and goffered green ruffs that frame the flowers after the fashion of Good Queen Bess. The flowers can be almost any color, which often extends to a stain on the green ruffs that persists long after the flowers themselves have faded.

Auriculas are also heritage plants, once the pampered darlings of the migrant weavers who made their way to England in the 16th century. Some are fabulously powdered, both flower and leaf, with a floury substance called farina. Bred for show, they can't tolerate garden life and require cosseting indoors. The thick, velvety flowers are vividly zoned in deep, mysterious shades that slip from tawny amber into copper, from black to midnight purple, crimson to blood red, lemon to white. Garden auriculas, also called dusty millers, are just as lovely, if less heavily floured. Not nearly so fussy as the show auriculas, these do just fine in ordinary garden situations. In my garden, they seem to prefer half sun or bright shade, and an open, humusy soil, but some people grow them beautifully in full sun and drier ground, so you may have to tinker a bit to find the best placement.

At first sight, *Primula kisoana* does not resemble a primrose at all. The hairy leaves are lobed and scalloped, much like those of coral bells (*Heuchera* species), but covered with short, woolly hairs. When these deciduous plants emerge from their winter hibernation, the tightly curled leaves look like roly-poly caterpillars. As the plants mature, the flower stalks sprout typical rosy pink primroses that unmistakably proclaim the family attachment. The leaves unfurl slowly, not reaching their full size until midsummer, long after the flowers have faded away. This makes these plants interesting during several seasons, for, thanks to their late arrival, the foliage continues to be handsome well into fall.

P. kisoana is native to the Japanese woods, and takes to woodsy Northwestern gardens with great enthusiasm. It prefers a rich, humusy soil that drains well, in light or bright shade. Given this situation (which often occurs beneath azaleas, rhododendrons, and similar shrubby spring bloomers), they will romp away, sending out fuzzy baby plants on underground runners. Within a few years, you can have a flourishing colony even if you only splurge on one mother plant. The white form, while rare, is slower, but still quite willing to spread. All you have to do is find a single plant, to be guaranteed success.

To meet the primrose family face to face, try to attend a meeting of the American Primula Society—there are branches all over the country, but the Northwestern chapters are particularly active. Each year Seattle's group hosts a stunning show and sale, where one can enjoy exhibits of prize-winning primulas in every imaginable category. The smallest varieties are arranged in bulb pans and stone troughs to emulate garden contexts in miniature. Both plants and seeds are for sale, and the deeply smitten may well decide to join the Primula Society right then and there, which at $10/year for a quarterly bulletin, regular meetings, shows, and a splendid seed exchange represents a true bargain.

In Search of Prettier Prunus

hat is prettier than a flowering plum in its fleeting season? Is there anything more enchanting than a frail cherry in full and fragrant bloom? What is lovelier in spring, and could anything be drearier for the rest of the year? Strolling through the changing urban neighborhoods, one finds that the only element common to all is the presence of prunus. In spring, it is all loveliness. In summer, one is still impressed, but only by the sheer quantity of the stuff. Considered by almost any criterion—numbers, weight, bulk, volume, whatever—the prunus tribe must be the most generously planted of all shrubs and trees. It seems curious that the most popular and frequently seen members of this enormous clan are rarely the most gardenworthy. If you are contemplating adding an ornamental stonefruit to your garden, consider the merits of some of the lesser-known varieties of prunus before plumping for yet another 'Kwanzan', or even, heaven forfend, the flashy, clashing 'Thundercloud'.

The charming Sargent cherry (*P. sargentii*) is seldom grown, yet is among the loveliest of its family. A regular and resplendent colorer in autumn, its many single flowers of soft pink appear early, amid bronzy-pink new leaves. Now, on paper, one could say the same thing about 'Thundercloud', but there is a crucial difference: in the Sargent cherry, the pink of the flowers is pale and pure, without a hint of blue; in 'Thundercloud', the pink is heavily tinted with purple, while the expanding foliage is copper red with hints of salmon. Red-pinks and blue-pinks never marry. The Sargent's leaves, translucent and suffused with chartreuse rather than red, are just emerging when the blossoms are in full spate, giving just a suggestion of pale golden bronze, which also helps make the effect harmonious rather than brash.

In form, the Sargent cherry is graceful where 'Kwanzan', say, is clunky; this takes on additional importance in winter, when all faults of outline are revealed. It grows tall in time, achieving perhaps 40 feet in as many years. In silhouette, it is upright rather than spreading, an appropriate choice for a large city lot or a country garden. All cherries tend to respond to excess pruning (amateur or professional) by sickening with bacterial or fungal diseases; when you see the hundreds of mutilated ornamentals throughout the city, it's hard to blame them. The sensible thing is to put a Sargent cherry—or indeed, any city tree—where it can develop its handsome natural shape unchecked. Should your chosen cherry not have a handsome, natural shape, don't plant it at all—choose another, or wait till the nursery has more in stock. This simplifies garden design and maintenance problems a good deal.

For smaller settings, *P. subhirtella* 'Autumnalis', the autumn cherry, will reward the gardener with showers of delicate white bloom beginning in October or November. In a mild year, it flowers more or less continuously through the winter, finishing up its long season with a final flurry in March or April. In colder years, there will be two distinct flowering periods, fall and spring, with scattered blossoms appearing at every thaw. The variety 'Rosea' carries a multitude of reddish buds which open to soft buff-pink flowers; this is the most common form around, but the species itself is worth seeking out for the delicacy of its snowy blossoms.

Both 'Autumnalis' and 'Rosea' can develop into good-size trees, though they are fairly slow to develop; both are quite suitable for a city setting. In England, they are frequently cut back hard when very young, and the resulting mass of shoots and suckers are thinned to produce a multi-trunked shrub. This does not seem to annoy the tree in the same way that hacking off large, mature branches does, perhaps because the effect is attractive—we all have our pride, after all. In any case, it is a practical solution to the prunus problem where space must be a powerful consideration. Mind, you probably can't do this to an established 'Autumnalis' with impunity, but the young are far more flexible about such things. If you want to underplant the shrub, once the basic framework of trunks has been selected you simply trim off the twiggy side branches to two or three feet above the ground, then plant away. Should the surrounding soil be too rooty, surround your shrub with a wheelbarrow load of fluffy new topsoil, taking care to leave the crown of the tree unsmothered, then add something nice—perhaps a clematis, some small bulbs, and a creeping ground cover.

Many prunus species do eventually create a dense canopy of rooty, dry shade, but the airy, rather open and arching branches of a connoisseur's flowering plum, 'Ukon', make a dappled pool of light shade in which many plants will thrive and bloom. Subtle not showy, 'Ukon' bears abundant crops of large, single flowers of palest yellow tinged with green, veined and stained with plummy purple at the heart. Against purple hazel or beech, or your neighbors' 'Thundercloud', 'Ukon' shimmers, cool and mysterious. Come fall, the leaves brighten to shades of red gold, brass, and copper, and when they tumble, reveal great beauties of line and form.

For the smallest setting, *P. cistena* is a dwarf red-leafed plum which can live happily in a big tub or planter box by poolside or patio. It makes a trim little standard, though seldom seen in this form (standards are trees with single trunks—often clipped into lollipops). Generally grown as a multi-trunked shrub, *P. cistena* may be considered a shapely miniature tree of character for tiny gardens, once trimmed of its lowest side branches. A small plant looks utterly distinguished in a big terra-cotta pot, underplanted with trailing silvery herbs—lotus vine or lacy artemisias—and long strands of the wandering Jew, a houseplant with folded, incurving leaves of velvety purple. Thread these streamers with plain-faced violas of apricot or terra-cotta, unless you prefer to match them to the clean, clear ruby of the leaves, and your sumptuous composition will sing all summer. The flowers are dainty, whiskery little things, ivory white with ruby red stamens that echo the leaf color. Dark leaves can become oppressive in summer, but these remain relatively fresh-looking, changing from claret red in spring to deep purple red over the summer, a pleasing backdrop for the chubby little fruits, glossy and almost black. In fall, the leaf color deepens once again and drops quite late, giving this prunus interest over an exceptionally long season.

April is a splendid time to plant trees, but if you don't manage it, give some time over the summer to consideration of where one of these plants might be best placed in your garden. Come fall, you will be ready to plant. If you already have an overgrown or unlovely flowering tree in place, this might be the year to rid yourself of it. Once the dud is gone, you can review your new yard with fresh eyes before deciding where its more deserving successor will go. The removal of a tree is a daunting task, and not one to take on lightly; mature trees give a neighborhood character and have qualities that are irreplaceable in our lifetimes. However, where those qualities are negative ones, where the health of the tree is in question, or where a large tree has been disfigured by ignorant pruning, removal is a valid option. Our urban gardens are so small, we can't afford the deadweight of plants which offer only fleeting charms yet take up so very much room. The selections above (and many others with similar strengths) offer us two, three, or four seasons of pleasure, and are reliable performers both in spring and again in autumn. Rather than moderate our desires (never!), it behooves us to be intelligent in our choices and give the edge to such garden treasures as these.

Wheeling Weeds

In some years, unseasonable siren weather lures us into the garden far too early, but those pools of sunshine that coax us out-of-doors promise more than they deliver. It's cold out there, and once the initial spring tidying is accomplished, little else is safe to attempt during these chilly days, beyond baiting for slugs, weeding, and watching spring arrive. Up leap the proud shoots from the mother bulbs below the ground. Many stalks are already big with bloom, and each must be ringed with slug death right now if we want those hopeful buds to achieve their full potential.

Most years in the Northwest prove to be banner years for slugs, thanks to the usual mild winters. The little gastropods take full advantage of any such clemency, multiplying from strength to strength before our wondering eyes. A veritable tiger of a slug, nearly seven inches long and fiercely striped and stippled all over, was nestled snugly in the warm compost bin. Sliced with the shovel and circled with slug death, he will serve as bait for his greedy cannibal relatives, who will flock to feed at the small corpse, exhibiting all the charming manners of their kind.

The nursery bed, where small divisions, seedlings, and cuttings grow on to flowering size in pampered and non-competitive comfort, is a favorite grazing ground for slugs, and doses of bran-based bait get sprinkled around the awakening infants. Though the plants placed here are often tiny, the nursery bed is apt to be foaming with freshest green as early as February. What happy plant is this, responding so lushly to the faint and feeble spring sunshine?

Nothing is so beautiful as Spring—
When weeds, in wheels, shoot long and lovely and lush...
What is all this juice and all this joy?

queries G. M. Hopkins, that earnest admirer of the natural world (and clearly a nongardener). Chickweed, that cheerful and untiring worker, is the usual source, busily covering the damp earth with tight little stitches of green, each clump embroidered all over with tiny white flowers. This eager spreader definitely needs to be kept in check, yet it is far from harmful in many situations, making a loose and moisture-conserving ground cover for daylilies or half-grown shrubs. It is less wonderful when growing over and through tiny seedlings, but it does offer splendid compost material, armloads of it, most welcome at a time when nitrogen sources are few.

There are far worse enemies about than chickweed; any of the taprooted hawkweeds and dandelions now wheeling their way into the garden will need to be pulled as soon as possible. Often the winter will have left the soil soft and open, and tremendous roots will come nicely up to hand. When this is not the case, try cutting off the tops every time they resprout. The most stubborn weeds can be vanquished by following each trimming session with a dose of high-strength fertilizer—as much as a teaspoon per plant, poured directly on the cut stem. This seems odd, perhaps, but if the fertilizer doesn't kill them outright, which it may well do, the combination of feeding and cutting will eventually exhaust the root. Since some taproots penetrate as much as 17 feet below the soil surface, this may understandably take some time. In spring, when all their energy is directed to new growth, the weeds are particularly susceptible to the cut-and-overfeed approach. Docks and dandelions present no special threat, but where bristling, prickly Canadian thistles abound, the gardener is well advised to use heavy gloves before trying to pull or cut the tops.

Another expansive rosette, dark green and studded and pimpled with needle-sharp prickles above and below the long, puckered leaves, belongs to the teasel plant. Its odd seedheads are the size and shape of an egg, covered with tiny bristles and encased in a setting of curving guard spikes, like a punk jeweler's cage for a gem. Dried teasel heads were used commercially until quite recent times to brush or tease the surface of woven cloth—thus the common name. Tall and dramatic, teasel is a splendid plant to enjoy where there is plenty of room, but in small city gardens the plants should be gingerly—gloves on—eased out of the borders and bid a firm farewell.

The ubiquitous annual spurge can be a dainty and attractive plant in a meadow or a wild garden, where it looks handsome for most of the year. Abundant stalks bear diamond-shaped leaves and numerous branchlets, every tiny stem bearing a paired set of bracts. Inside each is a curled leaflet and a minute, whiskery flower, typical of the euphorbia family to which it belongs. When it blooms, spurge is a fresh foam of lemon and lime as the bracts color gayly. However, if allowed to seed (and who can stop it?), annual spurge quickly becomes a menace among more polite plants. Pull all you see in early spring, even inch-tall seedlings, and you are well ahead of the game.

The Welsh poppy, *Meconopsis cambrica*, doesn't look like a weed, and its silky flowers of yellow or clear orange bloom bravely for months on end. It seeds itself equally well, however, and it is apt to become treated as a weed even in gardens where its presence was actively sought. Not a rampant plant, as a seedling it can be easily thinned or rooted out now. The foliage is light green and looks rather like Italian parsley; the leaflets are triangular, lobed, and scalloped. As soon as the new leaves emerge, tipping you off to their presence, you can pull out the long root of maturing plants. Shallow-rooted seedlings can be moved if you act fast, but once the roots strike deep, pulled plants or thinnings can only be composted.

Weeding is a companionable process, one that keeps our relationship with our plants intimate. Each emerging crown, each plump bud, each swelling shoot stands out clearly against bare soil or mulch, to be greeted or dealt with. We fondly greet old favorites, anxiously check for signs of late-developers, revel in the abundance of self-sown alyssum and forget-me-nots. These two plants form dense tangles of seedlings; thinnings removed now to other spots will bloom a little later than those left in place, their slight setback extending the show for some weeks. Despite the cold, the wind, and the occasional showers, there is great delight in renewing our acquaintance in the burgeoning garden, and there's no better time to get the jump on those wheeling weeds.

New Brooms Make Clean Sweeps

The Northwest is infested with hulking, angular Scotch broom, a weedy species with takeover tendencies that make its cheerful golden flowers less than welcome in a garden. None of its relatives share its reproductive skill, and among them are multitudes of year-round beauties that remain sadly underplanted. Few other shrubs can match the total abandon with which the brooms bedeck themselves, filling the garden with light. They pour out their blossoms as effortlessly as the blackbirds pour out their liquid, chunking spring music, and both are an essential, irreplaceable ingredient for spring magic. Widely used in Europe, brooms have never quite found their role in American gardens, and they tend to be relegated to rough spots where little else will grow—the verges of the driveway, the edge of the alley. This is a pity, for there are suitable brooms for every garden, no matter how tiny the available space.

Cytisus scoparius, that black-sheep Scotch broom, has few ardent fans, yet it is undoubtedly a plant with many strengths. Drought-tolerant, rarely requiring pruning, well able to fend for itself against all odds—short of a speeding automobile—Scotch broom has made itself thoroughly at home in the Northwest. When it seeds itself luxuriantly in the back yard, it seldom finds a warm reception, but gardeners who value stoutly self-supporting plants will want to make garden room for at least one of the mannerly scoparius hybrids. All are drought-tolerant after their first year, and quickly achieve maturity, yet most are compact enough to find a place even in small gardens. Best of all, they are carefree and virtually invulnerable to pests or diseases.

For 51 weeks of each year, brooms are neat, evergreen shrubs, a lovely place to hang a summer-blooming clematis or gaudy annual vine. They bloom in one concentrated burst, so that every twig is covered with bright blossoms in a display exceeded only by certain species roses. Their only graceless period immediately follows this tremendous output, but the browning blossoms drop as quickly as they unfold, and within a week the shrubs are once again groomed and dapper. Because brooms grow so quickly, they rarely hold a permanent place in the garden; you can count on having a broom in full beauty from the second through perhaps the tenth year of its life. By then, many will be shapeless and overgrown, ready for replacement with vigorous young plants. However, my island garden holds an ancient specimen of 'Moonlight' that has the height and character of a small tree, with a gnarled trunk fully four inches across. It seems in excellent health and continues to flower rapturously, though it grows in what has become almost total shade thanks to a maturing willow nearby.

If you have a small garden and want a shapely little shrub to fill an awkward corner, consider the charms of Cytisus scoparius 'Carla', a pretty creature with blossoms of rich crimson and silver pink. She seems to wear pure rose from a distance, a clear, warm rose without a trace of yellow in it. Viewed close up, each glowing red blossom is seen to be lined with palest silvery pink. 'Carla' looks especially handsome when surrounded by grey artemisias, the dark 'Palace Purple' heucheras, and soft grey-green mounds of the giant catmint, Nepeta x faassenii 'Six Hills Giant', which carries fountains of gentle blue flowers for months on end. Gentler color comes from 'Pink Spot', not a scoparius hybrid, but a form of C. multiflorus, the white Spanish broom, itself a handsome tall shrub for the larger garden. 'Pink Spot' gets rather taller, and blooms a week or two earlier than 'Carla', who joins in with the majority of the scoparius hybrids in late April or early May.

In gardens too small to hold a full-sized lilac tree or shrub, the scoparius hybrid 'Lilac Time' could take its place. This one is smothered with frothy flowers in faded grape shades, the smoky mauves and deep purples of watered silk. Actually, it makes a delightful companion for an older lilac, which will then spill down its fragrance on the less pleasantly perfumed broom. As the name implies, 'Lilac Time' blooms with the true lilacs, and a neat row of this broom below a hedge of lilac trees would be worth seeing. It also looks lovely against the silver-leafed shrub Senecio greyi, along with a sheaf of purple, feather-edged parrot tulips and creamy sprays of butter yellow Rosa primula.

C. scoparius 'Burkwoodii', almost a mahogany red from a distance, is actually a bi-tone with ruby-colored banner and wings and a deep gold keel. This one forms a cloud of dark, muted red that looks sumptuous when planted near a smoke bush, Cotinus coggygria, with purple-stained foliage, or the cream-and-rose variegated barberry, Berberis thunbergii 'Rose Glow'. Where a brighter red is wanted, the compact 'San Francisco' broom will be just the ticket.

Although the Northwest has seen relatively few of these fancy brooms in the past, they are widely used in California. Whenever they do turn up in local nurseries, they sell like hotcakes the minute their blossoms open. One frantic gardener showed up at her favorite nursery clutching a sprig of 'Lilac Time' and loudly demanding the rest of the plant. It developed that she had seen the swag of fat lavender flowers in a vase at a nearby restaurant and was swept clean away by the new broom. Fortunately, the nursery staff was able to produce the plant and the gardener went home happy. If you, too, feel the urge to make sweeping garden changes, consider investing in a few new brooms.

Breaking Up and Moving On

fter a year's absence, we returned to our Seattle garden, which had been in the care of friends. Much as they enjoyed the garden as we had left it, our friends were becoming interested in growing a few things of their own. Even after the wholesale removal of choice plants which took place when we moved, the garden was still grossly overfilled. Besides, practically everything left behind had doubled in size, taking up all the available space. Our friends were hard pressed to find room for a tulip or two, let alone the little herb garden they longed for. The garden was simply too full to allow the introduction of anything new. This frustration was all too familiar; indeed, the need for new ground was a major factor in our difficult decision to leave the city.

Making space in a crowded garden is no simple task. A single square foot of ground might house a dozen plants, sometimes more. Whenever we moved plants, each shovelful of dirt would yield a perennial, some bits of ground cover, and a handful of bulbs, all of which needed a new home as well as accurate labeling. Now the season was advancing, my time was limited, and any big removal was going to have to happen fast, so I recruited several big-hearted friends to help. I pre-labeled many of the plants we needed to move, but as always, others appeared as we worked that needed ad hoc tagging and bagging. "Androsace lanuginosa," I might cry out, handing over a lump of greenery to the bag lady beside me. Then a shrub, "Caryopteris clandonensis," or a handful of roots, "Schizostylus coccinea." My loyal buddies, stout nongardeners all, would respond with shouts of laughter and kindly write out the closest approximations they could muster. (The plantwise person who was supposed to be sitting comfortably making labels for everything had produced a healthy, handsome baby boy that morning, and decided not to show up after all.) When the time came to reset the plants in the new garden, it was astonishing to see what sea changes the names had undergone—some of the interpretations were ingenious indeed, and we will be sorting out varieties of iris and daylilies for years to come.

Those who find themselves forced to move established plants at a moment's notice will find the task easier if they are well equipped. Shovels, one large, one small; a variety of hand tools, including pruners; labels and pens; a huge supply of plastic bags and newspaper; plant pots and a few old boxes will about cover it, with a bucket or two of water on the side. Smallish perennials are easily moved, even by the inexperienced, for they can be taken up with a good-sized rootball, soil and all, and plunked into plastic bags. Form-fitting plastic holds the soil closely against the roots and keeps the drying air away. The bags may be layered in boxes to keep them separated and to avoid crushing anything; you can cram an incredible number of plants into a Volkswagen bus this way.

Bigger clumps of perennials are harder to move unless subjected to long and short division; each mother plant is broken up carefully, then the whole group is bagged and boxed together to keep the varieties straight. This may avoid an aftermath of total confusion, especially when working with iris and daylilies. I defy anybody to positively identify half-dormant divisions of either plant. There are thousands of named cultivars, and all are virtually indistinguishable when out of flower. For anything you don't want to break up—perhaps a maturing peony—pry the clump from the ground as best you can, then ease it into an oversize plastic bag. Slide that onto a flattened box, and you will be able to sled perfectly huge plants down steps or sidewalk with relative ease. Where there is wheelbarrow access, the flat box will keep things together while you slip-tug-push the plant into the tipped barrow. Once at least half the plant is on board, one person tips the barrow upright while somebody else shoves the plant the rest of the way in. By this time, you—or your friends—may well decide that two or three small peonies are actually nicer than one huge one.

In late winter or spring, daylilies won't mind a sudden move, but early-blooming iris might sulk a bit. Still, if they are replanted fast enough, they won't be set back much. Most perennials bloom in summer and fall, and if they are moved properly, they will rarely suffer. Both large plants and divisions should be whisked straight into their new homes, each tucked into a largish hole filled with plentifully amended soil and compost. Keep them well watered, but otherwise leave them alone to recover their equanimity. Once they develop new growth, give them a feeding mulch of aged manure, compost, peat, and sawdust or shredded bark.

Established shrubs and small trees need special treatment if they are to tolerate a move well. Ideally, one goes around and root-prunes them with a heavy shovel late in the fall, giving them a couple of cool months to get over that indignity before hoicking them out of their holes. Since none of us had planned that far ahead, I did the next best thing and went about giving notice of eviction with my little border spade about a month before moving day (the garden is so tightly planted that using a large shovel results in wanton destruction). With smaller shrubs, we teased the entire root system out of the crowded ground whenever possible, but some of the larger plants necessarily lost a lot of root in the process. Since all got good remedial treatment soon thereafter, none were lost, though some of the older shrubs were never quite the same again. Cuttings from resentful movers such as brooms, cistus, and ceanothus will develop quickly, and though it will be a few years before the youngsters can fill their places in the new garden, taking cuttings will probably be more satisfactory in the long run than trying to move an unwilling golden-ager.

There are two schools of thought on whether one should cut back the top growth of trees and shrubs before transplanting. Pruners figure that since much of the root system is lost or damaged and the whole plant is shocked, removing a comparable amount of the upper growth restores the root/branch balance and prevents the plant from killing itself in trying to support its outlying portions. The laissez-faire school assumes that part of the function of leaves is to supply the plant with nutrients, so the more the merrier. This school advocates transplant pruning only for aesthetic reasons. Any limb or portion of the plant which is clearly damaged or suffering may be cut off, but unless the need is obvious, you leave the whole thing alone to recover in peace. Any part that doesn't make it can be discreetly removed a few months down the road.

The next step is also debatable, for many experts will insist that trees and shrubs should be planted directly into the existing soil in the chosen spot, without benefit of soil amendments of any kind. This is the begin-as-you-mean-to-go-on school, which holds that a tree has a certain soil to live with, and it will do better if it gets used to that soil right away. Others, myself firmly included, feel that every plant benefits from improved soil, and we act accordingly. In my garden, each larger plant gets an enormous hole, the bottom of which is filled with a quart or so of peat moss, some well-rotted manure, and a whole bucketful of compost. This is all mixed up with the topsoil from the hole, then room is made for the rootball. The plant is introduced and the nice new dirt is heaped around the trunk, then tamped gently down. After the plant is well watered in, any extra soil is patted into a sort of moat a foot or so out from the crown or trunk; this keeps water where you want it, near the root zone. Again, no feeding mulch is added until the plant shows active growth.

As we finished up our last raid on the old homestead, the car was packed to the roof and the tired team was ready to depart. Our friend Sandy, now mistress of a half-empty garden, looked dazed and a little shaken as she bid us farewell. As we climbed into our seats, my husband of many years pointed out one little oversight; there was no room left for the children. And where were the children, anyway? A hasty search of the car produced a small one, tucked peacefully between a large rhododendron and a small Portuguese laurel. He had his blanket and his pink stuffed dinosaur, his seatbelt was fastened, and he was ready to roll. The other, I finally recalled, was waiting it out at a friend's house—and clearly, the friend's mom would have to bring the kid home, for you couldn't fit so much as a foxglove into that overloaded car. My hot, sweaty crew retired, several of them muttering darkly that they were definitely going to bag aerobics that evening and they had no idea that gardening could be so strenuous. Well, it isn't always, but everybody knows that breaking up is hard to do. Still, there's nothing like moving to get a gardener inspired to start all over again, aching muscles or no.

Passive Composting

A LOW-TECH GUIDE FOR BEMUSED GARDENERS

irt lacks glamour. Of all the many aspects of gardening, dirt-making gets the shortest shrift. This is ironic, for the best piece of advice a knowing gardener can give to a novice has got to be, "Make beautiful dirt." Think of dirt as the foundation of the garden; nobody builds a house on an unprepared site, and the same should be true for gardens. Making the garden before making gardenworthy dirt is like arranging fine furniture in rooms with plywood floors and unfinished walls. It makes a picture all right, but probably not the one intended.

Beautiful dirt feels, looks, and smells nice, and contact with it is a positive pleasure to both the gardener and the plants. It is perfectly true that turning raw dirt into rich soil requires some effort, but even that has its advantages. Dirtwork is cheaper than taking exercise classes, you don't need matching tights or fancy shoes, there is no disco music, and best of all, nobody is watching you in the mirror. Should your technique occasionally lack finesse, that remains your secret.

Granted the need to make pleasant dirt, why bother with compost? Experienced gardeners, even very busy ones, want compost because it is the soil builder supreme; better than manure, better than peat, far, far superior to any sort of artificial fertilizer, compost will actually alter the structure of your dirt. It turns dense, weeping clay into open, friable loam. It changes loose sand into retentive soil with body. Naturally enough, one batch of compost won't cause dramatic changes overnight, but the difference between improved and unimproved beds will be apparent almost at once.

Better texture, more worms, and sturdy, healthy plants are the initial benefits wherever compost has been generously incorporated. If you only have a little compost, lavish it in one small area at a time rather than giving the whole yard a tentative sprinkling. As the seasons roll around, the improved areas will show dramatic changes, egging you on to perform the same magic on the rest of the garden. In our small Seattle garden, beds which had been double dug a single time, then well mulched with compost for five

74

years had soil so open that you could plunge your arm into the dirt up to your elbow. By contrast, each new area we took on was solid yellow clay that formed a water-shedding crust when worked, baked in the summer, and held plants in such an unforgiving grip that some of them never got over the initial encounter and ended up disfigured for life. Even a single exuberant application of compost had a beneficial effect, and by the second year of compost mulching, the soil in the new beds was visibly better in color, texture, and tilth. What is this miracle-working stuff?

Compost is a simple but misunderstood substance. In a word, compost is humus. Rich, dark, and crumbly, it is the garden itself, recycled: plants and other organic components decomposed through microbial action. This can happen very slowly or in a matter of weeks, depending on what materials are used, their relative sizes and quantities, and how they are assembled. Making compost is really as simple as making bread or beer, and the process is not dissimilar. Soil-digesting bacteria, like yeasts, need warmth, moisture, air, and something to feed on to keep them alive and growing. Nearly all practical problems with making bread, beer, and compost stem from too much or too little of those basic ingredients.

The mystique of serious composting makes the whole business seem an arcane science, and an understandably intimidating one. For a lot of people, such chemical complications are an insuperable obstacle to regular composting. It is true that to do traditional—"hot"—composting effectively and consistently, one must be able to evaluate compostable materials in order to keep the all-important carbon/nitrogen ratio (a hotly debated subject in itself) just so. Fortunately, for practical purposes, it suffices to classify all compostable matter as wet or dry, green or brown, fresh or old, rather than as high in nitrogen or carbon. This simplifies decision making a good deal. It may not be science, but it works.

Warmth is another confusing element in the process. Many people have the impression that compost piles should be steaming hot, and indeed, a well-constructed pile can reach temperatures high enough to hurt your hand. It will also be hot enough to kill worms, a side effect that can be considered a serious drawback. Fewer people are aware that there is a simpler, slower composting method, usually called "passive" composting. It doesn't rely on heat so much as upon time; for those who neither need nor want large, continual supplies of compost, slow composting is an ideal solution. It involves very little work, recycles kitchen and garden wastes, and reduces the volume of outgoing trash as well (where trash removal is billed by quantity, as it is in Seattle, this is no small consideration).

Many gardeners are reluctant to give up precious garden space to a traditional composting system. To be successful, hot composting requires a good balance of nitrogenous and carbonaceous materials in large quantities, since hot piles must be ample to be efficient (a minimum size of three or four cubic feet is the usual recommendation). Few small yards produce large quantities of compostable waste on a regular basis, which is why serious composters glean their materials from all over the place. The bins used for storing and processing bulky materials must be big enough both to hold a good volume and to give the gardener room to turn the pile. Most often, a hot compost batch will be started at one end of a series of bins, turned and mixed into the second bin when the temperature of the pile falls, then removed to a third holding bin or used in the garden after a few weeks. Each time a bin is emptied, a new pile takes its place. This method involves a good deal of work, not the least of which is amassing the materials and learning how to blend an effective mixture, but it is a practical way to generate a lot of compost all through the year.

All this takes a lot of time, and demands space which few urban yards can easily spare. In contrast, passive composting requires only a single bin. Holding units can be relatively small, generally taking up less than a square yard of ground space. Most have a capacity of between 50 and 80 gallons, enough to work significant changes on most small gardens. The bin is filled with grass clippings, soft prunings, and other garden wastes whenever they occur, in no particular order. Kitchen scraps are tossed in as well, covered with a handful of grass or a thin layer of dirt to avoid smells. The energetic can use a composting wand to stir up their pile, while the less inspired can simply let things rip undisturbed. No matter what you do or don't do, you will eventually have usable compost, full of wriggling worms. How soon you get that compost depends on several factors.

A passive pile may take a couple of months or a couple of years to mature, depending on what you use and how you treat it. Woody prunings and dried leaves might require two full years to break down, and it would be worth setting up several bins if much of your garden waste is hard and dry. However, investing in even a modest shredding machine will speed things up considerably, since the smaller the pieces you put in your pile, the faster and finer the compost you get out will be. Chopping or shredding larger things like corn stalks, cabbage stumps, prunings, and beefy but aged annuals will reduce their bulk and will turn a dauntingly large mass into an astonishingly small pile to add to the bin. Shredded and mixed with grass clippings, that same woody pile would break down in months, rather than years.

Air is vitally important to any composting process (anaerobic composting is possible, but highly unpleasant). When a pile of rotting material starts to smell terrible, it is nearly always because there is too much nitrogen (read "fresh grass clippings") and too little air in the mixture. Heavy, compacted compost that clumps, molds, or turns slimy is simply oxygen-starved. All it needs to get it back on track is a breath of fresh air. Fortunately, there are several easy ways to provide for adequate oxygen without resorting to mixing things up with a pitchfork.

To avoid such clumping in the first place, always add roughly equal amounts of dry material and fresh greenstuff to your compost bin. Mix grass trimmings or fresh green leaves with shredded pruning material, fine wood chips, or hay. On its own, grass has a distinct tendency to form a big wad which can take a year to degrade. If your basic material is grass, grass, and more grass, dry half of each batch on the driveway or let it dry on the lawn before raking it up. Mix the resulting "hay" with the green clippings, and they will break down without putrescence. An even simpler solution is to keep a bag of sawdust or finely ground bark beside the composter. Fresh greenstuffs can be mixed with either one to advantage and with very little effort.

Once it hits the bin, compost can be left strictly alone for several months, after which time the eager gardener can begin to harvest the final product from the bottom of the bin even while continuing to add to the top. Should you wish to encourage the process in a mild sort of way, or want a load in a hurry, the bin contents may be periodically aerated. This is most easily done with a composting wand, a slender metal pole with collapsing wings at the working end. When inserted, the wings lie flat against the pole, making it easy to shove deep into the pile. When the wand is pulled back, the wings pop out like a molly bolt, leaving a good-size hole in the pile and mixing the bottom layer with recent additions at the same time. If your compost tends to be wet and heavy, a few good pulls with a composting tool every month or so will lighten things up considerably.

In Oregon, master gardener Peter Chan aerates his passive pile by keeping a stout pipe upright in the center. Each time new material is added to the pile, the pipe gets a good wiggle. He comments that in China gardeners use thick bamboo rods with the center sections split open as aerators.

Rotating tumblers or barrel composters are oxygenated by revolving the entire bin each time new material is added. If even that seems too much like work, a few twiggy sticks inserted throughout the pile as it is accumulating will create air pockets with no help from the gardener at all.

As long as compost gets plenty of air, it will seldom be too wet. Should a batch seem inert, however, it is probably too dry. If investigation reveals an unaltered mass of leaves and sticks, your best bet is to give the whole collection a good soaking, then toss in a generous amount of grass clippings or other greenstuffs. Confine future additions to 50/50 blends of fresh and dry materials, and keep any compost, active or passive, covered to conserve moisture. Tucking a heavy plastic bag over the top of the pile will help a good deal, even if your holding unit has a cover. When drought strikes and temperatures soar, give the compost an occasional hosing down—once or twice a summer will suffice in most cases.

Despite the initial cost, bins or holding units are a good investment for almost everybody, but they are of special value to those with small, urban gardens. Bins look tidier than random piles, and keep curious animals from investigating the contents. If possible, site the unit(s) conveniently near the kitchen, so that tossing in the cooking scraps is easy. Selecting the right container in which to save kitchen wastes can make a surprising difference to the way that little chore is viewed. After years of experimentation, we have hit upon our current ideal—a sturdy plastic juice pitcher which holds a gallon of scraps, has a deep, easily inserted lid with a broad handgrip, and doesn't retain odors. It stays under the sink when not in use. It is small enough that the contents don't start composting on their own, yet holds enough to make the trip to the compost bin worthwhile. The lid is tight enough that no smells leak out, yet it is easy to remove with one hand. These may seem like minor points, yet such minutiae can mean the difference between enthusiastic or grudging participation.

Kitchen wastes are unlikely to be the backbone of your composting effort, yet for many of us there is a psychological value to recycling what we don't eat. A friend to whom we had bequeathed our small Soilsaver unit when we left the city wrote a note to say that composting has changed her family's life and eating habits. "We hover over the fruitbowl now, and view our leftovers in a different light," she goes on. "Eggshell crushing, as you recommended, works nicely, feels satisfying, and makes a delightful crunching noise. We squabble over who gets to do it." Not everybody is going to get such rewards from the process, but lucky are those who do.

This same family raised a final and important point, for when they were ready to empty their composter, they slid open the doors at the base and found not black gold, not rich, crumbling earth with a texture like an angel food cake, but lumpy, coarse stuff with crushed eggshells very much in evidence and looking much as they had when inserted at the top. What had gone wrong? Well, nothing really. Quite often in life there is a jarring moment when the ideal becomes the actual. My friends' great expectations were as crushed as the eggshells, yet the apparent failure was easily remedied. For those like our friends, who view their first batch of compost with bitter disappointment, success is only a screening away. The truth is, compost is lumpy.

In order to get that lovely, finely textured seedling soil you dreamed about, you have to rub the compost through a heavy screen or sieve. They come in several sizes and weights, or can be made by wrapping coarse hardware cloth over the wheelbarrow and shoveling the compost on top. It isn't strictly necessary, though, for there are lots of good uses for unscreened compost. Dig it, lumps and all, into new garden beds. Use it, on top of a coarse gravel layer, as the bottom layer of soil in containers, urns, window boxes. Break it up a bit and treat your perennials to a light feeding mulch.

Should you want to empty your current bin and start over again, you can use the half-done compost in similar ways—just cover it with a layer of topsoil. It will break down nicely all by itself and deliver balanced, buffered nutrients to whatever you plant above it. The next time you dig in that bed, you will discover that your garden is well on its way to beautiful dirt. You may never come to think of dirt as glamorous, but your plants surely will.

Mail-Order Babies

was delighted to find a box of plants on the porch when we got home the other day. I usually forget exactly what I ordered, so there is something of the feeling of a birthday party on these occasions—what could it be? Inside this particular box were half a dozen rues, three each of *Thalictrum aquilegiifolium*, the columbine meadow rue, and *Thalictrum glaucum*, the dusty meadow rue. The columbine rue has finely cut, dainty leaves of steel blue, very like those of their namesake relatives, the columbines. Tall, slim stalks are topped with fluffy, puffy flower heads in lavender, purple, or white, from late spring into early summer. To my eye, the airy, bronzed seedheads which follow the flowers are attractive in their own right, making a light scrim or veil through which to view the farther reaches of the border. They do this very nicely both at the back of a small, narrow border, or near the middle of a big one; nearly three feet tall, they are delicate plants despite their bulk, well-suited to small gardens.

The dusty rue is taller, reaching as much as six feet in height, though it is only perhaps two feet wide. This one has broader leaves of deep blue-grey, handsome from earliest spring till blackened by frost. The flowers are spumy, abundant puffs of Chinese yellow, very long-lasting, and beautiful at every stage of their life. Plants in an open, sunny position will bloom in May or June, those in half shade in mid-June and July. They, too, make an insubstantial curtain through which the rest of the garden is seen dimly, suggestively. Placed just beside a gate or entryway, rue forms a delicate barrier which seems to expand whatever lies beyond it. The contents of even a tiny garden will seem mysterious when viewed through a haze of rue blossom or seedheads. Tall meadow rues are also very effective when placed behind or mingled with the stodgier rhododendrons, where their repeated, upright forms have a marvelously lightening effect on the surrounding shrubbery.

There are many other meadow rues, among them several charming wildlings found in alpine meadows throughout the Northwest. Many have dainty leaves much like those of the maidenhair fern, and though their flowers are less showy than the garden forms, they are often in subtle color runs of olive, khaki, and muted purples that flower arrangers would cheerfully kill for. Nearly all are quiet beauties which merit placement in woodsy Northwest gardens, blooming abundantly even in shade. Small plants may be found at the sales of our many local plant societies, and are well worth watching for.

The plants in my box were small ones, suitable for mailing. Their rootballs were wrapped in damp sphagnum moss, then in moistened newspaper secured with light rubber bands. The bundles were marked with labels and nestled carefully in plastic packing chips. When unpacked, each plant showed a dense rootball to which the soil clung, and the top growth, though short, showed vigor and healthy color. There are other packing methods which are just as effective as this, but only when the results are consistently this good can a mail-order company be considered a bargain. In general, it is preferable to buy well-grown plants at a local nursery, for these will transplant straight into the garden with little fuss. However, a distant mail-order nursery may be the only source for an uncommon plant, and then one has no choice but to take a risk with the traumas of travel.

For those who have only bought plants locally, it can be disconcerting to receive plants through the mail; some places send minute scraps, barely rooted, which need a great deal of nursing to grow to blooming size. Although small plants can be a good value, these mail-order babies almost always need a season in a nursery bed before being set into the garden. Some will want a full year of pampering before facing the mixed company of a boisterous border. Plants which suffered in transit or sat in cold storage for months before they were shipped may sulk for several seasons, and certain slow-growers that hate disturbance need the uncompetitive peace of the nursery in which to rebuild their strength. Usually, though, spring arrivals grown in the nursery all summer and then transplanted in fall will be established, productive members of the border by the following year. Fall additions may well be ready to move up to the big time by the following spring.

A well-made nursery bed will rival the vegetable garden for richness of soil, since it gets the same sort of treatment: lots of compost, rotted manure and stable sweepings, bone, soy and cottonseed meals, kelp and greensand, and a very thorough digging to incorporate all these nice things into the stiff native clay. All this must then be raked to a fine tilth, mulched well and left for a season to mellow. Persistent weeds are pulled and composted, and by fall, an impatient array of youngsters may be tucked in for a productive winter of root growth.

Where there is any possibility of choice in the matter, it is a good idea for at least part of the nursery bed to be in shade. High shade from tall trees whose branches are many feet off the ground is the most beneficial, allowing filtered light to reach the plants, yet shielding them from full sun and harsh winds. Shade cloth stretched over light wooden frames creates kindly shadows and shelter where nature doesn't, and such panels may be moved about the beds as the need arises. Deep shade, whether dank or dry, won't do; new plants are vulnerable to an excess of all the things they need. Plenty of light is good, but direct sun can kill. They need a consistent supply of water, but the soil must be well drained as well as nourishing. The free passage of air keeps molds and mildews at bay, but strong winds can damage or fatally parch young plants.

In our small city garden where ground space was at a premium, the actual nursery bed was minute, about 50 feet square. A tiered shelf-rack similar to those used for outdoor displays at garden shops held seed trays, four-inch pots, and bulb pans on slightly outward-tilting shelves. The lowest tray was three feet off the ground, while the tallest was at eye height; every plant was easily reached and cared for. The rack stood above a narrow bed along the back fence, its feet underplanted with hostas and small spring bulbs. As plants grew up, they were moved from seed tray to pot to nursery bed as quickly as possible, then whisked on to taste the fuller life in the borders. Their spaces were filled almost immediately by newcomers in need of intensive care, or faltering treasures which wanted fattening up before returning to the fray, in the familiar cycle of the gardener's year.

Terrorists in Tents

CATERPILLAR ALERT

ent caterpillars, those voracious little pests which can reduce a full-grown tree to tatters in just a few weeks, appear in varying quantities each year. The West is blessed with a number of natural predators, swallows and tiny parasitic wasps among them, and generally a banner year for caterpillars is followed by a tremendous influx of these beneficial predators. Even knowing that revenge is on the wing, a serious infestation is a painful sight. The caterpillars favor such garden plants as ornamental cherries and plums, crabapples—indeed, fruit trees of all sorts. They also like mountain ash, lilacs, and roses, among other things. In a bad year, they will eat hawthorn, willow, birch and alder, daylilies, honeysuckle, phygelius—in short, if you have a garden, sooner or later you will have tent caterpillars too.

That first sight of a grey, sticky web mass on a beloved plant comes as a shock, and for many people, the initial impulse is to reach for a spray gun. However, where there are just a few nests, the best option is to handpick the revolting little creatures to bag and burn. The squeamish will want to wear gloves, but those whose hatred is consuming may take pleasure in the hands-on process. The tents can be pulled off or gently scraped off using the back of a plastic picnic utensil (doing this through a plastic bag, as when scooping up dog droppings, preserves one's dainty hands from contamination and captures the tent neatly at the same time).

If, however, you are in the midst of a Total Experience, consider the wonderful ways of a deadly little bacterium known as *Bacillus thuringiensis*, or Bt for short. Many gardeners take their stewardship role seriously, preferring not to depend on malathion or worse chemicals to "fix" natural occurrences. Gardening itself is an unnatural act, yet we who love the smell and touch of the earth are unwilling to wreak environmental havoc simply to maintain our aesthetic control over the garden. Those of us with young children and family pets hesitate to poison the home ground where our small companions live and play. Bt, however, will not harm birds or bees. Both the children and little Fluffy are safe from it, but it will do in anything that feeds on leaves—including the sort of caterpillars that become butterflies, as well as those of cabbage loopers and other pests, so it behooves us not to abuse even this relatively innocuous chemical control. A handful of caterpillars does not an infestation make. However, when the life and health of the garden is at stake, the butterflies must take their chances.

In most gardens, it will prove easiest to use a liquid solution of Bt such as the one sold as "Thuricide." No matter what the brand, the label will read in part, "Active Ingredients: Bacillus thuringiensis, 0.8%," and may give you the Berliner potency rating as well. This is because a few years ago, when the use of Bt was somewhat experimental, the effective strength of the bacillus strain varied quite a bit from batch to batch. Now all makes are more or less uniform, but such labeling tells you what you can expect—dead caterpillars. Bt doesn't hurt beneficial bugs, because it only works when the pests eat leaves which have been sprayed with the stuff. Caterpillars, hornworms, and other nasties that dine on our dahlias soon find their digestive systems paralyzed. It may not look as though anything much is happening right away, but within a few days the caterpillars are making compost at the foot of your trees. One spraying may be enough to control a significant invasion, but when faced with a true population explosion, it is a good idea to spray two or three times, once a week or so. The caterpillars are most susceptible when in active growth, usually from late April through May.

The efficacy of Bt is thoroughly established, thanks in part to the residents of Ravenna, a Seattle neighborhood where local activists sought for years to have Bt sprayed on badly infested neighborhood trees. Seattle Parks Department personnel used a combination of Bt and a more damaging pesticide, but were loath to reduce or eliminate the dosage. When the city gave in a few years ago and began using Bt alone, the subsequent victory—total eradication of the tent caterpillar throughout the deep ravines of the neighborhood, as well as in the parks and back yards—made the national press.

If you have never sprayed anything before, invest in a sprayer that attaches directly to your hose—Lily-Miller has a good one, the "Six-Shooter," with a six-gallon capacity, for under $10. (It doesn't hold six gallons, just six gallons' worth of chemical concentrates. The sprayer is quite small, and comfortable even for a fairly wimpy person to manipulate.) What you do is dilute the Bt solution according to the directions—with Thuricide, you would put six tablespoons of Bt sauce in the sprayer, then fill it with water. The hose will draw off the proper amount to dilute what you are spraying to the optimal concentration. Hook the sprayer to the hose and wander through the garden aiming high and low. Refill as you go—a good-size city lot with a lot of plants might use a pint of the concentrate for a thorough saturation. Subsequent spraying will be lighter, so a quart would likely be sufficient for several sessions. Where mature trees make handspraying difficult, scale the roof—or porch, or garage. Those who don't do heights may prefer to hire a sturdy youth to spray from a ladder (though it is amazing how high you can spray with an ordinary garden hose and a lot of goodwill).

Giving the garden a dose of Bt is your best course of action in spring, but the best defense of all is carried out while pruning in late winter. Tent caterpillars will eat all sorts of things, for nearly any deciduous shrub may be a host plant. Indeed, they seem to share a lot of my tastes; my favorite plants are often their favorites too, yet somehow it doesn't make us friends. When you prune and tidy the garden in fall or winter, keep an eye out for signs of the enemy. Tent caterpillar eggs are laid in pearly little strips with a tough, glossy covering. Usually under half an inch wide, they look like narrow bands of Styrofoam encircling host branches. Strip the egg cases off carefully, then bag and burn them. No matter how cross you feel, exercise restraint when removing the egg bands, for if you scrape off a whole ring of the underlying bark in your zeal, you may well kill the branch. Destroying the incipient worms takes only minutes, but each nest broken is a victory for your trees and shrubs. Most trees and shrubs can survive an isolated defoliation, even a highly destructive one. However, if it happens several years in a row and if other environmental stresses—weather, pollution, poor soil —are also present, few plants have the reserves to survive repeated attacks.

If you have a yard full of mature deciduous trees and lots of large shrubs, think about clubbing in with neighbors to buy a large sprayer unit to share. (Be sure it is never used for weed killers, though, or you could end up accidentally damaging valuable plants.) Although there are many forms of pesticide which will kill tent caterpillars, most will kill a lot of beneficial insects as well, including bees and ladybugs.

Drought Crystals

s summer looms closer and global weather patterns continue to indicate a long-term warming trend and drought cycle, gardeners are on the watch for creative ways to deal with their changing macroclimate. Probably most have discovered the advantages of mulching, yet even that classic remedy is not without disadvantages. Those whose gardens harbor inordinate numbers of slugs (more than two), who garden chiefly in containers or on very sandy soil, will be pleased to know about alternatives. One of the newest, and by far the most fun, is drought crystals.

Relax—this is not a plug for a New Age attitudinal product. Drought crystals, for want of a better name, are not so much New Age as New Tech. Made of such odd and seemingly disparate substances as long-chain polymers, acrylics, and/or cornstarch, these little crystals—or water storage gel granules—share an unusual quality: the ability to absorb and hold enormous quantities of liquid relative to their size and weight. The discovery of a whole class of substances with this bizarre capacity was made years ago. Technical advances in recent years have made the polymers cheaper to produce, easier to control, and more stable, which set those busy industrial minds racing. Many and curious were the applications, perhaps the least aesthetically pleasing of which was that of plastic diaper liners.

Happily, more benign uses arose as well. The USDA, for instance, has patented a polymer derived from cornstarch which can hold several thousand times its own weight in water. Anybody who has ever played with a semisolid blend of cornstarch and water won't be a bit surprised to hear that the substance has another weird property. Initially used to bind water into overly porous field soils, the polymer product has now been developed into a "super slurper cocktail" containing millions of beneficial nematodes as well as lots of water. Even the sandiest, most sievelike soils can hold water when the hydrogel is mixed in, which is especially good news for farmers and citrus growers plagued by weevils and similar pests which thrive in dry soils. It is notoriously difficult—and expensive—to eradicate the weevils chemically, but highly effective natural controls exist in the form of beneficial nematodes which prey on the plant destroyers. Until now, it has been impossible to introduce the helpful nematodes in such infested soils, since they can't survive under drought conditions. However, when sandy soils are treated to an Aggie cocktail, the imported beneficials live long enough to do in the enemies. Furthermore, as the water-absorbing capacity of the soil itself is improved by the addition of the gel, the crops do better as well. In Florida trials, the cocktail has proven to be of enormous benefit, helping to control destructive weevils which beleaguered citrus growers have battled unsuccessfully for years. When orange juice prices return from the stratosphere, you can thank your lucky nematodes.

Many polymer gel products have been developed over the past few years, and they can be of marvelous assistance when you are establishing a new lawn, planting an orchard, or making perennial beds. However, most are available only in bulk from various agricultural supply places, are stable only for a few months, and can be hard to come by. One British-American company, Broadleaf, markets a long-lasting form of gel through garden centers. Broadleaf's P4 is the most stable polymer on the market, with a guaranteed useful life of at least five years. The curious can experiment with small packets containing about a teaspoon of granules, enough to make about a pint of hydrated gel. This is quite fun; you pour the crystals into a bowl, add the water, and wait. About 10 minutes later, the water is absorbed, the crystals have expanded, and you have a bowlful of goopy, slimy little cubes of gel. Mix these shimmering little chunks into dampened potting soil, using four parts dirt and two parts grit or coarse sand to one part super-gel, and you have super soil.

So what do you do with super soil? Some of the best places to use the stuff are in those plant containers that tend to dry out fast or get overlooked—those delightful but impractical planters shaped like animals, which bake dry in 10 minutes; the handsome but shallow wall-hung pots; the begonias in the guest room which you always forget to water. Empty and scrub out the container, then refill it with the P4-soil mixture and repot your plants. Within a couple of weeks, their roots will have found their way into the gel cubes. Once this happens, the plants are in the catbird seat. You can skip three or four of your usual waterings without harming the plants, for they now have their own little reservoirs.

Polymer gels will change the way you water, as well as the timing. As the plant rootlets take up water, the gel cubes shrink. Each time you water, they absorb and store it again; but this takes time, and a swish and a promise doesn't cut it. To rehydrate gel-enhanced soil, set smaller pots into a bucket of water for 10 or 15 minutes. Thoroughly saturate bigger containers with a slowly trickling hose in order to completely refill the crystals. You can't overwater unless you wander off and leave the whole container submerged, but the gel can only do so much, and you do still need to water every few weeks or so. Indoor plants belonging to forgetful types, or to those who travel a good deal, will benefit greatly from P4. No more returning home to a bunch of potted stiffs; you may find them a bit starchy, but they will still be alive.

Another excellent place to use P4 is in shallow seed trays, which can parch quickly in warm weather. A judicious addition of water-retaining gel can prevent the fry-dry-die syndrome that so often afflicts baby root systems each year. The crucial thing is to introduce the gel only in the very bottom of the tray or box, where the enlarging roots can seek it out. Seed that comes in contact with gel will usually rot, so a thin layer of gel-enhanced soil may be covered with an inch of fine potting soil. The seeds are sown on that, and covered with a fine layer of sand or vermiculite, then the whole tray is watered from the bottom to avoid washing the seeds out of place.

Cuttings are also prone to dry out, and for these, a slurry form of P4 is most helpful. This is powdery, rather than granular when dry, hydrating into a viscous goop that clings in a light coat to the cutting. Those who favor rooting hormones will discover that as little as five percent of the usual amount will be effective in combination with P4 slurry, because it stays right where it is supposed to and doesn't leech out into the surrounding soil.

Several adventurous gardeners I know swear by P4 manure tea; the crystals are hydrated with water that has had manure soaked in it overnight. Such "tea" on its own works wonders both with cuttings and pricked-out seedlings, and the manure-hydrated gel keeps a gentle stream of nutrients constantly available to young plants. However, the addition of any form of fertilizer, commercial or organic, significantly reduces the gel's water-holding capacity. This in itself is not a big problem, for the gel still holds enough to be helpful; however, it would be easy to use too much of almost any commercial fertilizer, which could prove fatal. Within a week of sprouting, young plants fix their developing roots deep into the gel cubes, as you can plainly see when transplanting time rolls around. Too much fertilizer can do as much harm as not enough, and only the mildest sorts would be appropriate. Still, there is clearly lots of room for experimentation here.

According to the manufacturers (including the USDA), all of these polymers are biologically inert. Though many have an active life of three to five months, others like P4 may be effective for years. When the gel finally does degrade, the end products are water, carbon dioxide, and a bit of nitrogen.

The most significant caveat with these gels is that they are most appropriate for light, open soils. In heavy, clay soils, an overdose of hydrophilic gel can lock in too much water, creating anaerobic conditions that lead to root rot. In dry, rooty clay soils, the addition of coarse sand or grit will keep the texture open and the soil aerated, and a small amount of gel will go a long way.

A second point to keep in mind is that although most manufacturers suggest incorporating gels into dry soil, then hydrating by soaking the ground, in practice, it is better to hydrate gels first. This insures both more thorough hydration and a more even soil-to-gel ratio. The gels take up the most water when wetted alone; a cupful of dry polymer can fill a wheelbarrow. It may take a couple of hours for the water to penetrate the gel completely, but once properly hydrated, the gel will rehydrate nicely even after it is mixed into the soil. In contrast, gel that is blended into the soil dry tends to clump, and quite a bit of it never hydrates at all.

If your soil is rich, loamy, and well drained; if your beds are deeply dug and thickly mulched; and if your plants are sturdy and well established, you probably won't want to fuss with this stuff. Should you be struggling with unimproved dirt in newish beds, this might be a good time to sow some drought crystals. When your friends' borders are full of flagging phlox, you can point to your straight and splendid clumps with pride. When they ask how you did it, mix them up a bowlful of P4 and let those clear, quivering cubes speak for themselves.

More Decorative Vegetables

dvancing gardeners are always on the lookout for something a bit different to knock the socks off their hort-head friends. We don't have to go any farther than the kitchen garden to find a wheen of likely candidates. It is amazing how a plant's physical context can alter the way we view it.

Last summer, a group of elevated gardeners strolled through our new garden eyeing everything with critical appreciation. All the newest and most unobtainable plants were identified in a split second, but a fine, lusty clump of something or other gave them pause. I couldn't remember just what it was myself (where *do* the labels go?), and there was much earnest pondering, much examining of leaves and stems, and some murmuring about *Labiatæ*, but no identification. Later that week I saw the same plant in a friend's garden and asked her what it might be. She stared at me oddly and finally said, "Oregano, dear. Just ordinary oregano."

Okra is hardly my family's favorite vegetable, but I grow the variety called 'Burgundy' anyway. I try to, at least; this is a heat-loving plant that does not take kindly to the cool, damp summers of the Northwest. In a good year 'Burgundy' okra passes for a stunning small shrub, its dark leaves, heart-shaped and scalloped, arching off lacquered red-black stems. The slim, tapered buds are wine red, slitting slowly to reveal silky petals of buttery moonlight yellow. When the flowers fall, the enormous pods form, dark as burgundy. In the rich soil of the border, the creature can be over six feet tall, and some inconspicuous staking of the nether regions is in order if the plant is exposed to wind.

Species rhubarbs, exotic and highly ornamental, get plenty of attention from ultra-gardeners, yet most are no handsomer than eye-catching escapees from the kitchen garden. Culinary rhubarbs can flaunt as dramatic a leaf, colorful, rippled, and flaring, as any horticultural rarity. The most common rhubarbs will send up noble stalks six feet high, capped with feathery flower plumes of white, creamy pink, or dull red. The uncommon species are occasionally available from seed, but until such treasures are in surer supply, we can profitably cast our nets closer to home. Superior strains or clones of any plant are simply those selected by observant gardeners and nurserymen. We can all do this in our own rhubarb patches, choosing especially shapely, large-leafed forms from among our pie plants. Rhubarbs with deep red flesh as well as dark skin tend to have the most strongly pigmented foliage, but even named varieties show considerable variation. The finest forms have a pronounced reddish cast to the whole plant, with bold ruby-tinted backsides. Plant these in damp soil where they will be backlit by late or early sun, and they will give as much pleasure as the least obtainable of wildlings.

Corn is sometimes grown as a foliage plant, especially the multicolored form called *Zea mays gigantea quadricolor*, with wide leaves striped in pink and rose, green and cream. Edible corn can be lovely, too, and a few forms deserve a place in the ornamental garden. 'Platinum Lady', a sugar-enhanced white corn with mulberry-stained husks, has allure for many long months, as does the even darker 'Burgundy Delight', a sweet bicolor with somber husks and leaves. Both forms hold their own from early summer, when the young plants look vigorous and promising, through the glory of high summer, when the silk spills from heavy ears. In autumn a small stand brings rustling wind music to gardeners who linger out-of-doors past Labor Day. Winter bleaches the broad foliage as pale as straw, and the gangling stems clack and rattle until they are at last cut down to make way for the first flowers of spring.

The plump globe artichokes prized by gourmets are also held in high regard by ornamental gardeners. Widely acknowledged as superior foliage plants, in practical terms these gorgeous giants have more than a few drawbacks. The felted and silvery leaves are armed with fearsome needles that make weeding nearby a loathsome chore. Furthermore, they require substantial staking, for a well-grown artichoke can top six feet in height. Once the tremendous leaves are spread wide and burdened with heavy pods, soaking rain or a buffet of wind brings them crashing down, and a more prickly, unpleasant mess to clear away is hard to imagine. A trio of thick stakes can anchor the base of each plant, but tall specimens require a system of guy wires to keep them upright. Where they touch the plant, the wires must be wrapped with soft cloth or sections of old rubber hose to keep from cutting stalk or stem. Italian purple artichokes have silver-black foliage and dark purple pods, and since they are more compact than the commoner culinary plants, they do not need such unwieldy staking. The closely related cardoons (*Cynara cardunculus*) are an even better choice for most gardeners, for although their leaves are similarly pewtery and sculptural, the plants rarely top four feet and seldom need staking at all. All of these creatures require significant amounts of space, and are less than kindly to small neighbors planted in their rain shadows. This doesn't mean that only holders of grand estates can aspire to such heights; there are several wonderful sidewalk plantings of artichokes in Seattle's Capitol Hill and Queen Anne neighborhoods. Most miscreants would think twice before trampling such well-armed adversaries, and even roaming dogs are daunted by their hardware. A tall hedge of artichokes would look alarmingly fierce yet splendidly architectural, and few burglars would care to tangle with them. They are, in sum, terrific city plants; tough, unapproachable, and lovely. Set swathes of oregano about their feet and you will have something magnificent indeed.

Snob Plants of the Decade

very year, new flowers and vegetables make their curtsies and waltz through the rounds of the magazines on the proud arm of their doting dads, the promoting nurseries or seed companies who introduce these blushing creatures to a mostly yawning world. It is important to remember that even award-winning belles have been judged not against the old standard plants, but against other new introductions. This may not seem like much of a distinction, but it really is; the sweetest corn of the year might not surpass 'Sugar Dots', or even 'Silver Queen', and the biggest new rose is unlikely to match the vigor of 'Peace', the scent of 'White Wings', or the hips of *Rosa moyesii*.

Often the showiest of the new plants become temporarily trendy. Suddenly one sees them everywhere, planted by the thousand. A few years later and with equal speed, these flash plants plunge into obscurity as newer, more dazzling creatures come along. Only time can prove which of the debutantes are destined to be keepers, though there are several outstanding introductions of recent years that I'm willing to bet on. As yet in limited supply, snapped up as fast as they appear in catalog or nursery, here are some incipient classics, plants of character which will lend cachet to any garden—and gardener, which after all, is often half the point.

New and very much in demand is the smooth, cream-yellow *Coreopsis* 'Moonbeam', a sunflower relative that takes drought in stride, yet does an excellent job even under good garden conditions—not always the case. Don't think of towering stalks; 'Moonbeam' rarely gets over 18 inches tall, forming bushy, mounded rounds liberally covered with dainty daisy-flowers. As the years pass, the mounds become small thickets, making lovely carpeting beneath rhododendrons or yellow shrub roses. It is not thuggish, and any extra bits you might pull off will always find a welcome in the gardens of your friends. This plant comes from exceptionally sturdy, hardworking stock—a racehorse from a line of cart haulers. Its relatives bloom in darker, fairly harsh and obvious shades of yellow, cheerful but not exactly the thing for gardeners who favor the subtle. Before the flowers appear, its foliage makes a fine backdrop for bulbs, for the leaves are much divided, almost threadlike, and of a deep, dark green which sets off the chalky flowers to advantage. It dies down to a creeping mat in winter, when a light blanket of sawdust might replace snow cover in the mild maritimes. Reports from back East indicate that 'Moonbeam' may not prove lastingly winter hardy, but in the Northwest, it takes Zone 7 winters in stride. Even if relegated to replaceable annual status back East, 'Moonbeam' will remain horticulturally hot, for few plants are similarly reliable, pouring out pale flowers generously through the backstretch of summer and on into fall. Pale they are, moonlight pale, but pale with punch—and this is one of the most important colors in the garden. There is nothing better than the soft yellows, creams, and off-whites for emphasizing the brights; these gentle colors can effortlessly unify brilliant color mixtures which refuse to work together. Blend in 'Moonbeam' with foliage and flowers of silver, darkest purple, ember red, even black. This is also the plant to clarify and soften restless, insistent plantings of clear blue, white, and acid yellow. Mix it in with sharp orange-yellow combinations, too, to gentle and mellow the harsh contrasts. You can deadhead spent blooms every month or so, cutting spent shoots right down to the stem rather than leaving the stubble poking up. If you do, you may be enjoying blooms into November, but even if you never lift a secateur, this giving creature will put on a continual display. If you don't plan to deadhead, a light mulch of aged manure and compost mulch in July will keep 'Moonbeam' shining on through the summer and well into fall.

Heuchera 'Palace Purple' goes on everybody's 'must get' list the instant they see it. A chance hybrid of two American natives, *H. americana* and *H. villosa,* the original 'Palace Purple' was found growing in a nursery bed of seedlings at Kew a few years back (why does it take the Brits to discover the beauties of our native plants?) and was named to honor the Queen Mother, whose own gardens are just over the back fence. Both of the parent species are themselves pleasing in a subdued sort of way, modest plants of simple charms. 'Palace Purple', like 'Moonbeam', is a swan among ducks, for this plant would be a stunner in any company.

Thanks, perhaps, to the proximity of Royals during its conception, 'Palace Purple' is a dapper toff of a plant, its glossy leaves so dark a red as to be nearly black in certain lights. They are broad and ruffled, deeply veined and crinkled, their flaring undersides lined in brilliant burgundy red. It carries slim wands of little white bell flowers, and if cut back hard after the spring bloom session, will repeat the effort in the fall. Again, a light compost mulch and a hearty high tea of manure-ade in midsummer will renew the luxuriance of the foliage and promote repeated bloom in autumn. This is not a plant for deep shade, where it lapses into sullen darkness, nor for full, hot sun, where the leaves scorch and curl. It is at its best in dappled shade, needing the play of light to reveal its full beauties. Try it in a raised bed, backed by sheaves of hardy arum, the weirdly dramatic *Zantedeschia aethiopica* 'Green Goddess'. Encircle the hazy violet daylily 'Russian Rhapsody' with a ruffled skirt of 'Palace Purple', placing them atop a sloping bank where they will be viewed from below. Use it, too, as an edger for raised beds, especially where afternoon sunlight streaming across a lawn will make it catch flame.

Should you happen to fall for both of these plants, resist the natural urge to plant them beside each other. That purple-with-yellow stuff is OK for Easter eggs, but seldom flattering when garden plants are involved. 'Moonbeam' blends orange-sherbet daylilies with vivid blue gentians or campanulas masterfully. It gleams behind a stand of black lily turf, *Ophiopogon planiscapus* 'Ebony Knight' or 'Nigrescens', particularly when both are backed with a smoke bush, either the purple-leafed kind or the plain green *Cotinus coggygria*, which produces more luxurious smoke than the darker ones. 'Moonbeam' deserves the supportive company of other stellar autumn performers. Group it with the broad, coppery leaves of *Crocosmia* 'Solfatare', its small, brassy flowers less showy than the foliage. Back both with a mass of feathery *Solidaster* 'Lemore', another cross between two American natives, this time an aster and a goldenrod, which blooms in butter and egg yellows. Toss in some steel blue rue, *Ruta graveolens* 'Blue Beauty' or the lighter, smaller 'Jackman's Blue', and you have an exceedingly good show for several months.

Put your 'Palace Purple' in front of a fuzzy grey shrub, perhaps the crinkle-leafed *Cistus creticus* with chalky pink flowers like single roses. Thread the space between them with clumps of ruby-colored Japanese blood grass and shocking pink belladonna lilies for a satisfying grouping with multiple seasons of beauty. The blood grass *Imperata cylindrica* 'Rubra' is another recent arrival that is spreading in gardens as fast as Bermuda grass (though it is far more welcome). It is small enough for any garden, usually under two feet in height, with upright, broad-bladed leaves, the upper portion of which become intensely, richly, sumptuously red, fading down the stalks to yellow and green. Each small division will fatten up nicely, making a good clump in short order, yet it is not invasive; if you are going to invite grasses into your beds, this is the first point to clarify. Blood grass is not as effective when grown in a mass—few things are, actually—but it is a knockout when used sparingly to punctuate carpets of juniper or heather, or beneath dark-leafed hazel, prunus, or Japanese maple.

These new beauties are still snob plants at present, which can make them both expensive and hard to track down. But since all are sound of constitution, and willing garden workers under a variety of conditions, it won't be long before they transcend trendiness and take their rightful place as essential garden ingredients. They may in time become as common as roses or irises, but like both those queenly creatures, they have qualities which must lastingly lift them above the common run.

The BORDER in EARLY SUMMER

EARLY SUMMER

 May takes spring splashing into summer, full and laughing merry. The air is full of apple blossoms, the petals strewn over the long grass like cupped pink shells. Blossoms fall like wandering, fragrant snow-blows from the pear trees, and litter the trampled brown earth beneath the children's swing. Pools of petals, pink, white, and rose, lie in overlapping circles under a row of ornamental fruit trees, apricot and peach, plum and cherry. At night the dark grass is lit up by these circles, the petals softly reflecting the greenish moonlight of early summer, a light like old ivory yellowed with age.

Warm rain carries the spiced apple scent of the sweetbriar, a rose with perfumed leaves. Another such, *Rosa primula*, snug against a south wall, has ferny, lacy foliage that wafts a sweet smell of incense through the garden on sun-warmed breezes. Early peonies catch the tumbling petals of rain-shattered roses and bee-plundered fruit blossoms. May mingles the last of April's rains with the first of June's roses; through May the promise of spring comes to fulfillment in the maturing bounty of summer.

June is the loveliest month in the garden; all of spring's freshness is tenderly coupled with the waxing strength of perennials and the triumphant glory of roses. In June spring overflows into summer; the rush and flurry builds, peaks, and is still for a long, quiet moment. June is a hush, a month out of time. The mornings are pearled in mist and spangled with dew, the long days are blue and gold. The twilights are late and lingering, full of bird music and the creaking of tree frogs. The nights of June are short and saturated with the scent of roses. Other scents move on the warm night air: the smells of mint and thyme, the pure fragrance of orange blossom from the philadelphus, the healthy, earthy essence of newly mown grass. In June the garden's night breath is light and fresh, its sweetness clean and new. *Nicotiana*, the flowering tobacco, the homely sweet rocket and night-scented stocks, mignonette and sweet peas contribute their part to the inimitable perfume.

If April is generous, June is a superabundant giver. In gardens where roses reign, this is the moment of total abandon. Every surface, every pillar and post, every trellis and fence, every tree and shrub is laden with roses. Clematis scramble with them hand in hand, tossing long arms full of flowers over arbor and gate. Delphineums send up their aspiring spires, a run of heavenly blues held high against the serene blue of the heavens. The garden of June is youthful with no regret for childhood; it is youth moving joyfully, confidently, toward maturity.

The end of the month brings the triumph of the border, now full to the very brim and spilling over into the house. There are flowers in every room, flowers behind the children's ears, flowers in their pockets. In the border not a scrap of bare earth remains visible. Fresh foliage wheels in lovely but unappreciated patterns, secondary to the flowers. White Madonna lilies bloom supernal amongst spider-fingered hellebores. Daylilies blow in wide sheaves, lilac and grape, apricot and grapefruit, lemon-lime and green-gold, plum red and plum black. Irises open, the bearded ones which are yet wholly feminine; frilled and goffered confections of ecru, lavender, and mauve, some only inches tall, others towering above sturdy stakes. Blue-black *Iris chrysographes*, the plum-scented *I. graminea*, tussocks of Pacific Coast iris, each petal touched with delicate tracery. Tall, slim Siberians wash through the gardens in runs of blue: sea blue and sapphire blue, watercolors of turquoise and teal, smoke and slate, and opalescent, cloudy white.

White gardens are full of hydrangeas and roses, lilies and peonies, white 'Claryssa' sage (*Salvia horminum*), and white petunias with their odd, raspy scent that catches at one's throat. By night white gardens have a muted, wavering light of their own. The foliage disappears into shadow and only the flowers are visible, catching the moon and holding it, pale and glimmering in the endless half-dark of a June night. Quick on their heels come the mild dawns, magically soft, dawns of dew and sparkling rainbows on the grass, all the trite trash of Victorian poetry made new. It is so silly to talk of dew-spangled grass, so incredibly lovely to see it. It is enchanting to lie in the cool wet grass, to feel the heat of the earth beneath it, still warm from yesterday's sun, and to examine the minuscule garden pictures, upside down and quivering, mirrored in each glittering droplet. From a distance each dewdrop holds a prism fleck of broken rainbow, but close up these resolve into tiny duplicates of the larger scene.

Bask. This is it. Bask, revel, and don't lift a finger you don't have to. Soon enough it will be time to groom and fiddle, but this is the garden's golden hour—take it while you may.

Peonies and Hostas

PLANTS WITH TWO STRINGS TO THEIR BOWS

 hen we first moved to this old farm, a small orchard of aging fruit trees next to the house seemed the ideal site for a winding peony walk. The dappled shade of the arching, umbrella-pruned trees would allow the flowers, so tantalizingly fleet on the single peonies, to persist just a bit longer than they do in full sun. The grass there was already spangled with white wood anemones, and we could easily envision a thick band of bold-leafed peonies rising through sheets of violets, shooting stars, and primroses. In summer, when the bloom was past, there would still be lovely textures in a rich palette of greens, for peony foliage is beautiful in its own right and far more lasting than the flowers.

When we started clearing the area and marking off the proposed border, we discovered several clumps of old peonies already in place. Neglected for years, mown regularly with the grass, these old girls were still putting forth wine-stained stems through a tangle of blackberries, nettles, and a rampant pyracantha. Their presence confirmed the rightness of the peony walk, and the ancient plants were carefully divided and reset in renewed soil. It will take a few years to find out what they are, and we may never know exactly, for peonies have not been high in horticultural favor for many years, and many hybrids are now lost or unrecognized. However, their many strengths are creating a new respect for these old-fashioned plants, the finest forms of which have been preserved in connoisseurs' gardens across the country.

Like rhododendrons, peonies are generally chosen for their flowers, but both are best considered as foliage plants, since they carry those stunning blossoms for just a few short weeks. This need not discourage anybody from planting peonies; although they are not evergreen, they are hardy, tough, reliable plants that are in beauty for a good eight months each year. The emerging shoots seem glazed with lacquer, the shining stalks are colored in burgundy or dark purple, ember red or a metallic bronzy green. The leaves unfurl dramatically, their slender lobes dark-edged like the stems. The buds swell enticingly all spring, and explode into bloom as summer draws near. As the blossoms fall, the leaves continue to grow in size, deepening in color until autumn calls out glowing tints of pink and salmon, copper and gold.

Peonies are often planted in the sun, and that works fine, but they will also tolerate a fair amount of open, high shade, especially when given free passage of air (not hampered by thick shrubs) and a retentive but well-drained soil. In the Northwest, this means amending clay soils with grit or sand, and adding daunting quantities of compost or other humus to sand. It is worth taking the time to amend the peony's soil pocket well; make the hole huge, add well-rotted manure, compost, grit or sand, then mix in the garden soil. It may seem like a lot of work, but if you do it right the first time, you will never have to do it again, nor will your children, nor even your grandchildren; a happy peony can stay in the same spot for a century without requiring division or replanting. Think about that as you swing your shovel high. This is for the future!

You don't need to worry about pruning or shaping peonies, either; it is enough to cut and clear away the old stems in early winter. Some of the double flowers (they are called "bombs" for good reason) are very heavy, especially when wet. These tend to drag their stems to the ground, giving the plant a flopsy look. Staked peonies look worse than trussed chickens, but such flopsiness is very easily corrected in a completely invisible way by putting circles of chicken wire over the base of each plant when the shoots first emerge. The wire rises with the stems and is quickly hidden by the unfolding new leaves. Even a hard rain won't knock the plants down once the wires are in place, and chicken wire doesn't damage the stems as wrapped twine sometimes does. Tiered hoop supports of galvanized steel are also practical and look less objectionably homemade to some, though they are more obtrusive than the chicken-wire circles until the plants have fully leafed out.

When we planted the peony walk, our foundling peonies and their newer relatives were interlaced with a number of hostas to make attractive foliage combinations that will last through the summer. I always think the hostas are dead, so late do they poke their fat snouts through the soil, but once awake, they lose no time in unrolling their huge leaves. Some are like smoky blue seersucker, others are ribbed and corded in cream and sage, or deeply veined and splashed with gold. Most bloom rather late in the summer, sporting perfectly nice bell flowers in muted blues, lavenders, or soft white. It is not the flowers for which we plant hostas, however, and if they were to skip a season or two, few gardeners would notice or mourn. Their greatest beauty is in their foliage, and the great wings of their leaves make an ideal counterpoint to the fine lacework of the peonies.

When the soft pink single peony 'Audrey' fills her wide goblets with falling apple blossoms—exactly the same color, and not far off in fragrance—the picture seems perfect. In a few short weeks, however, 'Audrey' will be a lovely small foliage shrub, and the torch will pass to the grey-blue leaves of *Hosta* 'Brigham Blue' and the rounded little 'Blue Cadet' at her feet.

One of the charms of peonies is their tantalizing swiftness; the buds burgeon, burst, bloom, and fade as quickly as fleeting spring itself leads us on to high summer. Gardeners who want more can choose early and late varieties as well as the more common June bloomers, and can plant their peonies in partial shade to prolong the flowers as well.

An early-bird peony called 'Halcyon' is outstanding; it is a white poppy-flowered single peony with a bright fringe of violet petaloids at its heart. Plant *Viola cornuta* hybrids, clear-faced pansies in violet or pink, to clamber into the leaves of this one. The bushy, low-growing peony 'Seraphim', covered with starry, glossy single white flowers, is also quite an early-bloomer, and looks wonderful with the creamy pink rosebuds of Rosa 'The Fairy', a foam of forget-me-nots, and a silvery threadlike tangle of Artemisia canescens at its feet.

The ruffled, silky petals of 'Sea Shell', another early single peony, are a warm, clear pink that looks marvelous among grey and silvery herbs like artemisia, lavender, and catmint. 'L'Etincelante' ("the sparkler") is another sumptuous, silvery pink peony with a shimmering reverse of deeper rose; this really deserves planting in a row of at least three plants (a hedge of 10 plants along a walkway is traffic-stopping) to get the full effect of this fluttering, dazzling flower. Even after the flowers fade, the plants are shapely shrubs stout enough to play host to annual vines, a purple-leafed grape, or a summer-blooming clematis.

'Lois Kelsey' is an unusual flower that is a knockout both in the garden and in a vase. This one is a full, puffy lactiflora with laciniated, fringed petals of clean white, centered with a thick fringe of golden yellow stamens sparked by flame red anthers. A connoisseur's plant, to be savored alone in a leafy setting, 'Moonrise' is a creamy moon-colored single, subtle and delicious. No peonies have more fragrance than the double rosebud blossoms of 'Gardenia', a white that is well placed beneath climbing roses or clematis.

'White Innocence' is very tall, close to five feet, a fountain of a bush, all covered with large, silky single petals of icy white centered with a curious ball of staminodes like carved coral in cream and pink. This was fascinating, but not as tempting to me as the species plant, *Pæonia officinalis* 'Rubra Plena', which has hummingbird red petals centered with a ruby red pistil and heavy, dangling stamens crusted with gold; it looks like an offering on a sushi tray. The foliage is excellent too—lacy, almost ferny—and beautiful for months.

Many peonies are very difficult to breed, some the result of literally millions of crosses, which may result in but a handful of viable seed. Germination is slow and erratic, and if successful, the seedling can take 12 years and more to reach blooming size, and must be carefully evaluated over a number of seasons after that to boot. Clearly, peony hybridizers are a patient lot.

Peonies are best transplanted when dormant, September and October being the usual months for the performance of this exercise. Potted plants should be set in the ground with the crown at the same level as it was in the pot. With bare root plants, be careful to position the bud eyes (little knobs which project from the heavy upper part of the root) about an inch below the surface. If they are buried too deeply—more than a couple of inches —the plant may be "blind," blooming shyly or not at all.

Peonies resent disturbance, and will practically never bloom the year or two following transplanting, so don't panic and replant the thing. Give it some time, and appreciate the bronzy green new growth, the plum black sheen on the new stems and opening foliage, the graceful, lacy mature leaves. If after a few bloomless years you still suspect that you planted too deep or that heaped mulch has covered the eyes better than you intended, gently brush the soil away from around the crown of the plant till you can see where the shoots emerge. Tenderly recover the buds more shallowly, even if it leaves a depression around the plant. That won't hurt anything, and will help get water (one of the plant's greatest requirements) to the roots. The impatient do well to perform this delicate excavation work after the leaves emerge, for nothing is easier than to accidentally destroy the emerging shoots during a hasty sortie. Once the blossoms begin, pick them with restraint until the plant is mature enough that your raids pass unnoticed. That day will come surprisingly soon, for time is the gardener's friend. For us, each flying year brings long-awaited pleasures as our choicest plants achieve triumphant maturity.

Colorful Quickies for New Borders

hough patience is an important part of making a new garden, patience alone is not enough. Paths and patios can't satisfy the gardener's longings for plants; even if you choose to build a new garden by the book, laying out the architectural features before setting any plants in the ground, remember to set aside an area for immediate bloom. Once the borders and beds are ready, they too may be planned to give the impatient gardener a satisfying frisson even in their first season.

Just four months after planting, our new perennial and shrub border looks full and cheerful, thanks in part to the use of some ardent early bloomers. Matricaria (feverfew) is an old standby of cottage gardens and always a hard worker, but when its roots meet the manure in a well-prepared bed, it takes on unsuspected qualities of both beauty and staying power. Single plants may be four feet tall, bushy, symmetrical, and absolutely laden with fresh white daisies. After this first bloom wanes—which can take a good two months—cut the plants a few inches above the ground, give them a refresher of manure and compost and a good drink, then jump back to be out of the way when they take off again. Their second wind will carry them well into fall, sometimes even to Christmas. There are numerous forms, tall and dwarf, single or double, crisp white or golden yellow, and all are useful and obliging plants with simple charm. 'White Stars' and 'Golden Ball' are the nicest of the small ones, and, to my eye, the plain type plant, single and graceful, is the best of the big.

Some of the border salvias make excellent filler for a new garden, quickly forming enormous soft clouds between youthful shrubs. Any of the clary sages (*Salvia sclarea*) are easy to grow from seed, and will fill out fast, reaching three feet or more by midsummer. They bloom long and hard through the summer, usually in soft lavenders, palest blue, cream, and a gentle mauvy pink. If you let them go to seed (they are quite attractive even when faded), they will often self-sow, giving you a whole new crop for next year. A particularly good hybrid strain from Thompson & Morgan called

S. horminum 'Claryssa' is available as separate colors or in a mixture. Claryssa's foliage is a healthy green, and she sends up large spires of colorful bracts: spanking white netted with green, deep pink with violet, or a dark and glowing midnight blue. The color range is closely selected, giving a number of plants of each color, but little or nothing of shades in between—a very desirable trait for those who want uniformity for planned effects. Potted seedlings show color when quite small, which makes it easy to sort them out for garden placement. Every white garden I've seen this summer has white 'Claryssa' in it, and rightly so.

A splendidly baroque clary sage is available from Canyon Creek Nursery. The seed of this one was collected from an outstanding stand of plants found in the wilds of Turkey. The leaves are dark green, huge and hairy, and the plant itself is enormous, standing some five feet tall. The fat flower buds are so heavy that they flop down over the leaves, looking rather like reticulated fish. As they open, they rise dramatically, opening into tremendous jets of tiny flowers with large, showy hoods of lavender, cream, and soft blue. This plant has presence for months, and is soundly perennial. Though short-lived, it self-sows enough to ensure a steady supply, both for you and for your friends. The seedlings make resting rosettes in the first year, and will bloom generously the following summer.

Some of the most brilliant garden color comes from annuals, many of which self-sow willingly if the season's last flush of flowers is left to set seed. California poppies are especially cooperative in this regard, and a recently developed strain called 'Thai Silk' is among the loveliest things in the garden. The color runs are those of sari silks, hot pinks and cool reds mixed with coppery oranges and bronzy golds. Some shades are muted, others clarion clear, and their mingled blossoms are absolutely gorgeous. Scattered among clumps of ornamental grasses—especially blue-grey oat grass, festuca, and phormium—'Thai Silk' transforms the restrained (not to say humdrum) appearance of the average grass garden into something incredibly sumptuous. Let 'Thai Silk' ramble through a hillside of junipers, transforming the dull into the daring. Lace it along the driveway, beside a path, or through a young but hopeful border. Sharing the good-natured constitution of its parent plant, this mixture is robust enough to use in exposed, dry positions in full sun, where it may mingle to mutual advantage with silver-leafed artemisias, velvety *Senecio greyi*, and rockroses (*Cistus* species).

The artemisias are another good bunch to know, for there is a plant for any place you can think of and nearly all of them are quick workers that play supportive roles in young borders. Most are sun-lovers, sporting silver or grey foliage and stems covered with downy white hairs. Some of the commonest are too pushy for long-term relationships—including the best-known cultivars, 'Silver King' and 'Silver Queen'. The far less rampant cushions of *Artemisia* 'Silvermound' may be bought at the supermarket these days, so common has it become. This is a nice little plant, but there are many other artemisias worth searching a little harder for.

The wiry stems and scrappy little leaves of *Artemisia canescens* look like tangled, lacy steel wool, frosty and refreshing as an underplanting for roses or the hot scarlet trumpets of *Phygelius capensis*, the cape fuchsia. Source of the fatally potent French absinthe, *Artemisia absinthium* 'Lambrook Silver' makes an airy, open shrublet two or three feet tall, with thin, fine foliage heavily dusted with silver. It soon makes its presence felt in a young border, forming a whorling counterpoint to upright sheaves of broad-leafed New Zealand flax (*Phormium* species), Siberian iris foliage, or grey-green yuccas. 'Lambrook Silver' makes a wide, sprawling shrub which fills in the bare places below lanky roses and tall ornamental grasses, or skirts a young weeping silver pear tree to perfection.

'Valerie Finnis' is an upright, spiky artemisia with large, fuzzy-napped grey leaves and frizzy little flowers of old gold. Bolder and less bushy than 'Lambrook Silver', 'Valerie Finnis' makes a nicely textured backdrop for dwarf daylilies, whether the intense purple of 'Little Grapette' or the buttery rosebud blossoms of 'Double Cutie'. Ms. F. is also a great companion for marine blue agapanthus and the dark, sulky blue of the farinaceous sage, 'Victoria', which she sets off to perfection.

Perhaps the best artemisia of all for new borders is a form of *A. arborescens* named for the famous garden in which it was found. This is 'Powis Castle', a strongly shaped, dramatic plant with shrub stature. Almost ever-green, it has terrific garden presence from a very early age. Placed behind young tea roses, it makes a silvery background that gives every flower a powerful boost. Rowed behind young shrubs which need time to fill out, 'Powis Castle' will form a billowing hedge in just a few months, providing stalwart support to the perennials and annuals nearby. Threaded with clematis, it makes a tapestry wall against which smaller plants are seen to great advantage, any deficits of size or vigor kindly masked. By the time those maturing shrubs are hungry for more room, the artemisia will be past its prime and ready for removal, its silver making way for slower-growing garden gold.

Ornamental Herbs to Savor

*J*ust as a dash of fresh rosemary or lemon thyme can wake up a workaday salad, so an infusion of herbs brings snap to a humdrum border. We don't have to ransack the specialty catalogs to find good-looking, aromatic candidates for such a role; some fine and highly attractive plants are probably blushing unseen in the kitchen garden already. Anybody's list of the choicer salvias will certainly include some of the culinary sorts; the fuzzy grey 'English Broadleaf' sage, for example, will slip unobtrusively into any color scheme, making stronger colors all the brighter for its quiet presence. Rippling mats of curly golden marjoram make a lovely, close carpet for edging path or border, and the golden-leafed form of feverfew (*Chrysanthemum parthenium*) refreshes the eye and brightens shady corners; it also cures migraines and brings a pungent bite to mild salads.

Choosing among the many flowering alliums in the garden catalogs can while away a wet week, but some of the nicest won't even be in the running. Common chives are a lovely foil for *Diascia rigescens*, a long-armed twinflower with lipped flowers of a curious metallic pink. Chives can be planted to good effect near one of the hardiest flowering maples, *Abutilon x suntense*. The deep, fluted cups of rich lavender are a perfect match for the fluffy purple chive blossoms, and the grassy foliage of the chive looks nice at the shrub's feet. (This abutilon has proved hardy to 5°.) Garlic chives, *Allium tuberosum*, are similarly grassy, if larger overall, but this one opens flat umbels of sweetly scented white flowers that look especially pretty emerging from the skirts of the low polyanthus rose 'The Fairy', with its muted pink blossoms. The tall, grey-green blades of common culinary leeks have distinct garden presence, and their massive flower heads in faded mauve and cream are architecturally attractive for months after the flowers have faded. The flower stalks droop with age, tumbling companionably into whatever sits in front of them. They look especially nice growing through roses underplanted with masses of oregano, which also holds its seedheads in good condition for months. Alliums are easily grown from fresh seed, though divisions taken from the vegetable patch will have greater garden impact right away.

The many forms of sweet fennel, *Fœniculum vulgaris*, are all more or less decorative. Finocchio, or Florence fennel, with a bulbous base and an odd aniselike flavor, has proved perennial in the Northwest, returning placidly after single-digit winter lows. Early spring awakens a froth of bright green that elongates into slender stems. These can reach five feet by mid-summer, forming shimmering towers of fine, hairlike foliage. Spangled with rain or dew, this fennel sends scintillations of light through the garden. In fall it passes away in a burst of copper and gold, lovely and aromatic to the very end. A constantly coppery cousin of common fennel is called variously bronze, black, purple, or red fennel. The color is a smoky admixture of them all, with the olive bronze tones ascendant in shade (which this plant tolerates very nicely), and the warm purple-black tints more pronounced in full sun. This is a stunner, especially when grown in a good-size clump. Paired with the red European wood spurge, *Euphorbia amygdaloides 'Rubra'*, backed by thickets of *Macleaya cordata*, the plume poppy, and given a front row of something silvery like lamb's ears (*Stachys olympica*) or steel-woolly balls of *Artemisia canescens*, the coppery fennel adds an unmatchable lightness to the textures and tones of its companions.

Most dramatic of all is the European giant fennel, *Ferula communis*. One does not toss its wiry, netted foliage into the salad bowl, but nothing looks fresher than the spumy young shoots of this energetic fennel when they spring eagerly from the cold soil in the last days of winter. It takes several years for a plant to reach maturity, but once established it will send lusty bloom stalks as much as 15 feet in the air. Each is capped with a well-wrapped yellowish knob that splits to reveal a huge, wheeling umble of coarse white florets. All fennels seed generously and sprout freely from fresh seed, though the seedlings transplant well only when quite young. If you find lots of seedlings in the garden, you can transfer tiny clumps to four-inch pots, then grow them on for a bit before setting them in their final spot. Plants larger than seedlings rarely survive transplantation.

Stars of the Potato Patch

hile browsing through a local nursery, my oldest son noticed a small sign marked "potato vine" above a humble group of pots ranged almost out of sight amid a host of flowering zinnias and marigolds. Dark green leaves, long, narrow, and notched at the base, looked familiar—just like deadly nightshade. Here, unsung, was a marvelous climber, *Solanum jasminoides* 'Album', alias the white-flowered potato vine.

The unprepossessing name gives no clue of the splendors of this plant; when suited, it will swiftly make its way up netting or a trellis, through shrubs, into an ornamental plum or crabapple. Sooner than one might expect, it begins pouring down shower after shower of silver white star flowers in clusters of eight or ten. Despite the specific epithet "jasminoides," these vines are not scented, but, porcelain pale and delicately modeled, the flowers have no need to apologize for their lack of fragrance. Each floret is close to an inch across, centered with a sharp beak of golden yellow, quite similar to the blue deadly nightshade flowers but rather larger.

The similarity between nightshade and potato vines is no accident; both plants are members of the solanaceae family, as are the eggplants. The potato vine, and several others much like it, are the climbing stars of the family, the Luis Herrera of the plant world. Like Sr. Herrera, they hail from South America, though they are found more frequently in Brazil than in Colombia, and are only rarely found on bicycles. In the Pacific Northwest, the white potato vine is capable of reaching 20 or 30 feet in time, covering the side of a house completely in a few years (there is a fine example of this industrious activity to be observed in Seattle's Montlake neighborhood). Those who have a sturdy specimen of the evergreen *Clematis armandii* already in place are in a position to create a smashing duet simply by adding a young white potato vine at its feet. The vine is not heavy, and makes a good companion to ceanothus, photinia, Portuguese laurel, or sweet bay, any of which it will use as a trellis up which to wend its starry way.

The potato vine begins to bloom while still just a pup, and once it's launched, you can expect continuous showers of bloom from late spring until sharp frosts. A well-grown specimen is guaranteed to do great things for your gardening reputation, but in fact this is one of the easiest plants to please. Completely indifferent as to soil (as long as drainage is sharp), the potato vine wants only sun and adequate water through our summer droughts to do you proud. In colder parts of the Northwest, it is apt to act like an annual, but given a sunny, open exposure, some protection from drying winds, and a thick winter mulch of compost and aged manure topped with chopped straw or bracken, it will return to warm, sheltered gardens for many years. Plants which are mingled with the evergreen clematis may last even longer, given the extra companionship and protection. Though several majestic specimens in Seattle were cut to the ground by the Zone 7 freeze during the black winter of 1988-89, most recovered their poise by the summer's end, and those in our island garden came through almost unscathed, thanks to the protection of the evergreen viburnum they call home.

A slate-blue-flowered potato vine is not as showy as the white one, but a wall covered with its hazy French blue blossoms makes a wonderful backdrop for old-fashioned shrub roses, especially the hot magenta ones which can be awkward to place well. Blue potato vine also looks terrific when combined with velvety purple Jackman clematis, or the clear rosy pink of *Clematis* 'Hagley Hybrid'. Either pair will make a winning effect if allowed to ramble through a wisteria arbor or clamber into ornamental fruit trees, bringing long months of color where little is left.

More relatives wait in the wings, all of them more or less hardy throughout Zone 8. A connoisseur's charmer, *Solanum crispum*, has olive green leaves, their edges waved and slightly ruffled. The named form 'Glasnevin' carries lavender blue flowers in especially fat clusters that look almost like grapes, so generously are they produced. Though reputedly tender, 'Glasnevin' also made it through the Great Frost of '89, and lives on to tell the tale in more garden than one.

Next time you see a pot labeled "potato vine," think twice before you pass it by. These plants may have earthy roots, but given half a chance, they will gladly climb to the stars.

Collecting Columbines

One of my favorite plants is blooming just now, a small columbine given to me by an elderly neighbor who has grown it for many years in her Seattle garden. The flowers are upfacing, the color of crushed raspberries, and although each is small, they are as closely packed as the crammed blossoms in a Victorian posy. Next to the modern hybrids I grow, this small one looks solid rather than airy, partly because it lacks wings. The typical columbine has five wide-sweeping "wing" sepals and five tubular petal "horns" which taper to curving spurs. This old-fashioned flower is double, having 10 sets of horns which are themselves tripled, three horns tucked in each set rather like the old hose-in-hose primroses. Some garden visitors have identified them as "grannies' bonnets," but an old-fashioned seed strain of columbine called 'Biedermeier' yields plants with similarly tiered blossoms in warm shades of pink and purple.

Single columbines will often arrive in a garden unannounced, and while few are outright homely, the garden wildlings are often coarser, shyer to bloom, or less interestingly shaped and colored than selected garden forms and collectors' species. One curious kind of columbine that always arouses interest is the tattered double form, a variable, mop-headed creature with a flurry of spurless petals. The best known of this type is 'Nora Barlow', with deep red petals streaked with green and pink. It comes mostly true from seed, especially if it is not grown near other columbines, but even when produced in strict isolation, seed from 'Nora' is apt to yield raggedy children in plain colors, some of whom are plain indeed, as well as look-alike offspring. For this reason, plants of 'Nora Barlow' offered for sale (in certain upscale East Coast nursery catalogs) as field-grown seedlings "which may vary" can be expensive dogs; save your money and order a seed packet from Suttons or Thompson & Morgan, or buy a potted one in bloom at a local nursery.

The anemone-flowered columbines also come mostly true from seed and make showy yet distinguished plants. They are often quite large, the plants reaching three or four feet in height and the flowers as much as three inches across. They, too, are double, but look as if stamped out by a cookie cutter. Neat stacks of petals frame a bristly heart of gold stamens, and the flowers often face up rather than drooping as Nora's do. The seed exchange of the Hardy Plant Society includes seed of anemone-flowered forms in eight colors, including a purple so dark as to seem black. Even if you don't live near an active branch of this dedicated group, access to this seed list is reason enough for membership, though the quarterly bulletin is another draw.

When you visit nurseries in May and June, keep an eye out for unusually colored columbines. Few nurseries will offer more than a few varieties, but some staggering beauties have come from the commonest seed strains. For long-lasting bloom and showboat flowers, the 'McKana Giant' strain is unbeatable. These are scaled for the border, the plants two or three feet high and nearly as wide, with big, long-spurred flowers dangling from wandlike stems above the mounded grey-green foliage. The leaves of all columbines are lacy and attractive, whether fine or bold. Some are fresh, parsley green, others sea green or blue-grey. They hold their own even without flowers, useful filler for indoor arrangements throughout the year in our mild climate. The leaves of the McKanas are especially large, which helps balance the huge flowers, nearly the size of the hummingbirds which flock to them. The color ranges from lovely pastels of pink, blue, and cream to pale primrose yellow warmed with deeper tones of rose and lemon. One plant will bring you a gardenful of glorious progeny in short order, all of them beautiful, but there are never too many, since your friends will swoop down and bear them away. I try to save the prettiest for my own garden, but this is not always possible since the hand is quicker than the eye. If you can hold on to them, the offspring make excellent bargaining material; even quite sophisticated gardeners go for these big beauties in peach and butter yellow, palest rose and white, or a mysterious, dusky purple touched with silver and green. Well they might; a gorgeous plant is hardly made less desirable by obliging, easy ways, and most columbines are trouble-free plants.

One of the earliest to bloom is the very small *Aquilegia flabellata*, a six-inch dainty that looks quite delicate but is as hardy as they come. The chubby little flowers are a miraculous, intense blue, looking like pools of summer sky amid ruffled grey-green leaves. In the form *A.f.* 'Nana', outer petals of that same amazing blue are lined with inner petals of clean white, and 'Nana Alba' is all white, a pale, milky color faintly washed with blue. All three are delicate, choice understory plants for the garden, and all are at home in large containers or window boxes. They are also delightful companions in bed or pot for late-blooming small narcissus like 'Baby Moon' or 'Hawera', with blue or white alpine forget-me-nots for a fine-textured accompaniment.

Columbines are great mixers, very willing to fill the garden with handsome children. Individual plants may only last for five or six years, but they unfailingly leave a generous legacy of progeny. The more kinds you grow, the more varied the offspring are likely to be. Some hybrids are relatively stable —the McKana children are quite uniform, as are the pretty, compact 'Music' hybrids—while others are so variable (or so promiscuous) that their children are seldom worth keeping. Members of the *Ranunculaceæ*, the large and vigorous buttercup family, columbines are hardy, easygoing plants that come in a multiplicity of sizes, colors, and forms. If you don't find just what you want in local nurseries, check the seed catalogs for some of these special kinds. Most columbines are very easily grown from seed, whether in small pots or directly sown into a nursery row in the vegetable garden. A late spring or summer sowing does very well, needing only regular watering in the first year. Columbines generally flower their second year; when they do, mark those you want to keep with color-coded yarn or a detailed label to remind yourself what they look like. When fall transplanting time rolls around, a few notes like "dark pink petals, cream horns" or "primrose yellow self" will be invaluable.

To plant—or transplant—columbines successfully, dig wide and fairly deep holes, adding compost, aged manure, some peat, and a bit of bone meal to the soil. Allow the sturdy roots lots of room, since they hate to be cramped. Water in well, and keep them moist (but never soggy) until new growth proves them established. Once settled in, they need only water and an occasional grooming to keep them fit. Once the flowers fade, trim the bloom stalks to the ground, along with any ratty-looking leaves, and water generously to encourage a new flush of foliage (and often more flowers as well). Save only a few seedpods on any single plant, for ripening a full seed crop can quickly exhaust a heavy bloomer. From late spring through full summer, the fluttering dove-flowers of some member or other of this peaceful, lovely family will grace your borders, the foliage contributing color and texture to the scene for most of the year. How often can you get all that from a $.60 seed packet?

Seductive Weeds

hen gardens are abandoned, the woody shrubs and trees hardly notice, fending for themselves for years on end, but only the toughest perennials can persist without assistance from the hand of man. Anybody who takes on the renovation of a neglected older garden quickly enters a new world of weeds —introduced garden weeds, otherwise known as old-fashioned favorites. Some of them, certain primroses, wood anemones, filipendulas, and even hostas, have thick or deep-running roots that may compete successfully with wild grasses. Other garden plants have such aggressive root systems as to make them a menace to their neighbors. These are often the sole survivors in gardens that have been preserved in form only, tended casually and by nongardeners.

A friend who recently moved to such a garden wrote of her pleasure when first she walked through her new yard. Big old trees shaded mossy lawns, and though the flower beds had lost their crisp lines, they were still obviously part of a real garden. Best of all, she said, they were full of pretty flowers. Tall blue bellflowers nodded everywhere, orange daylilies bloomed along the drive while white daisies, lavender poppies, and orange alstroemeria packed the beds. A year or two later, the blue bellflower had been identified as *Campanula rapunculoides*, one of the most pernicious garden weeds that exists. Rough rosettes of dull green, slightly toothed leaves give rise to slender stalks well covered with drooping, rich blue bells. Very pretty, but not fit for mixed company; it has racing roots and an unerring killer instinct that prompts it to infiltrate the crowns of less robust perennials. Like certain running grasses, its roots can pierce a fat iris tuber, puncture a hardy cyclamen corm, or penetrate the thick storage roots of a daylily. So invasive is this plant, and so similar to more desirable campanulas, that it may unwittingly be sold by nurseries—and some good ones, too—under a misleading variety of names. Many knowing gardeners hold all suspicious-looking new campanulas in pots for a season, just to ensure that this relentless destroyer not be released among their treasured plants under an alias.

My friend's joy was distinctly tempered by the time she realized exactly what she had in those promising beds. Her field daisies were not in the same class with this campanula, though they too can cover a lot of ground in time, seeding and spreading about with ease. Still, they can be controlled by pulling out the plant, root and all, which relegates them to a far more benign category. Her lavender opium (*Papaver somniferum*) poppies, like all poppies, will reproduce freely from seed, which, once in the soil, will guarantee a fresh crop every time the soil crust is disturbed. Still, these too can be pulled, and though they are plentiful, they can in time be overcome or restricted to manageable quantities.

Alstroemeria is another story, for once established, these South American natives send storage roots as much as five feet below the ground, and can be nearly impossible to eradicate. The lovely Ligtu hybrids are not so stout as all that, but the orange- or yellow-flowered species, *Alstroemeria aurantiaca*, is the worst pest of the family. Impervious to weed killer (as are all of these cheerful thugs), these tuberous plants can be controlled and even eliminated by regular pulling of the stalks. It is most effective to allow the plants to bloom and begin to set seed, as this requires them to make an outlay of significant energy. Don't delay till the seeds actually ripen, however, or you will simply perpetuate the problem, for fresh seeds germinate with great freedom. If you keep on the job, the storage roots will eventually be exhausted, though the process can take years.

A lovely creature that has destroyed untold thousands of rock gardens is the innocent-looking silvery creeper, *Cerastium tomentosum*. Sometimes called snow-in-summer because of its winsome white flowers, this busy dwarf leaves Flo-Jo in the dust, roaring through garden beds, under cement walks, infiltrating stonework and infesting walls while leaving scores of strangled and dying plants in its wake. It will happily worm its way into the heart of any plant that stands still, but has a winning trick of adopting its owner's taste; it will unfailingly prefer the same plants that you do. It is hard to know why such plants are still in commerce, let alone available from some otherwise reputable nurseries.

We have a generous planting of a handsomely variegated plant in our farmhouse dooryard. The lobed and toothed leaves are a smooth sage green strongly edged with cream. In late spring, frothy flowers something like short Queen Anne's lace rise above the foliage. Although we recognized the creature as the all-but-ineradicable bishop's weed, we assumed that since it was enclosed in solid cement on all sides and had clearly been in position for many long years, we could leave it there with impunity. Unfortunately, the old cement walk developed a crack. Before we knew it, the bishop had trickled away and is now heading around the side of the house at top speed. Fortunately, his path is restricted to an area that is slated for house-expansion construction in a year or two; it is to be hoped that the bulldozers will manage to stop his progress before he works his way into the new gardens.

Not all garden weeds are to be avoided at any cost. I knowingly introduced a group of the tremendously tall, splendidly showy plume poppy, *Macleaya cordata*, to the rough border that edges the children's playing field. Plume poppy boasts huge, heart-shaped leaves of deep, coppery green lined with pewter. It also carries shaggy, loose panicles of rosy brown florets atop stems as much as 12 or 15 feet high, and a well-grown clump is a breathtaking sight. It has the richly deserved reputation of being the prettiest weed in any garden, and indeed, it has decidedly pushy ways, running from one end of a large border to the other before the unsuspecting gardener realizes what is going on underground. It is most prolific in light soils, however, and our heavy clay, combined with drought conditions—we never water the rough border—combine to keep the macleaya in its place. More or less. Actually, it does stray a bit, but since there is plenty of room in that border, we don't much mind. Besides, since there are always lots of visitors who want a piece for themselves, the wandering shoots come in handy.

This brings up an important moral question: is it right to pass garden thugs along, to deliberately contaminate other gardens with maddening and destructive plants? Even though you warn the recipients, are you sure that they fully understand what will happen if you allow them to take home a scrap of the plant they so foolishly desire? With obstreperous but not actually noxious weeds, plants like plume poppy or Ligtu alstroemeria, it would not be wrong to give away a start, along with a stern and vivid caveat. With rampant raiders like *Cerastium tomentosum* and *Campanula rampunculoides*, however, such a gift is a Trojan horse, deceitful and deadly.

Beyond Petunias

SELF-PERPETUATING ANNUALS FOR THE HARRIED GARDENER

My husband and I are knee-deep in the process of renovating an enormous, overgrown garden, restoring some beds and building new borders amid the ruins of the old. Unfortunately, the only plants we can afford in the necessary quantity are youngsters that won't fulfill their promise for several years. New beds can look pitifully empty, so we strewed annual seeds with generous hands to fill our raw garden with color. We chose hardy annuals that perform well even on unimproved ground to give ourselves a spirit-lifting display in these difficult first years. Since those annuals may be needed for four or five years in some areas, we favored sturdy self-sowers that help crowd out weeds and don't need to be watered or fussed over.

For quick and long-lasting brilliance in any kind of garden, nothing can replace annuals, those bright and willing bloomers that perform their entire life cycle in a few colorful months. Because this cycle matches the typical American gardening pattern so neatly, even the most utilitarian gardens are apt to have a few examples; the tomatoes, corn, and beans may alternate with a flurry of marigolds, a ruffle of petunias, a scream or two of salvias. As novice gardeners are quick to discover, the vegetable patch is a good place for exotic annuals like these, for all hail from warmer climes and all can turn distinctly temperamental if they don't get generous and steady supplies of sun, water, and fertilizer.

Annual gardening can be both more and less than the ordinary cycle of peas and petunias; by putting in a bit of painless, even pleasurable research, we can have far more to look at than is offered by the average garden-center six-pack. Annual flowers—and herbs, and even vegetables— can provide a complex and varied garden tapestry in vivid tints and subtle tones unknown to crayon manufacturers. Not only that, but many annuals are far less demanding in their requirements than those petulant exotics, content to bloom their hearts out in dubious soil, without benefit of fertilizer or supplementary water. Best of all, many will return to our gardens of their own volition, self-sowing freely and generously.

Certain annuals naturalize with particular ease and grace, adapting to their surroundings with the aplomb of natives. Patches of silk-petalled portulaca reappear each summer in old beach gardens on Cape Cod. One may find nigella and feverfew in Ohio farmyards, or red flax and borage in an abandoned lot in Denver. Willing workers such as poppies and pansies will often hybridize, their unsolicited offspring appearing in many a back alley or old garden across the country. To discover which annuals are likely to behave in this heartwarming way, it is necessary to gather together a few seed catalogs and to spend some time browsing through them. (This is what passes as research.)

As you flip through the pages, it may strike you that the annuals are amusing somebody. "HA!," the catalog writer will comment, or even "HHA!" Actually, this is not because these plants are a giggle; those cryptic marks indicate frost tolerance. Anything marked "HHA" is a half-hardy annual, intolerant of many things, frost among them. By and large, the half-hardy bedding beauties are a demanding bunch; living in the fast lane, they want the best, right now. These seedlings must be cosseted in warm greenhouses, and the plants mustn't venture out-of-doors until frosty nights are just a memory. Their faithful fans perform yeoman service, digging deep to make loose, fluffy soil, supplying quantities of fertilizer and water early and often, and keeping competitive weeds away. Like vegetables, when their growth is checked by insufficient water or nutrients, half-hardy annuals respond with what amounts to a plant tantrum, drooping, dropping buds, or refusing to grow. Frequent shortages can lead to prolonged and sometimes fatal sulks. This isn't just theatrics; unlike perennials, shrubs, or bulbs, they have no reserves. A stressed annual is often a dead annual.

If you have secretly been ashamed of your poor luck with bedding annuals, relax; you are in good company. Many avant gardeners wouldn't dream of fussing with bedders, yet they don't eschew annuals altogether. All those pretty creatures marked "HA" are hardy annuals, made of tougher stuff. Even in youth they can take considerable cold, and are apt to flower earlier than their tender cousins. Many bloom straight through the summer, some continue into fall, and a few will still be hard at it when cut down by the killing frosts of winter. Calendulas (the shaggy pot marigolds) and honey-scented sweet alyssum are two old favorites that bloom endlessly where winters are mild (some hardy annuals are fitfully perennial in temperate climates). Even where winters are harsh and the snow falls early, the seedling children of these stalwarts may rise to greet you in spring.

Unlike the seed of half-hardy annuals, which require greenhouse temperatures or warm summer nights to germinate, the seed of hardy annuals actually germinates better if exposed to frosts. Although few garden books mention it, the optimal time to sow hardy annuals is in late fall, after a killing frost. October is the usual month in the northern states, though in mild winter areas gardeners may wait until November or early December. As you do your last chores around the garden, scatter the seeds where you want them to grow. The ensuing weather won't hurt them a bit; some will germinate during the cool, slow days of autumn, put on root growth beneath the winter snow, and bounce into bloom with the first burst of spring. Others awake in earliest spring, passing quickly from seedling to flowering plant. These early birds may pass through several generations before those Memorial Day six-packers hit their stride.

If this seems farfetched, try a little experiment: sow half a packet each of three or four hardy annuals in late fall. Shirley poppies, sweet alyssum, feverfew, and annual larkspurs are all good candidates for late sowing. Save the remaining seed in a closed jar or tightly sealed plastic bag to keep it as fresh as possible. (Some books recommend that seed be stored in dry, dark places, but I usually leave mine with the garden tools in the sun porch, and it comes to no harm despite the light.) Come spring, sow the remaining seed. Chances are good that when you do, you will discover that the autumn-sown batch has already made vigorous plants.

Busy gardeners already hard pressed to squeeze in yet another chore will welcome another piece of advice: leave the annuals alone. In order to self-sow, plants must be allowed to set, ripen, and scatter their seed. That may seem obvious, yet zealous garden writers are always reminding us that constant deadheading—grooming plants of all spent blossoms—is the key to long bloom in annuals. Deadheading does prolong bloom, but many annuals will flower over a long period without any intervention at all. What's more, no plant can set seed if each fading flower is promptly removed. The whole garden need not go to pot for the sake of next year's seeds; often it suffices to leave the seedheads on a few mother plants, tidying up the rest all you like to encourage further flowering. Where annuals decorate the vegetable patch, think of these mother plants as a seed crop, something like dry beans. Though certain annuals are almost guaranteed to return, until your chosen ones are firmly established, it pays to let nature work unhindered.

In both urban and country gardens we have found that self-sown annuals really shine in mixed beds or borders. Here evergreen shrubs are softened by herbs and perennials, masses of bulbs encircle bushes and small trees, and no one type of plant predominates. The lasting pleasures of a well-assembled mixed planting cannot be overstated, for there is always something to delight the eye, in winter as well as during the clement months. Tucked amid plants of greater substance, self-sown annuals can reproduce endlessly, contributing their effortless effects year after year without impairing the garden's looks.

In our city garden, for six years we relied on self-sown annuals to decorate several areas that were in the public eye yet out of range of the hose. Where our lot borders the alley, a narrow strip of dry soil held a few columnar junipers, some clumps of blue flag iris, and a sagging old bay laurel. We shaped the shrubs, thinned and reset the iris, introduced sweet woodruff and ajuga for ground covers, and planted hundreds of spring bulbs. We then sowed hardy annuals throughout: godetia and forget-me-nots, Shirley poppies and bush morning glories. All of these return cheerfully, often joined by volunteers, escapees from other gardens.

Our compost bins were in this narrow alley strip, and when we tossed garden gleanings into the bins, we made a point of shaking spent annuals over the strip as we passed. Now those first few varieties mingle with over a dozen others, some of which we did not introduce. The lovely annual larkspurs with branches of blossoms like tiny perched birds in deep blue, soft pink, and white arrived without active encouragement on our part, as did a host of pale yellow snapdragons, the narrow spires of faded pink and lavender linarias, and tall, silver-pink opium poppies. This alley area is never watered and only gets weeded once or twice a year, yet there are always flowers here from earliest spring until hard frosts.

The front of our small urban lot is a steep hill open to the south and west. Here the self-perpetuating planting is based on hardy annuals that thread through low shrubs, Mediterranean herbs, and prostrate junipers. Once the evergreen shrubs matured, the bank remained attractive all year without much help from the hand of man. The soil here, an infertile yellow clay, initially supported a meager crop of weeds and a languishing lilac and was clearly not capable of much more. One summer we mulched the entire hillside with 18 inches of shredded bark mixed with cottonseed meal, then ignored it. By fall the sorry grass was smothered, earthworms were hard at work, and the top inch of soil had turned a couple of shades darker. In went the junipers, some grey-tipped, others blue-green, as well as the evergreen herbs—rosemaries, thymes, lavenders, and sages. These would become the backbone of the planting, but as we worked we also added generous quantities of hardy annuals, shaking the seed in circles around each shrub and covering the entire bank with interwoven drifts.

The following spring saw the junipers double in size, their plumate branches rising like retrievers' tails lifted in greeting. The herbs were settling in nicely, too, but all were still quite small and it would have looked a bit sparse were it not for the foaming froth of flowers that filled and overflowed the bank. The ivory daisies of chamomile covered the ground below the sparkling white ones of feverfew. Cobalt blue borage blossoms gleamed above carpets of California poppies in cream and pink and soft gold. A trickling stream of baby blue eyes ran between hummocks of white sweet alyssum and forests of chalky pastel candytuft. Here and there bold patches of warmly tinted calendulas made sunny spots amid the cooler colors. Since we have dry summers, things can get a bit tatty by high summer, but freshness is quickly restored by cutting the hardy annuals back hard, to stubble a few inches high, in July. If we then supply a mulch of compost and aged manure, and a long soaking drink, we are rewarded within a couple of weeks by renewed bloom that carries on through the fall.

The bank now supports colonies of 20 kinds of hardy annuals. Their seeds have traveled down the slope and taken over the parking strip—with a little cooperation from us. Farther down the sloping sidewalk, the apartment building next door now boasts spreading colonies of calendulas and poppies, feverfew and borage. Some of the residents have started to plant a few perennials among them, in a small streetside strip which hitherto housed only blue flag iris and weeds. Seeds from our bank have blown across the street to beautify an abandoned lot, been hand- or bird-carried into yards and alleyways all over the neighborhood, filling ragged, empty places with flowers. This house is now rented to friends, both artists, who have expanded our original planting with colorful additions of their own, and the garden continues to brighten the neighborhood throughout the year.

Not long ago, we traded the pleasures of our urban garden for a delightful old farm on an island a short commute by ferry from the city. Here, too, we are incorporating hardy annuals into the beds and borders. Along the drive, a tall hedge of ancient, arching spireas left only a thin, dry strip of ground for planting. We wanted a welcoming wave of flowers here, dark blues washed with every shade of cream through warm orange, all sparkled with white. It made sense to use plants that could come back from being inadvertently crushed by uncertain drivers, were drought tolerant, and only required planting once; hardy annuals filled the bill. We blended a blue mixture of larkspurs (using some hybrid strains as well as the local volunteers), both spring and summer forget-me-nots, tall, fuzzy-leafed borage, and a lower-growing borage relative, *Echium vulgare*. For the creams, yellows, and orange tones, we used California poppies, adding a dwarf strain of calendulas that ran heavily to buffs, straw yellows, and sorbet oranges. Feverfew in several varieties, dwarf and tall, as well as white larkspur and white forget-me-nots heightened and lightened the color blend.

Soon the driveway was edged by a thick ribbon of flowers that faded back into the field behind the hedge in a natural-looking way. Indeed, it looked so natural that it made us start to think about a wild-flower meadow. We had enough experience with both wild flowers and meadows to realize that far more was involved than merely tilling up a field and dumping a can of fancy meadow mix over it. Furthermore, there were other complications, like two small boys who felt that the field had their names on it. Our compromise solution, which pleases us all, was to till up strips around the edges of the field and introduce perennials such as ox-eye daisies, Queen Anne's lace, butterfly weed, and native lupines. These strips are liberally laced with hardy annuals, many of which are the same wild flowers that come in the fancy mixes. By the second season, all our introductions were seeding themselves into the meadow. Some got trampled in the wake of an errant soccer ball now and then, but most bounced back quickly. The few that didn't went as unmourned as those squashed by imperfect drivers on the other side of the hedge; there are always plenty more where those came from.

Lots of people with a large lawn or field are tempted into meadowmaking, but meadows can be minute, fitting into the smallest yards. A friend in Ohio made a delightful pocket-handkerchief meadow, inspired by European farm fields where the Shirley poppies and cornflowers blow amongst the rustling golden wheat. He sowed hardy annuals along with the wheat, and varied the texture by working in annual ornamental grasses, most of which are also good self-sowers. Cloud grass, cotton grass, and pale pink, fluffy love grass, animated oats and quaking grass, squirrel tail and hare's tail grasses made a gilded, shimmering fabric that whispered with every wind. Punctuated by the brilliant poppies in scarlet and crimson, eyed and fringed with black, the sky blue cornflowers, and a few moonflower field daisies, the little plot offered rich color and lovely, shifting textures right through the winter.

The trick to using hardy annual grasses in such a mixed planting is to label each starter patch or to sprout them in pots, since they will otherwise get weeded out along with escapees from the lawn. In the infant stages, any kind of grass looks pretty much like grass, and it takes the eye of experience to detect which are wanted and which are interlopers. Many annual grasses flower and set seed generously, so once your patches are firmly established you can simply thin them annually to allow room for their companion flowers. You will have to weed once or twice in early- and midspring to keep the unwanted competition down, but once that's done you can let the whole works take care of itself. Grasses, too, must ripen and set seed before being mown; many gardeners like the looks of the sun-bleached grasses in the snow and leave them standing until late winter or early spring brings up the next year's crop.

Experiment a bit, trying half a dozen new annuals each year to discover which will return to your garden. Designate an area where you can sow likely candidates both in autumn and in spring, and where the soil won't get worked over or disturbed—many seeds require light to germinate well. If they are accidentally covered, you may not see your flowers again until another bout of weeding or tilling returns them to the surface. Once the seedlings appear, weed and thin them, then sit back and watch, for these are plants that give the most when left pretty much to their own devices. As your successes mount, move your lab around the yard. Continuing trials, on however modest a scale, will reveal which plants favor poor, rocky soil in full sun, which thrive in clay, or sand, or boggy ground, and which prefer the richer soil of the garden proper. It's perfectly true that we reap what we sow; those who sow their hardy annuals wisely and well can go on reaping for years to come.

The Grass Could Be Greener

The Pacific Northwest is the only place I have ever lived where the grass is green all winter and brown all summer. This is due partly to our recurring summer droughts, and the nature of the particular grasses which make up our lawns, but also to the way in which our lawns are mown and watered. The current prohibitions on lawn sprinkling need not mean a sere and crisped brownsward, since a healthy, properly trimmed lawn does not need to be watered for two hours a week in the first place. If your lawn looks and feels swell, and you are watering less than once a week in under two hours, turn to the sports page. You don't need this column. If your grass crunches underfoot and shows signs of premature balding, read on. Here's what you can do right now to reverse this unseemly trend without resorting to illicit soaks.

Short term, the best choice is to stop mowing during the hottest months. Cut grass high and seldom, rather than close and often, from late June till the rains return in late summer or fall. Once the spring ebullience wears off, grass growth slows down quite quickly and we need mow only once every four to six weeks in high summer. The edges of the lawn may require more frequent trimming, but the open areas should be allowed to reach $2\frac{1}{2}$–3 inches (most lawn mowers are set at $1\frac{1}{2}$ inches, but can easily be set higher). This added height is valuable for several reasons: first of all, grass wants to go dormant when the weather is hot and/or dry. Longer grass shades its own crowns, which helps keep at bay the sleepiness that overcomes crew-cut grass when the heat is on. Longer grass blades also conserve moisture; a lawn shorn at $2\frac{1}{2}$ inches will consistently need less water than a closer-cropped one from which water losses to evaporation are considerable.

Another trick to try probably involves changing your watering habits (should you have any). Small urban lawns can often be watered most effectively with soaker hoses made of canvas or plastic. The double-barreled kind with pin-prick holes is cheap, fairly flexible, doesn't rot, and can be made shorter very easily. Faucet attachments allow ganging up to four hoses, and at such low speed, all may be run simultaneously without losing water pressure or flooding the cellar. Overhead sprinklers can be quite wasteful, but soaker hoses work on the trickle-down theory, and we all know how effective that can be. Lay the hose hole-side down with the water on as low as it can go, and leave it in place for an hour. Early morning is a fine time to water, and if the hose is laid out the night before it just takes a minute to turn it on when you get up, and off before heading to work. This waters a relatively small area deeply and thoroughly, rather than broadcasting to the entire neighborhood, but the job is done right. In our city garden, one hose lay is sufficient, but larger yards may require several. Soaker hoses may not be practical for the biggest lawns, but will still be more effective in the problem places which aren't well served by the sprinkler.

Where the earth is really parched and the grass is dead or very soundly sleeping, a little aeration can help; get out your garden fork and jump on the shoulder, forcing the tines a good couple of inches into the baked clay. Even if you don't fill the holes with sand and fertilizer, just getting some air and water to the root zone will be helpful. There is a fun gadget, called an air and water aerator, which uses water power rather than muscle power; I don't know of any local source, but they can be ordered from a reputable horticultural supply firm, A.M. Leonard. The price is reasonable, and Leonard gives good discounts even for small quantities, so get the neighborhood involved in your order.

Grass can't grow well if it's underfed, but the bizarre American syndrome of force-feeding it only to sheer off all its luxuriant locks contributes nothing to its health and is wasteful to boot. Slow fertilizers, such as bone meal, cottonseed meal, and soy meal, are ideal for lawns, and may be sprinkled on with a light hand when the rains resume. (No fertilizer, however gentle, should ever be applied to dry plants or dry soil.) If you add a tablespoon of kelp meal for every cup of bone meal or soy meal, many of the trace elements lost with the grass clippings (and rarely supplied by commercial fertilizers) will be restored. Fall feeding with these low-key ingredients won't promote sudden or excessive growth, but will give roots something to chew on during the cool months when they do a lot of developing hidden away from sight. Compost is a nutritious mulch, especially good where bare dirt shows between unhappy crowns. If the earth is well scratched with a rake, some mild fertilizers are strewn about, and a light blanket of compost is applied, the rain will do the rest, and in the spring, the benefits to the grass will be obvious to all eyes.

Reckless Roses

ot summer days are for lounging, a time to avoid strenuous activity by any fair means. Only in earliest morning is it cool enough to venture out, hoe in hand, to weed and study and savor the garden. Sleepy birds call their reveille, and the first light of the waking day is tender, resting gently on tightly tucked buds and the shut flowers which belong to the sun. At this early hour, the scents of summer are softened, the odors of mint and oregano, honeysuckle and jasmine are separate, each coming clearly as we pass them by. Later, the building heat will blend them with the day scents of lavender and rose into a heady perfume no money can buy, the smell of the June garden.

Of all summer scents, this essence of June is unique, unmatchable, for June brings roses in its wake. They come almost overnight, in reckless profusion that fills the garden with color, the air with enchantment. On still mornings, the wandering gardener who is up before the sun finds the folded buds flushed with color and fat with promise. Most hold the merest suggestion of fragrance in the cool dawn, but as the sun climbs, the sliding sunlight catches and warms the unfurling petals, coaxing the fullest perfume from the newly opened flowers.

Some roses have only an elusive scent, but one which gives its fragrance freely is the statuesque 'Lawrence Johnston', a splendid hybrid of *Rosa foetida*. The flowers, which appear in force in June, then intermittently until late fall, have the excellent attribute of shattering cleanly as they fade, the new unmarred by the passing of the old. The ruffled, tumbling blossoms unfold from buttery buds to big silken cups of lemon cream. In form, they are semidouble (carrying a few more petals or petioles than a single rose would), rather loose and flaring, with a fluffy central knob of celadon green surrounded by clustered stamens of old gold and soft brown. The fragrance is also lemony, with a faint herbal overtone, very light and clean. A spray of 'Lawrence Johnston' is most refreshing in a bedside nosegay, and the scent carries wonderfully on the warm evening air. An upright, vigorous shrub, it can reach 10 feet in height and spread, making a staggering ornament for a large border. In our meadow border, it is matched with a flowering maple, *Abutilon x suntense*, which produces loads of lavender mallow flowers somewhat like single hollyhocks. They are the color of chive blossom, with which both the abutilon and rose are thickly underplanted, intermixed with the lacy silver-grey sprawler, *Artemisia absinthium* 'Lambrook Silver'. Where room is restricted, 'Lawrence Johnston' may be trained over an arch or encouraged to cover a fence or wall, where it will take up surprisingly little ground room, though filling the vertical space handily. This is not a rose to fuss over, seldom troubled by pest or disease and needing only an annual thinning of the older canes to keep it shapely and productive. The original plant was selected from a French nursery by the American-born creator of the famous Gloucestershire garden, Hidcote. Grown for many years in that garden as 'Hidcote Yellow', it was introduced to the trade in the forties by Graham Stuart Thomas and given Major Johnston's name at his own request—a fitting tribute to both man and rose.

Where a brighter color is wanted, the equally healthy 'Sunny June' will cover pillar or post with glossy, dark green leaves and quantities of sun-colored flowers, single and huge. The petals are crisp, with the stiff feel of enameled paper, saturated with a rich, clean yellow that is brilliant without being harsh. This is one of those invaluable shades (another is chalk yellow) which complements almost anything. The blossoms are centered with long, curling red stamens the color of Chinese lacquer, each ending in a tiny flat circle of gold; when backlit, these ignite, giving the flowers a glowing intensity. It looks all the more vivid with an underplanting of dusky copper fennel, a pewter grey hebe called 'Boughten Dome', and a backdrop of plummy, purple-leafed cotinus or a burgundy purple shrubby hazel.

An old-fashioned favorite, the sweetbriar (*Rosa eglanteria*) is a happy spendthrift with its fragrance, pouring it out from blossom and leaf alike, thus heavily scented even when not in bloom. After a warm rain, its perfume pervades the whole garden, persisting for hours on the fingers of those who handle the leaves. It is an unusual odor, wholesome and homely, curiously like that of stewed apples and quince. The flowers, which thickly cover the wide-flung arms of this hardy old shrub, are simple and fresh, wide-eyed single blossoms of warm pink fading to white at the central boss of frilly golden stamens. Each petal is heart-shaped, rather thin of substance, and faintly veined with violet-pink. Eglantine, or sweetbriar, looks sentimentally perfect scrambling over a log fence around an old homestead, covering an arched gate in a sunny farmyard, or clambering up and through an evergreen hedge. No trespasser will try twice to penetrate a barrier hedge of sweetbriar, and this easiest of roses might well be planted along the edges of inner-city lots, where it would do Doberman duty even without benefit of obedience school.

Most roses demand a good deal of sun, and *R. glauca* (*rubrifolia*) grows very well in a sunny situation, where the dark green leaves become backed and stained and tinted with deep reds and purples. In partial shade, the foliage is even more glorious, for it takes on a gunmetal sheen like a dusting of silver through which the somber colors glimmer. The flowers are fleeting, smaller, more delicate and wild-looking versions of the eglantine. They are succeeded by sprays of little round hips, red-black and glossy, which last through the autumn, when the foliage turns brighter red before falling at last. This, too, is a terrific hedging plant, dense, well-armed, and spangled with ruddy ornament. In favored sites, the red-leafed rose can achieve the proportions of a small tree, and may be confused at a distance with the smoke bush, *Cotinus coggygria*, in its purple form. When it blooms, the satin pink blossom against the dusky purple leaves is every bit as pleasing as a flowering plum, though it lasts far longer in beauty.

Where space considerations affect the choice of a rose, *R. moschata nastarana* (often sold as 'Nastarana') is a sound candidate. Small and delicately formed, this little shrub is an almost endless bloomer, particularly in a sunny, sheltered spot. Its foliage is finely textured, and the long, slim shoots are burdened with hundreds of plump pink buds. These open in clusters, each branch a bouquet of semidouble white rosettes spilling their perfume with prodigal abandon. It is happily partnered with an American wild flower, *Gaura lindheimeri*, a whippy, whorling upright perennial with the look of a wiry shrub. Gaura, too, blooms forever, its tight buds packing the tips of its long wands. They are the same warm pink as nastarana's buds, and open into silky little butterfly flowers of the same cool white.

In a little bouquet on my desk, the citrus scent of 'Lawrence Johnston' blends with the fruity odor of the sweetbriar, the pungent fragrances of golden curly marjoram, ornamental oregano, and copper fennel blending with the brisk, almost medicinal smell of lavender. Gathered early, these flowers sat inert until wakened by the heat of the day. Now the fragrance of June, the haunting, nameless smell of early summer, is concentrated in this glass, spilling first through the room, then moving lightly through the whole house, carried on the small wind of twilight.

The BORDER *in* HIGH SUMMER

JULY ▪ AUGUST

HIGH SUMMER

The gardens of July and August have the beauty of maturity. Like ladies of a certain age, their charms are most obvious when lightly veiled. Cool, foggy mornings fill the garden with neutral oyster light, kind and flattering to all colors. The border glows intensely, its brilliance emphasized by the slanting shadows and soft, diffused light. At high noon all color is drained of power, and shapes and patterns are blurred by rippling heat and harsh light. Late afternoon brings the garden back into focus. Plants are attractively backlit, their colors deepened, their relationships clarified. During the extended twilights the air itself is blue and silver. The garden glimmers softly in this mysterious half light that brightens with the coming of the moon. The nights are always hot, but the night scents are variable—now sensual, explicit, and charged with insistence; now dreamy, allusive, and languorous.

Though the bright flames of rose and peony have burned low in the border, the wand of color has passed into competent hands and summer's race is on. The time for promise is past; all is fulfillment or failure. Great spiked spears of torch lilies in burning colors split the hot sky. Tall grasses spread in magnificent gilded sheaves, their shaggy bloom stalks tasseled and heavy with seed, soaring even higher than the kniphofias. Daylilies are everywhere, the spidery lemon-lime 'Lady Fingers', 'Water Witch' in a haze of mulberry, French grey, and plum, and always the indefatigable 'Stella d'Oro', golden girl of the garden. The slim, whorling stalks of true lilies are laden with long, heavy buds that open daily. The great waxen trumpets of the Aurelians blow gold and green, rose and ribbon pink, purple-black and moon white, their saffron pollen spattered by ardent bees. Tiger lilies, tawny and butterscotch, chalk yellow and sun yellow, silver pink and copper, proliferate in every corner. Upfacing Asiatics pack their short stems with blossom, their curling petals cheerfully freckled. Buff and burgundy, cherry and bronze, blackish red and copper, they give weight and substance to washes of silver artemisias and masses of gentle pink sundrops (*Oenothera berlandieri*). Slowly the arching, fern-fronded *Lilium speciosum* comes to perfection, spreading fans of flowers the color of raspberries and cream. Magnificent Oriental hybrids open improbably huge, splayed bells seven or eight feet above the ground, their rippled, lace-edged petals rose and white, silver and gold.

Forsythia and weigela are long gone, replaced by buttercupped hypericum and silk-petaled cistus, lavateras like single hollyhocks, hardy hibiscus, and hydrangeas with creamy mounds of bloom. Prickly ornamental thistles and soft lamb's ears, solid mounds of hardy geraniums and airy puffs of baby's breath, flopping wands of dancing gaura, pink and white, and upright, architectural euphorbias fill the beds. In the cutting garden, swirling zinnias and painted daisies, flax and balsam, larkspur and love-in-a-mist mingle with purple peas, red kale, and green romanesco in a gay and useful mishmash of mismatched tint and tone.

In July one should only savor the garden. Dry, hot days are made for enjoyment; we taste now the fruits of earlier labor, making notes all the while toward future ones: "Shift new *Rhododendron oreotrephes* two feet to the left; underplant with blue rue—'Blue Beauty'? 'Jackman's'?—and some ice blue, tufty grass—*Festuca glacialis? glauca?*" In another spot we might note, "Rose 'Kathleen Mills' and hydrangea 'Pretziosa' need to change positions—rose is too shadowed in summer now that the buddleia 'Lochinch' has filled out. Fill gaps between all with white hellebores."

Such planning seems effortless—or at least physically passive, as is appropriate when temperatures climb—but it calls for concentrated mental application. Take all the time you need to look and

ponder, returning to a trouble spot often through the day to evaluate the group in different lights. Beyond this, a little desultory
grooming will always be in order. One can weed a bit in the misty
mornings, or deadhead here and there in the cool of the evening,
but more than that is de trop. The only constant is water, which
must be applied wisely and well in order not to waste resources—
yours or the water company's.

As August slips toward September, the chores begin again in
earnest. The border blaze of August dies down at month's end, and
if the flames of fall are to be properly appreciated, some serious
prinking is in order. Trowel and trug are in daily use, for like those
ladies of a certain age, borders don't preserve their summery charms
without considerable effort. Willingly we spend ourselves in watering and grooming, pruning and feeding, cutting back and filling in
any gaps with chrysanthemums and asters. All this effort pays a
hefty dividend, for given proper care our borders will hold considerable beauties for several months to come.

A Green-Gold Garden

oughly half of the gardens I have seen recently boast a white section: either a little garden room filled with white flowering things, a white border, or at least a white bed. This is a pleasant affectation, the dream child of the redoubtable Ms. Jekyll, popularized for another generation by Vita Sackville-West, but let's do branch out a bit. What about a red garden, a purple one, a peach, salmon, and apricot one? If that all seems a shade obvious, why not attempt something subtler: a green-and-gold group in which flowers and foliage alike will fit our theme.

Here our conceit will be that all the flowers must either be green, that lovely citric yellow which holds a good deal of green, or gold. We will avoid a harsh, brassy effect by tempering the bolder golds with softer ones, and using foliage of blue, gunmetal, and pewter as buffers. Green flowers are not fascinating to everybody, but those of us who collect them sometimes do a lot of head-scratching before finding just the right way to demonstrate their subtle graces. The charming little viola 'Irish Molly' catches the eye of many a gardener, but few can place her to their satisfaction. Her blossoms are of a curious shade of green, almost a bronze green shading to khaki and pale golden yellow. Her eyes are black-lashed, as proper Irish eyes must be—a fetching creature, but where to put her? She suffers from an unfortunate tendency to look dirty in most company, but when her skirts are interlaced with that flat and willing creeper, golden moneywort (*Lysimachia nummularia* 'Aurea'), Molly comes into her own. Behind her, and only slightly taller, stands *Patrinia triloba*, an uncommon but easygoing perennial with shapely leaves, dark and deeply lobed and ornamental for most of the year. In summer the small, fragrant flowers form large flat umbels of greenish gold, and in autumn the foliage warms to purple and red.

The great clans of *Coreopsis* and *Helianthus* provide dozens of golden flowers, and when well grown and tempered with plenty of green and grey, these rather coarse plants can achieve a charming, billowy effect. The exception to the family rule is provided by *Coreopsis* 'Moonbeam', an ethereal plant with superb, delicate flowers in changing shades of goldy green—there is nothing coarse about this creature. The curry plant, *Helicrysum italicum* (*angustifolium*) is a perfect mixer for this group, where its soft grey foliage exercises a calming effect on all the hot, bright golds. Its bloom is equally low-key—small, subdued daisy florets in old gold, which associate nicely with green flowers.

Are there really green flowers? Frankly green blooms are rare, but green roses exist (in the species *Rosa viridis*), and a green hollyhock—which is reportedly immune to rust—has recently arrived from China. Closer to home a friendly annual, bells-of-Ireland (*Moluccella laevis*), builds sturdy green-flowered towers. The new delphinium strain 'Green Expectations' produces spikes of florets in a good range of soft greenish tints. Among daylilies, 'Green Balloons' carries round, fat grass green buds that open into chartreuse yellow flowers—not wonderfully distinguished, but a pleasure all the same. 'Green Flutter' and 'Green Fringe' have much the same cool, un-ripe-lemon coloring, and deep, glowing green throats. An elegant, spidery daylily called 'Ladyfingers' is chalk yellow tinted green with a grass green throat. 'Green Magic', a trumpet lily, blows white with green shadows. It is especially fragrant at night, as is the faded greenish white flower, not unlike phlox, of *Hesperis matronalis*, the sweet rocket of the Elizabethans.

Flowering tobacco is often night-fragrant—the starry green and white blossoms of *Nicotiana affinis* are famous for it. There are lots of green flowers among the ornamental nicotines, from the moonlight green of *N. sylvestris*, the woodland tobacco, to the bronzed, olive green of the languorous, tubular *N. langsdorfii*, each floret enriched with an eye of navy blue. *N. alata*, the common annual nicotine, boasts several truly green hybrids, including 'Domino Green', 'Nicki Green', and 'Lime Green'.

The masterworts (*Astrantia* species) often run to the green. They are meadow flowers from the Swiss and Carpathian alps, but they take kindly to lowland garden conditions, where they are outstanding both for ease of cultivation and for showiness. Perhaps that is too strong a word, for the individual flowers tend to be small, yet the plants have undeniable garden impact, their airy mass of pincushion flowers rising on sturdy stems two or even three feet above the handsome, palmate leaves. The blossoms are most often white or palest pink, all touched with silver and strongly infused with green; each petal is netted, veined, and tipped with it. The flowers them-selves are unusually formed; flat disks of daisy rays, centered with puffy tufts of fluffy stamens. They bloom in midsummer and again in autumn, often continuing in beauty until hard frosts cut them down.

Proud stems of the statuesque summer hyacinth, *Galtonia candicans*, are loaded with drooping, dangling green-tinged ivory bells. On a smaller scale, a ruffled little heuchera called 'Chartreuse' sends up slim wands of tiny greeny-yallery bells. Lady's mantle (the alchemilla) will prove most useful, especially *A. mollis*, with wide, scalloped leaves, as pleated as a lady's fan, and fat plumes of tiny, spumy green flowers which flop irrepressibly to grovel in the gravel of the nearest pathway. The effect is really quite pretty, as the bold leaves make a plump cushion above the foamy cloud of bloom. On a smaller scale, *Alchemilla conjuncta* will make a very pretty filler between larger perennials or beneath shrubs. This is usually sold as *A. alpina*, which is a dowdier little thing; you can tell at once which your plant is, because the lobes of *A. conjuncta*'s leaves are fused at the base—conjoined, in a word. Isn't Latin wonderful?

In any garden, perennials look their best when given some solid support from background plants. A splendid choice for this garden group is the cut-leaf golden elder, *Sambucus racemosa* 'Plumosa Aurea'. This can reach 10 feet if you let it, but when pruned to the ground in late winter it remains a compact shrub, its foliage finer, larger, and more brilliantly colored. Among smaller shrubs, *Euonymus fortunei* offers several appropriate forms: 'Emerald and Gold' is a neat little thing with lovely fresh green leaves edged with golden yellow; 'Emerald Gaiety' is a bit bigger and splashier, its leaves edged in creamy white; while 'Silver Queen' will slowly build into a good-size shrub, its leaves variegated in a subdued golden yellow that turns to ivory in midsummer, and blushes pink in winter.

The familiar golden privet 'Vicary' has a brazen color, but the proper companions will make it look vivid rather than hectic. If you have only seen this plant hacked into a hedge, you will be astonished by the character it shows when grown as a trim standard or small free-form shrub covered with spiky little bunches of fragrant white flowers. Newer to our shores, an English hybrid bush honeysuckle, *Lonicera nitida* 'Baggeson's Gold' has foliage of a deep, almost bronzy gold, a handsome plant that is clearly destined for a wide distribution.

For silver things, we will want more helichrysums, artemisias both lacy ('Silver Bouquet') and bold ('Powis Castle'), dusty miller and lamb's ears. Blue-grey comes from a pair of compact little shrublets, *Hebe southerlandii* and *H.* 'Pewter Dome', both fine-textured plants. Grey-green spires of *Ballota pseudodictamnus* and the pale gold of another hebe, *H. armstrongii*, a whipcord with tiny, adpressed leaves like overlapping fish scales, bind our theme party together. Grey herbs, like lavender and sage, and blue-green ones, like rue and certain alliums, will balance and cool hot, heavy golds.

Textures of leaf and twig take on extra importance in a single-color garden, and the foliage plants require equally careful consideration as the flowering things, for most effective placement. In our gold-and-green garden, many of the flowering plants will have a similar leaf form. To create more interesting textures we might introduce feathery, gold-tipped junipers as a handsome background for smoother, bolder leaves. Wiry, stiff-twigged Mount Etna brooms (*Genista aetnensis*) have a light, airy feeling for all their impressive size—they can reach 20 feet in time. Within the border, the velvety herbs soften the harsh, flat greens of helenium, helianthus, and coreopsis. Meadow rue and columbine both have lacy, glaucous leaves of blue or grey, notably the native Western columbine, *Aquilegia formosa*. It has swinging pagoda flowers of lacquer red which would provide an igniting spark of deeper color in our scheme.

Ms. Jekyll rightly railed against those who get prissy about purity in color-theme gardens like this one. Lavender will of course bloom in dark blue spires, but we won't exclude it on that account; many a theme garden fails to make its point precisely because of this timid attitude on the part of the gardener. Use your eyes and your best color sense, and dare to add that touch of blue, that splash of peach, to pull the whole composition together. Too strict a color interpretation can make for an insipid picture. How many of these white gardens would be improved by the inclusion of the pinkish-cream rose 'Penelope', which has pastel coral pink hips in fall. 'Nevada' is a very good rose, let's admit that freely, but when any plant becomes ubiquitous it needs reexamination (and that goes double for grass). Pick a theme and play upon it, but don't hesitate to bend your chosen rule if your garden picture would be the better for it. A correct and safe composition will never offend, but it will rarely achieve splendor, either. Far, far better to be spectacular—even spectacularly mistaken—than tamely, sorrily safe.

A Few Cutting Words

ull summer brings respite to the busy gardener. All the chores and activities of spring are finished (or left for fall...or next year). Trees and shrubs have leafed out, baskets are full of bloom, wave succeeds wave of color and scent in the full, fat borders. Time to sit back, relax, and enjoy the progression of bloom. Time for me to make a few cutting remarks.

There are always a few diehards who can't stop and don't even want to. For such as these, "relax" is an active verb. Some lucky souls are content to take a well-earned rest, smell the flowers, wander about the garden snipping buds for the house. Others, however, relate most happily to their gardens in an active way. I personally am not capable of looking at my garden for more than perhaps three minutes without fidgeting, pulling a weed here, nipping an obtrusive branch there, pinching a shoot or precocious bud in yet another spot. One of the best ways for such gardeners to see the garden is to water it; hose in one hand, pruning shears and/or a drink in the other, there is no pleasanter way to while away a summer evening. For any such nonstop gardeners, I would like to recommend a small but exceedingly pithy little book put out by the Arboretum Foundation, called *Cuttings Throughout the Year* (see Appendix D).

If you have run out of things to fiddle with, have sown all your biennials, potted up all your choice seedlings, emptied your refrigerator and freezer (mine are generally full of small self-sealing plastic bags of peat moss and certain seeds that like extended periods of cold), and are ready for a new project, do get this amazing book. It consists of a series of monthly listings of plants from which one can take cuttings, hardwood, softwood, and root cuttings. There is a good section explaining just how this is done, with diagrams and pictures, and a key to indicate which sort of cutting to take.

This invaluable source has been compiled over a number of years, based upon the local experience of many of the finest gardeners in the area, including that of two past directors of the Washington Park Arboretum, both internationally recognized figures in horticulture. In short, it is information one may safely act upon. In June there are 80 plants from which one may—indeed, ought to—take cuttings. In July and August there are 150; something is listed for every month of the year. The application is clear; when you cruise your friends' gardens, keep your eyes out for stunning things to take bits of—and of course, offer bits of your own plants in return. Fair is fair.

What if you want more of something, but just can't cut it? Take a leaf cutting, a root cutting, layer a low limb, get into grafting; directions for the performance of these interesting operations are also included. Propagation of plant parts is a very useful horticultural tool, and this book goes a long way toward making the various processes simple. It is a most handy book and may well be unique; as far as I know, there is nothing like it anywhere in the country. Lots of good gardeners are intimidated by propagating, and the authors of *Cuttings Throughout the Year* work hard to alleviate such fears, partially through stimulating the gardener's natural greed; who wouldn't be enticed by the offer of more for practically nothing? It is also deeply satisfying to watch a plant which you have raised from seed or cutting grow to ripe, majestic maturity. Once you taste success of this kind, plant propagation becomes irresistible in its own right.

Not tempting you? Perhaps you have located a source for a wonderful plant you have wanted for years, but it is very expensive and you need six or eight of them to fulfill the dream scheme you have in mind. Perhaps a friend has succeeded in raising a difficult or unusual plant from hard-to-come-by seed and you must have one too. Perhaps you would like to offer a favorite but unnamed backyard rose to a number of your friends. Perhaps there is an old camellia tree with particularly lovely flowers, and perhaps the land it grows on is slated for construction. If any of these situations speaks to you, perhaps you could use this book.

PLANTING DIAGRAMS

A Multiseasonal Border

The border represented here is a small one, designed to fit into a typical urban yard. The dimensions are 40' × 20', and the garden is oriented toward the south and west. Fencing of some kind would provide support for screening vines, define the garden's boundaries, and keep stray animals and people more or less at bay. The plants are arranged to create a sheltered, private enclosure in which the gardener may putter undisturbed throughout the year. The paved seating area is large enough to be used by several people, yet there is enough space left for a full range of plants.

The planting scheme is a tight one and, if followed, will make a very full, not to say luxuriant, planting in a fairly short time. If very small plants are used, the garden will look settled in in two or three years, mature in six or seven. If larger plants are used, the time required for a mature appearance will naturally be shortened, but it is likely that rather fewer of them will fit the space.

Despite the common wisdom, it is a good idea for new gardeners to overplant; quick success is always gratifying and helps smooth the sometimes bumpy garden path for nervous neophytes. Packing them in may be horticultural heresy, but overabundance is easily corrected and looks exciting right away. A sparse, stingily planted border of shrubby buns and shredded bark may indeed look terrific in 10 or 12 years, but in the meantime the erstwhile garden has gotten bored and wandered off to play racquetball.

New gardeners should indulge their plant lust freely, sandwiching everything together in as pleasing an array as they can muster. They will soon know their plants intimately, and if a few should be lost along the way, there are plenty more where those came from. Even great gardeners lose plants, and shamelessly admit to black thumbs with this plant or that. The plants themselves appreciate the company of their own kind; widely spaced specimens often look uncomfortable, while companionably placed ones will flourish. Plants that grow up in close proximity learn to live with each other, and so long as the soil is well prepared and the nutrients replenished regularly, dense plantings can be healthy and attractive. Occasional shaping and pruning will keep the plants in balance, but it as well to choose dwarf or compact plants in the first place. Placing a few stepping-stones in the wider reaches of the border will facilitate pruning and other chores.

PLANT LISTS

KEY:

A = Annual	E = Evergreen	HB = Hardy Bulb	T = Tree
B = Bulb	F = Fragrant	P = Perennial	V = Vine
BN = Biennial	H = Herb	S = Shrub	* = Not Shown

The BORDER in WINTER

Evergreen elements dominate in the winter border. Plants that form a quietly supportive background to summer's brilliance come into their own when temperatures drop. Mild days will induce furled buds to open, as many as a dozen kinds at a time. Quite a few of winter's flowers have captivating fragrances, which may be savored pleasantly in a little suntrap like this.

PLANT	TYPE	NO. USED
1. *Bergenia* 'Bressingham White'	P, E	3
2. *Sarcococca ruscifolia*	S, E, F	2
3. *Kalmia latifolia* 'Shooting Star'	S, E	1
4. *Mahonia aquifolium* or *bealei*	S, E, F	1
5. *Fatsia japonica*	S, E	1
6. *Helleborus, orientalis* & *foetidus*	P, E	3 each
7. *Iris foetidissima*	P, E	1
8. *Pulmonaria* 'Sissinghurst White'	P, E	2
9. *Pulmonaria* 'Roy Davidson'	P, E	3
10. *Rhododendron* 'Lady Rosebery' or 'Lem's Cameo'	S, E	1
11. *Juniperus virginiana* 'Skyrocket'	T, E	1
12. *Pieris* 'Forest Flame'	S, E	1
13. *Ruta graveolens* 'Jackman's Blue'	P, H, E	1
14. *Salvia officinalis* 'Purpurea'	P, H, E	1
15. *Heuchera* 'Palace Purple'	P, E	2
16. 'Rubine' Brussels sprouts	BN, Semi-E	3
17. *Cytisus* 'Pink Spot' or 'Carla'	S, E	1
18. *Azara microphylla*	S, E, F	1
19. *Hedera deltoidea* 'Sweetheart'	V, E	3
20. *Schizostylus* 'Sunrise'	P, E	2
21. *Ballota pseudodictamnus*	P, H, E	3
22. *Arbutus unedo* 'Compacta'	S, E	1
23. *Thymus lanuginosus**	P, H, E, F	3
24. *Cyclamen hederifolium**	HB, F	3
25. *Sarcococca humilis*	S, E, F	5
26. *Camellia* 'Donation'	T, E	1
27. *Euphorbia wulfenii*	P, E	1
28. *Iris unguicularis*	P, E, F	1
29. *Rosmarinus officinalis* 'Prostrata'	S, H, E, F	1
30. *Prunus subhirtella* 'Autumnalis'	T	1

PLANTING DIAGRAMS

PLANT	TYPE	NO. USED
31. *Hamamelis mollis* 'Pallida'	S, F	1
32. *Laurus nobilis* 'Saratoga'	T, E, H, F	1
33. *Fothergilla gardenii*	S, F	1
34. *Juniperus virginiana* 'Skyrocket'	T, E	1
35. *Ruta graveolens* 'Jackman's Blue'	P, H, E	1
36. *Lavandula angustifolia* 'Hidcote'	S, H, E, F	3 each
or 'Munstead'		1 each
37. *Jasminum nudiflorum*	S, E	1
38. *Hedera helix* 'Buttercup' or 'Gold Heart'*	V, E	3
39. *Rhododendron* 'Hotei' or 'Yellowhammer'	S, E	1
40. *Viburnum tinus* 'Eve Price'*	S, E, F	1
41. *Clematis calycina* or *C. cirrhosa balearica*	V, semi-E	1
42. *Woodwardia fimbriata* (giant chain fern)	P, E	1
43. *Sarcococca confusa*	S, E, F	3
44. *Thymus citriodorus* 'Aureus'	P, H, E, F	6
45. *Cyclamen coum*	HB	2
46. *Daphne odora* 'Marginata'	S, E, F	1
47. Winter pansies	BN, E	12

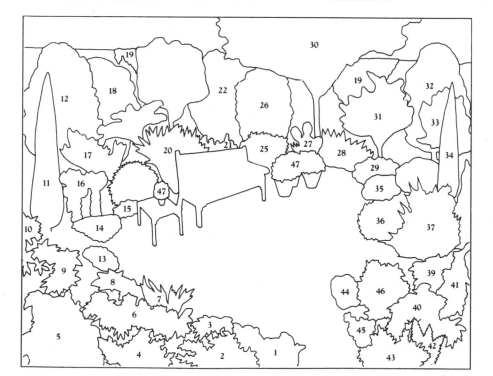

The BORDER in SPRING

Winter wanders away slowly, leaving a sea of waking perennials in its place. Many spring flowers appear as early as January, while winter flowers may persist through March, tying the equivocal seasons together. Bulbs, the essence of spring, are here in profusion, interspersed among the larger, more permanent plants. Deciduous shrubs and late-leafing perennials with small crowns share their territory readily, and the determined gardener will find that an astonishing number of bulbs may be packed into our small space.

PLANT	TYPE	NO. USED
1. *Bergenia* 'Bressingham White'	P, E	3
2. *Nepeta mussinii**	P, H, F	1
3. *Kalmia latifolia* 'Shooting Star'*	S, E	1
4. *Pulmonaria* 'Sissinghurst White'	P, E	2
5. *Pulmonaria* 'Roy Davidson'	P, E	3
6. *Rhododendron* 'Lady Rosebery' or 'Lem's Cameo'	S, E	1
7. *Ruta graveolens* 'Jackman's Blue'	P, H, E	1
8. *Salvia officinalis* 'Purpurea'	P, H, E	1
9. *Heuchera* 'Palace Purple'	P, E	2
10. *Fritillaria persica* (interplanted with 'Rubine' Brussels sprouts)	HB	5
11. *Pieris* 'Forest Flame'	S, E	1
12. *Cytisus* 'Pink Spot' or 'Carla'	S, E	1
13. *Clematis macropetala* (pink form)	V	1
14. *Cornus florida* 'Cherokee Daybreak'	S/T	1
15. *Helictotrichon sempervirens* (blue oat grass)	P	1
16. *Euphorbia myrsinites*	P	1
17. *Ballota pseudodictamnus*	P, H, E	3
18. *Arbutus unedo* 'Compacta'	S, E	1
19. *Camellia* 'Donation'	T, E	1
20. *Euphorbia wulfenii*	P, E	1
21. *Clematis alpina* 'White Moth'	V	1
22. *Iris unguicularis**	P, E, F	1
23. *Rosmarinus officinalis* 'Prostratus'	P, H, F	1
24. *Ruta graveolens* 'Jackman's Blue'	P, H, E, F	1
25. *Fothergilla gardenii*	S, F	1
26. *Rosa primula*	S, F	1
27. *Cornus florida* 'Cherokee Sunset'	S/T	1
28. *Rhododendron* 'Hotei' or 'Yellowhammer'	S, E	1
29. *Viburnum tinus* 'Eve Price'*	S, E, F	1

PLANT	TYPE	NO. USED
30. *Daphne odora* 'Marginata'	S, E, F	1
31. *Thymus citriodorus* 'Aureus'	P, H, E, F	6
32. *Pæonia officinalis* 'Alba'	S, F	1
33. *Nepeta mussinii**	P, H, F	1
34. Primroses	P, F	15

Areas marked "B" are planted with spring bulbs. (Bulbs are placed under deciduous shrubs and among perennials.)

PLANT LISTS

KEY:

A = Annual	E = Evergreen	HB = Hardy Bulb	T = Tree
B = Bulb	F = Fragrant	P = Perennial	V = Vine
BN = Biennial	H = Herb	S = Shrub	* = Not Shown

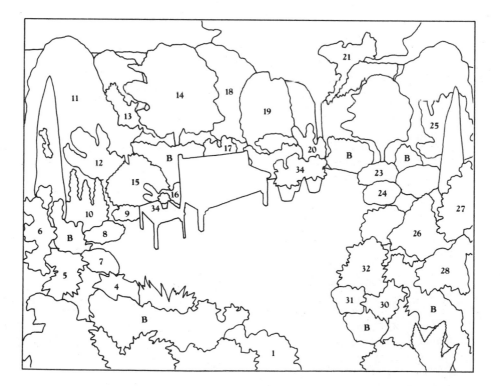

The BORDER in SUMMER

Several spring-flowering plants leave handsome foliage in their wake. Pulmonarias and peonies contribute all through the fall, as will the evergreen hellebores and sarcococcas. Less decorative foliage, like the withering bulb leaves, is hidden by the fresh froth of new growth that rises to take its turn upon our little stage. The summer color is arranged so that purples, mauves, and pinks meld into silvers, creams, and yellows, which build in turn into blues and golds. Naturally, these choices are open to substitution, as indeed are the plants themselves. The point of any plan like this is to suggest the range of possibilities offered by any site—but the end result ought to suit the gardener as much as the site.

PLANT	TYPE	NO. USED
1. *Astrantia maxima*	P	1
2. *Nepeta mussinii*	P, F, H	1
3. *Iris fœtidissima*	P, E	1
4. *Salvia horminum* 'Claryssa White'	A, F	1
5. *Lilium* 'Regale' (interplanted with pulmonaria)	HB, F	6
6. *Ampelopsis brevipedunculata* 'Elegans'	V	1
7. *Buddleia* 'Pygmy Purple'	S	1
8. *Thalictrum aquilegiifolium*	P	1
9. *Vitis vinifera* 'Purpurea'	V	1
10. *Ruta graveolens* 'Jackman's Blue'	P, H, E	1
11. *Salvia officinalis* 'Purpurea'	P, H, E	1
12. 'Rubine' Brussels sprouts*	BN, Semi-E	3
13. *Heuchera* 'Palace Purple'	P, E	1
14. *Helictotrichon sempervirens* (blue oat grass)	P	1
15. *Euphorbia myrsinites*	P	1
16. *Cornus florida* 'Cherokee Daybreak'	S/T	1
17. *Clematis* 'Hagley Hybrid'	V	1
18. *Ballota pseudodictamnus**	P, H, E	3
19. *Kniphofia* 'Little Maid'	P	1
20. *Helichrysum petiolare**	A	3
21. *Rosa* 'Penelope'	S, F	1
22. *Hemerocallis* 'Little Grapette'	P, F	1
23. *Salvia horminum* 'Claryssa Pink'*	A, F	1
24. *Rosa* 'The Fairy'	S, F	1
25. *Iris sibirica* 'Flight of Butterflies'	P	1
26. *Hemerocallis* 'Ice Carnival'	P, F	1
27. *Jasminum officinalis*	V, F	1

PLANTING DIAGRAMS

PLANT	TYPE	NO. USED
28. *Rosmarinus officinalis* 'Prostrata'*	S, H, E, F	1
29. *Clematis* 'Will Goodwin'	V	1
30. *Artemisia* 'Powis Castle'*	P, H	1
31. *Rosa* 'Just Joey'	S, F	1
32. *Ruta graveolens* 'Jackman's Blue'	P, H, E	1
33. *Coreopsis* 'Moonbeam'	P	1
34. *Lavandula angustifolia* 'Hidcote' or 'Munstead'*	S, H, E, F	3
35. *Lilium* 'Golden Splendor'	HB, F	6
36. *Cornus florida* 'Cherokee Sunset'	S/T	1
37. *Miscanthus sinensis* 'Zebrensis' (zebra grass)	P	1
38. *Kniphofia* 'Primrose Beauty'	P	1
39. *Thalictrum glaucum*	P	1
40. *Hemerocallis* 'Stella d'Oro'	P, F	1
41. *Pæonia officinalis* 'Alba'*	P, F	1
42. *Nepeta musinii*	P, H, F	1
43. *Salvia horminum* 'Claryssa Blue'	P, F	1
44. Culinary herbs	A, P, H, F	12

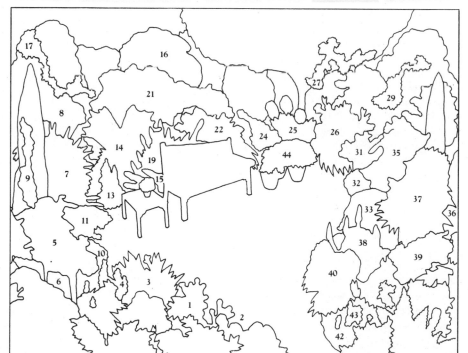

The BORDER in AUTUMN

Foliage color contributes powerfully to the brilliance of the autumn border. Several of the plants which took a back seat during the summer return to center stage, notably the spring-blooming fothergilla and hamamelis. Vivid strands of purple grape and variegated ampelopsis weave through background shrubs, lighting up quiet corners for a fall finale. As the summer flowers dwindle, the surprising pink nerines emerge to glitter improbably in the chilly morning mists. A few winter bloomers begin to perk up, sensing that their time is drawing near. Though there are relatively few flowers, it is impossible to mourn for summer when autumn's largesse is offered so freely.

PLANT	TYPE	NO. USED
1. *Bergenia* 'Bressingham White'	P, E	3
2. *Astrantia maxima*	P	1
3. *Nepeta mussinii**	P, F, H	1
4. *Iris fœtidissima*	P, E	1
5. *Fatsia japonica*	S, E	1
6. *Ampelopsis brevipedunculata* 'Elegans'	V	1
7. *Callicarpa* 'Profusion'	S	1
8. *Salvia harminum* 'Claryssa White'	A, F	1
9. *Ruta graveolens* 'Jackman's Blue'	P, H, E	1
10. *Salvia officinalis* 'Purpurea'	P, H, E	1
11. *Buddleia* 'Pygmy Purple'	S	1
12. *Lespedeza bicolor*	S	1
13. *Vitis vinifera* 'Purpurea'	V	1
14. 'Rubine' Brussels sprouts	BN, semi-E	3
15. *Heuchera* 'Palace Purple'	P, E	1
16. *Helictotrichon sempervirens* (blue oat grass)	P	1
17. *Euphorbia myrsinites*	P	1
18. *Cornus florida* 'Cherokee Daybreak'	S/T	1
19. *Clematis* 'Lady Betty Balfour'	V	1
20. *Schizostylus* 'Sunrise'	P, E	1
21. *Ballota pseudodictamnus**	P, H, E	3
22. *Arbutus unedo* 'Compacta'	S, E	1
23. *Rosa* 'Penelope'	S, F	1
24. *Cyclamen hederifolium**	HB, F	3
25. *Kniphofia* 'Little Maid'	P	1
26. *Helichrysum petiolare**	A	3
27. *Nerine bowdenii*	HB	12
28. *Hemerocallis* 'Little Grapette'	P, F	1

PLANT	TYPE	NO. USED
29. *Salvia horminum* 'Claryssa Pink'	A, F	1
30. *Rosa* 'The Fairy'	S, F	1
31. *Euphorbia wulfenii*	P, E	1
32. *Iris unguicularis*	P, E, F	1
33. *Hemerocallis* 'Ice Carnival'	P, F	1
34. *Prunus subhirtella* 'Autumnalis'	T	1
35. *Hamamelis mollis* 'Pallida'	S, F	1
36. *Rosmarinus officinalis* 'Prostrata'*	S, H, E, F	1
37. *Ruta graveolens* 'Jackman's Blue'*	P, H, E	1
38. *Clematis* 'Will Goodwin'	V	1
39. *Fothergilla gardenii*	S, F	1
40. *Artemisia* 'Powis Castle'*	P, F	1
41. *Rosa* 'Just Joey'	S, F	1
42. *Lavandula angustifolia* 'Hidcote' or 'Munstead'*	S, H, E, F	3
43. *Crocosmia* 'Solfatare'	HB	12
44. *Solidaster* 'Lemore'	P	1
45. *Coreopsis* 'Moonbeam'	P	1
46. *Hemerocallis* 'Stella d'Oro'	P, F	1

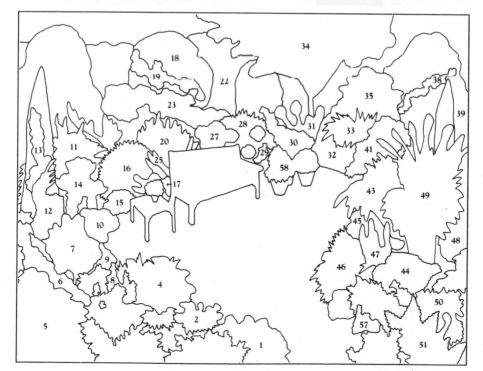

PLANT	TYPE	NO. USED
47. *Kniphofia* 'Primrose Beauty'	P	1
48. *Cornus florida* 'Cherokee Sunset'	S/T	1
49. *Miscanthus sinensis* 'Zebrensis'	P	1
50. *Viburnum tinus* 'Eve Price'	S, E, F	1
51. *Woodwardia fimbriata* (giant chain fern)	P, E	1
52. *Daphne odora* 'Marginata'	S, E, F	1
53. *Cyclamen coum**	HB	2
54. *Thymus citriodorus* 'Aureus'	P, H, E, F	6
55. *Pæonia officinalis* 'Alba' (foliage color)	S, F	1
56. *Nepeta mussinii**	P, H, F	1
57. *Salvia horminum* 'Claryssa Blue'	P, F	1
58. Culinary herbs	A, P	15

PLANT LISTS

KEY:

A = Annual	E = Evergreen	HB = Hardy Bulb	T = Tree
B = Bulb	F = Fragrant	P = Perennial	V = Vine
BN = Biennial	H = Herb	S = Shrub	* = Not Shown

The BORDER in BLOOM

Combined List of All Plants in the Multiseasonal Border

PLANT	TYPE	NO. USED
Ampelopsis brevipedunculata 'Elegans'	V	1
Arbutus unedo 'Compacta'	S, E	1
Artemisia 'Powis Castle'	P, H	1
Astrantia maxima	P	1
Azara microphylla	S, E, F	1
Ballota pseudodictamnus	P, H, E	3
Bergenia 'Bressingham White'	P, E	3
Buddleia 'Pygmy Purple'	S	1
Callicarpa 'Profusion'	S	1
Camellia 'Donation'	T, E	1
Clematis alpina 'White Moth'	V	1
Clematis calycina	V, semi-E	1
Clematis cirrhosa balearica		
Clematis 'Hagley Hybrid'	V	1
Clematis 'Lady Betty Balfour'	V	1
Clematis macropetala (pink form)	V	1
Clematis 'Will Goodwin'	V	1
Coreopsis 'Moonbeam'	P	1
Cornus florida 'Cherokee Daybreak'	S/T	1
Cornus florida 'Cherokee Sunset'	S/T	1
Crocosmia 'Solfatare'	HB	12
Culinary herbs	A, P	15
Cyclamen coum	HB	2
Cyclamen hederifolium	HB, F	3
Cytisus 'Pink Spot' or 'Carla'	S, E	1
Daphne odora 'Marginata'	S, E, F	1
Euphorbia myrsinites	P	1
Euphorbia wulfenii	P, E	1
Fatsia japonica	S, E	1
Fothergilla gardenii	S, F	1
Fritillaria persica	HB	5 HH
Hamamelis mollis 'Pallida'	S, F	1
Hedera deltoidea 'Sweetheart'	V, E	3
Hedera helix 'Buttercup'	V, E	3

PLANTING DIAGRAMS

PLANT	TYPE	NO. USED
Hedera helix 'Gold Heart'		
Helichrysum petiolare	A	3
Helictotrichon sempervirens (blue oat grass)	P	1
Helleborus fœtidus	P, E	3 ea
Helleborus orientalis		
Hemerocallis 'Ice Carnival'	P, F	1
Hemerocallis 'Little Grapette'	P, F	1
Hemerocallis 'Stella d'Oro'	P, F	1
Heuchera 'Palace Purple'	P, E	2
Iris fœtidissima	P, E	1
Iris sibirica 'Flight of Butterflies'	P	1
Iris unguicularis	P, E, F	1
Jasminum nudiflorum	S, E	1
Jasminum officinalis	V, F	1
Juniperus virginiana 'Skyrocket'	T, E	1
Kalmia latifolia 'Shooting Star'	S, E	1
Kniphofia 'Little Maid'	P	1
Kniphofia 'Primrose Beauty'	P	1
Laurus nobilis 'Saratoga'	T, E, H, F	1
Lavandula angustifolia 'Hidcote'	S, H, E, F	3 ea
Lavandula angustifolia 'Munstead'	S, H, E, F	1 ea
Lespedeza bicolor	S	1
Lilium 'Golden Splendor'	HB, F	6
Lilium 'Regale'	HB, F	6
Mahonia aquifolium or *bealei*	S, E, F	1
Miscanthus sinensis 'Zebrensis' (zebra grass)	P	1
Nepeta mussinii	P, H, F	1
Nerine bowdenii	HB	12
Pæonia officinalis 'Alba'	S, F	1
Pieris 'Forest Flame'	S, E	1
Primroses	P, F	15
Prunus subhirtella 'Autumnalis'	T	1
Pulmonaria 'Roy Davidson'	P, E	3
Pulmonaria 'Sissinghurst White'	P, E	2
Rhododendron 'Hotei'	S, E	1
Rhododendron 'Yellowhammer'		

PLANTING DIAGRAMS

PLANT	TYPE	NO. USED
Rhododendron 'Lady Rosebery'		
Rhododendron 'Lem's Cameo'	S, E	1
Rosa 'Just Joey'	S, F	1
Rosa 'Penelope'	S, F	1
Rosa primula	S, F	1
Rosa 'The Fairy'	S, F	1
Rosmarinus officinalis 'Prostrata'	S, H, E, F	1
'Rubine' Brussels sprouts	BN, Semi-E	3
Ruta graveolens 'Jackman's Blue'	P, H, E	1
Salvia horminum 'Claryssa Blue'	P, F	1
Salvia horminum 'Claryssa Pink'	A, F	1
Salvia horminum 'Claryssa White'	A, F	1
Salvia officinalis 'Purpurea'	P, H, E	1
Sarcococca confusa	S, E, F	3
Sarcococca humilis	S, E, F	5
Sarcococca ruscifolia	S, E, F	2
Schizostylus 'Sunrise'	P, E	2
Solidaster 'Lemore'	P	1
Thalictrum aquilegiifolium	P	1
Thalictrum glaucum	P	1
Thymus citriodorus 'Aureus'	P, H, E, F	6
Thymus lanuginosus	P, H, E, F	3
Viburnum tinus 'Eve Price'	S, E, F	1
Vitis vinifera 'Purpurea'	V	1
Winter pansies	BN, E	12
Woodwardia fimbriata (giant chain fern)	P, E	1

The Art of Watering

remember visiting a famous English garden, admiring the wide borders full of lush phlox in late July. Few plants show the lack of water faster than phlox, and I complimented the gardener on discreet placement of the watering equipment, for there was none in sight. He looked blankly at me, and I thought perhaps it was one of those American phrases incomprehensible to the English, like saying "flashlight" for "electric torch." He shook his head thoughtfully and trotted to the garden shed, where he showed me a solitary tap, two buckets, and a couple of watering cans. That was it, the "watering equipment" for a 10-acre garden. Not a single hose anywhere. Amazing.

Of course the English climate differs from ours in one important aspect: their summers are generally a good deal wetter than ours. They have their years of drought, but thanks to a very high standard of soil building, the gardens generally take it in stride. In the Pacific Northwest we can expect very little rain between June and September. It may be overcast and grey more often than it's hot and sunny, but it rarely rains to any extent during the summer. Experienced gardeners are among the few people who have made this simple climatic observation, and I don't know of any who have had serious losses during the recent drought. I, however, have had considerable losses, and I know exactly why.

When we moved, many (too many) plants were dug up hastily and shoved into inadequate pots—temporarily, of course. Had they been tucked in a nursery bed right away, this might have been a different story, but time was short and there were a million things that needed doing. A few holding beds were dug, but the soil here reminds me of my high school dates—either fast and loose or stodgy and tight. It goes from pure clay to sifting sand quite quickly, with very little in between. Mourning the soft, open loam we had built in Seattle, we dug in barrows full of manure and stable sweepings, and mulched the transplants well—at least in the beginning we did. By late spring, things were heating up, we were running out of time, and the last beds in the lower garden above the stream were only sketchily amended.

The previous tenants assured us that the garden area had been well tilled and manured the spring before, so we weren't very careful. That was an error.

One person's generosity may be another's stinginess; quantities must be observed, or judgment withheld. Whatever had been done to that soil was not enough, and we—or at least our plants—are paying the penalty. The lower garden is on sloping land facing south and open to the west. It falls gently to a small stream, currently a small mudhole. In past years the stream was evidently adequate to water the whole area, judging by the size of its pump and the number of irrigation pipes running out of it. This year it dried up almost completely by early July. Of the hundred or so plants put in that garden in June (not the best time for transplanting anyway), perhaps half are dead or severely maimed. The corn the boys planted was properly knee-high by the fourth of July, but never got any higher, and now in late August it is drying up, a few feeble ears showing a scattering of small, hard seeds.

There are a few bright spots, however. The scarlet runner beans and morning glories are having a field day. The hollyhocks, though short, are blooming well, and the sunflowers look terrific. Coreopsis, those cheerful fluffy daisy-flowers, are blooming hard. Late-sown cosmos look fine, deep green and full of buds. The daylilies are parched, but blooming well anyway. All the Mediterranean herbs are luxuriating, the lavender silver white and loaded with blue flower stalks, the rosemary glossy and compact. Several kinds of oregano and marjoram have become bushes, alive with bees, and the garlic has never been so big (it got plenty of water back when it wanted it).

One of the best groups down there is positively unruffled by the drought: a small group of agapanthus that never really flowered generously before has been throwing up stalk after stalk this year. *Macleaya* (*Bocconia cordata*), the plume poppy, flutters its big, curiously shaped leaves of silver-plum and pewter, quite happy to be soaking up all that sun. An Australian silk oak (*Grevillea robustad*) has put on a foot of bronzy green new growth and has never looked so content. It is only borderline hardy—I bought it as a houseplant—but has survived several winters so far. I wasn't too sure about transplanting it, but it looks better pleased down in our little Sahara sun belt than ever it did in Seattle.

Up by the house the picture is not bad at all. These were the beds that got some attention, and everything has settled in well, blooming and putting on new growth nicely. These beds get watered by soaker hose for an hour every other week, which has been perfectly adequate so far. I water everything in pots by hand, always the most efficient way with containers, unless there are too many. There *are* too many, but with good technique (drenching everything really well, and promptly removing the telltale empty pots when something kicks off) we get by, fooling most of the people most of the time. Up here things *look* good, but the sad pile of labels tells its own tale of loss and destruction. The worst part is that all of it could have been avoided. All of it. Preparation pays off, and the better the preparation the better it pays. Even with very little water the amended and mulched beds are holding their own. The moral? Make Beautiful Dirt. That's all there is to it.

Cats and Catmints

uxley's Encyclopedia of Gardening begins its lengthy entry on cats with a crabby diatribe against the garden depredations of domestic cats. Mr. Huxley waxes eloquent on that ubiquitous animal's propensity for using freshly worked earth—read seedbed, nurserybed, newly potted plants—as a feline lav. He describes various Victorian anticat devices which in no way resemble antimacassars, and mourns their passing. He reminds us that it is illegal to harm wandering cats; that cats, like dogs, are not legally responsible for the damage they may achieve in a neighbor's garden; that the animal's owner will not be held liable for same; and that cats may be expelled from one's garden with only such propulsive force as is strictly necessary. The entry ends with a studiedly neutral warning that bran-based slug baits may be mistaken by prowling cats for pet foods, often with tragic results. "Pity," he seems to say, and continues briskly on through "Cell" and "Centipede" before the full implications of this subtle suggestion sink in.

City gardeners often come to view marauding cats with extreme prejudice. Tempting as it may seem, catnapping with intent is probably not the optimal response to feline raids. Since we can't legally beat them, we might as well enjoy them. If your imagination will not strain so far—the thought of frolicking cats at happy play arousing only a brooding fury—you may console yourself with visions of reeling cats cavorting clumsily under the influence. In a word, divert them from their merry mischief with cat narcotics.

If such an ill-tempered response rankles, concentrate on the indisputable fact that catnips and the related catmints are widely admired border plants. Indeed, members of the *Nepeta* family appear in every self-respecting border from Land's End to John O'Groats. Americans have been slower to embrace these low-key plants, but once their true value is recognized, they will become common stock among urban garden guerillas from Boston to Seattle, from Minneapolis to Texarkana. The most familiar *Nepeta* is probably *N. cataria*, better known as catnip. Oils produced by this plant have a powerful psychoactive effect on most cats; they are a feline marijuana. Toys stuffed with the dried leaves make sedate older cats as silly as kittens, but fresh leaves, like those of the potent opium poppy, make them sleep. Grow enough of this stuff and the former terror of the neighborhood will be found prostrate and snoring, dreaming twitchy, drug-induced dreams on the border's edge.

When I first heard about drug therapy for Bad Cats, I set out a small plant and waited for action. It quickly materialized, leaving a valuable lesson in its wake; you need to plant lots of it. One catnip is no match for a cityful of cats. In truly infested neighborhoods, a minor investment in chicken wire pays a handsome dividend, for little handmade cages, however homely, will protect young plants nicely until they are big enough to fend off their admirers themselves. Chicken wire supports are left in place and keep the flopsy plants more or less upright when they put on summer bulk. Wire baskets or tomato cages are also effective cat controls, and both are easily removed when the plant begins to grow strongly. The protection is needed only briefly, for established plants display all the tenacity of the mint family to which they belong.

Catnip and its ornamental cousins, the catmints (hybrid forms of N. x faassenii), appreciate the same garden conditions as the cats do; warm, sunny exposures and ordinary soil will keep them happy for years. It may seem contradictory to suggest mass plantings of cat attractants, but there is logic behind the thought: by filling cats' favorite places with their drug of choice, you can keep them out of sensitive areas. Mostly.

Catnip itself is not a showy plant, making a felty greyish mound some two feet tall (or across, when crushed into a spreading mat), with stalks of softly colored flowers in lavender, pale blue, or white appearing in early summer. Catnip mingles comfortably with other herbs and low shrubs, performing well in hot spots along driveways and sidewalks. The catmints, selected forms of N. x faassinii, make larger, fuller plants which are natural mixers that blend pleasantly with everything else and fill empty young borders attractively at top speed. Handsome forms with descriptive names—'Blue Beauty', 'White Wonder', 'Early Wonder'—are available from various commercial sources, and occasionally appear in local nurseries. A personal favorite, 'Six Hills Giant', is both beautiful and vigorous—no mere cat could successfully demolish this one, which can reach four feet in height and close to five feet across. It carries masses of deep blue flowers over a long season, and is quite willing to rebloom all fall if sheared back in mid-July. Like all the catmints, it is readily divisible; one plant set out in fall can be pulled into 50 pieces, tiny but rooted, a year later. One can, however, have too much of this particular form, especially in a small border. It isn't a rampant runner—it spreads only modestly at the roots—but the exuberant top growth knows no bounds and may overwhelm its companions before you realize what is happening.

The largest catmints are at their best hiding the knobby knees of climbing or old roses and leggy buddleias, frothing out between large shrubs, or making wide drifts in sunny new gardens. All the catmints are terrific companions for spring bulbs, for they die down to nubbins over the winter, then billow out to conceal the decaying detritis left in the wake of careless spring beauties. Late bloomers are also complemented; the cool blues and greys of catmints are a splendid foil for glittering Schiaparelli pink nerine lilies. These die down early in the fall, then send up long, sinuous stalks topped with heavy buds which burst open in October and may carry on into November, when their spidery, twizzled petals provide a thoroughly surprising burst of color. Arrange the catmints and bulbs amongst a few bushlets of tidy grey 'Munstead' lavender, pink and purple tricolor sage (*Salvia officinalis* 'Tricolor'), and a long-armed immortelle (*Helichrysum petiolare*) with round, grey leaves like silvery coins, and you have a picture which satisfies for eight or ten months of the year.

While my garden suffers its share of indignities, most are undoubtedly perpetrated by our own cats, whose collective name would appear to be Legion. We moved to a larger property with the expressed intention of restoring a small farm, making a large garden and offering open space where the children could play. Catastrophic numbers of cats were not part of the plan. The accumulation came about in various ways—we believed that two kittens are happier and less troublesome than one (which proved true—several times). We turned out to be suckers for homeless and unwed mothers-to-be. The increasing numbers of food bowls became a magnet for the strays of the neighborhood, many of them survivors of the herd run by the aging former owners of the place. However, with ranks of catmints edging the borders and sprawling mats of catnip strategically placed throughout the yard, I think we can finally coexist in peace.

Red-Hot Pokers

THE LONG AND THE SHORT OF IT

ugust is a bosomy month in many gardens, a month of swelling, sumptuous mounds and magnificent, rounded billows formed as the perennial beauties reach—and pass—their apex. It is very delightful, all this feminine shapeliness, but as with anything in this complicated world, it requires a counterpoint. Indeed, such soft cushiness will appear all the more luxuriant for a bit of contrast. To this end, we must look for something tall, spiky, and swashbuckling; in short, we want the masculine element. Isn't this thrilling? And right in our own gardens, too.

One vastly underrated group that might fill our requirements is the poker family, the best-known member of which is a staunch old-fashioned plant regarded with almost universal disdain—but wrongly so. This is *Kniphofia uvaria*, the red-hot poker of Victorian gardens that still blazes sturdily away in neglected old gardens across the country. Properly grown and groomed, red-hot poker can make a sparkling show in a boldly colored border, sending up rocket after rocket five or even six feet in the air. Gardeners who are longing for carefree long-blooming border plants will do well to give this old war-horse a second glance, for few plants will do so much for so little. Divide that huge old clump behind the garage, surround the divisions with daisy-flowered billowers—perhaps heleniums like 'Copper Spray', a robust auburn beauty, and 'Waldtraud', a tawny-bronze sibling, both heavy bloomers over an extended period. The hardy sunflowers (*Helianthus* species) offer equally good contrast, and mix well with both pokers and heleniums; consider the rich yellow, double-flowered 'Morning Sun', or the classic 'Lodden Gold', bouncing but never brash. If you wonder at the preponderance of "hel-" words, think of the sun ("helios," if you recall your Greek) and put them there. The pokers will like that too.

Those who cultivate more refined color schemes may look with increased favor upon some of old red-hot's sisters. There are quite a few named varieties floating around, though few nurseries carry more than two or three.

Hunting them down can be part of the challenge, and the reward will be there for all to see for long years to come. A particularly stalwart bloomer in gentle shades of yellow is called 'Primrose Beauty'; this one has two or three bloom sessions each year, and can carry on straight through a mild autumn. The tall wands are well displayed against a background of green and silver such as is provided by the statuesque *Buddleia nivea*, with gigantic embossed leaves. Surround both plants with daylilies, perhaps the elegant, spidery blossoms of 'Lady Fingers', the cool, greenish yellow of unripe lemons, or the huge, powder pale blossoms of 'Aquarius' in a quietly pleasing combination.

A bolder-colored poker, 'Earliest of All' carries two-foot spikes of warm, rosy salmon in June, while the taller 'Parmentier' sends up skyrockets of salmon and coral in July and August. Both enliven a dull herb garden no end, bringing zip to an overly tasteful collection of greys and silvers. Taller still is 'Goldmine', which can reach four feet and blooms through late summer. Its coloring is a subtle run of yellow to old gold with amber highlights that complement the coloring of roses like 'Graham Thomas', 'Amber Queen', and 'Wild Ginger', and mixes well with tall gilded grasses and lemon-and-lime variegated sage. There are a number of vivid pokers in coppery reds, brilliant dark oranges, or heavy, hot tomato reds, all of which can create a stir in the high summer garden. Try them ranged against a red barberry, a purple hazel, or a silver-plum backdrop of that imposing and beautiful weed *Bocconia cordata*, the plume poppy. With these strong and curiously colored pokers, it helps to grow the plant in a nursery bed, pick the first blooms, and carry them through the garden looking for the right supportive setting. If you are swapping plants with friends, beg a bloom stalk in midsummer and wander with it, sticking it in this shrub or that border to try the effect. Poker plants grow fast and transplant readily any old time, so sitting on the sidelines for a season or two won't hurt them a bit.

Certain exotic species kniphofias deserve wider garden placement, some quite small and well behaved enough for the most restricted beds, others enormous with rambling ways. Perhaps the most dramatic is *K. northiæ*, named for the botanical illustrator, Marianne North, who both shocked and impressed the Victorian world with her work (that she did it at all was the shocking part). This one spreads broad, grey-green leaves in stiff, almost formal rosettes, topped by tall spires of coral and greeny-gold. The dainty little *K. galpinii* would certainly find a spot in smaller gardens were it more widely available. It forms a graceful, slight rosette of slender, swordlike leaves, sending up diminutive spires of soft tangerine-colored flowers in mid-summer.

A whole race of miniature hybrid pokers is being developed, useful for those with tiny gardens, and a welcome element in mixed borders of any size. Most of them come from England, where poker plants are held in high regard for flower arranging, and several companies offer a lovely seed series called 'Border Ballet' which produces dwarf plants with sizable bloom spikes. These are best grown in a nursery bed and selected for proportion and tir for they are as variable as any seed strain. Selected miniature hybrids are becoming available in America, notably 'Little Maid', a tiny replica of the lusty poker called 'Maid of Orleans'. 'Little Maid' is a pokerette workhorse, sending up several batches of greenish ivory bloom stalks two feet tall, delicate and well balanced with the fine, grassy foliage. 'Vanilla' is a bit taller, and carries creamy yellowish blossoms the color of egg custard. It too produces batches of bloom over a long season, as does the paler 'White Fairy'. Seed from the Hardy Plant Society exchange is yielding lovely dwarfs in peach, pink, and apricot, bloom-size and garden ready the second year.

Kniphofias of all kinds come quite easily from seed, and can reach blooming size in as little as six months, so it is worth seeking out seed of species and hybrid series should they prove difficult to locate in local nurseries. If you don't find them, the thing to do is ask, early and often, for there is nothing like a customer request to get more unusual plants grown and shown. These uncommon pokers are always admired and much requested when seen in bloom, and since they are practically indestructible, subject to no known pests, remarkably disease-free, and need only the most minimal care, they are a natural for American gardeners.

Should you be lucky enough to bring one home, keep its modest requirements in mind, for properly treated plants are very generous creatures. All pokers will do best in sunny areas of the garden, and will live for years in ordinary garden soil, though the better the soil you give them, the more and bolder they will bloom. Their only fussiness is not liking damp feet; pokers must have excellent drainage to succeed. Once established, they laugh at drought, but the first year, like any other plant, they must be kept from drying out. Trim back the tatty old leaves at the base of the plants very early each spring (you can do it in the fall if you like, but there will always be a few more by spring, so why bother to do it twice?). They may look bare and leggy for a while, but new leaves will quickly cover those gawky ankles. When the bloom stalks brown off, cut them clean away at the very base, as low as you can, to keep things looking trim and to encourage the formation of more spikes.

Pokers are very long-lived, and old clumps will go on blooming and building for years without intervention from the gardener. Should you want a few divisions to offer friends, take them in the fall. Each rosette or clump of leaves must have a corresponding chunk of root, but even quite small bits will develop into blooming plants quickly, often during their first garden season. These handsome pokers are slowly achieving broader recognition, for, once they are seen, avid gardeners eagerly embrace them, gathering them, tall and trusty, into the bosom of the garden.

Some Like It Hot

As you thumb through the nursery catalogs, pay special attention to descriptive passages. Note items like "tolerant to drought," "loves a hot, dry position," "needs little irrigation," or even "resents summer watering," especially if the plants are mid- to late-summer bloomers. Even in a dry year, the spring garden will pretty much take care of itself, but as the summer rolls on, moisture-loving plants begin to suffer. If your garden let you down badly in the last drought, think back to what looked terrific in someone else's yard. Some of the best performers I have noticed were hardy native or species plants, built to take dry heat in stride.

In August, when many plants were flagging, *Oenothera berlandieri*, the Mexican evening primrose, bloomed undaunted. This is a stunning plant that loves hot weather, opening its big rosy pink blossoms in profusion. These large flowers are the size of teacups, delicate Chinese porcelain teacups, with the delicate texture of watered silk—there is nothing coarse about them except their energy. Despite their family name, the flowers are open all day long. About a foot tall at bloom time, this evening primrose spreads from basal rosettes into bushy, compact plants bubbling with bloom. It has running roots, so each plant will spread over time into a sizeable colony. To make a satisfying picture, place it in front of a silver-rose daylily like the ruffled 'Vivacious', or the rich burgundy-rose 'Summer Wine'. Surround these plants with sprawling, lacy artemisias—perhaps the threadlike, dissected leafed 'Powis Castle', or the glistening, glossy variety 'Lambrook Silver'. Place a few plants of the stately Texan, *Gaura lindheimeri*, to wave their graceful white-tipped wands behind the whole, which they will do nearly all summer, rain or no. This is an airy plant, so back it up with several clumps of a robust red-stemmed eupatorium—not the familiar fireweed, but a splendid relative, *E. cannabinum plenum*. This East Coast native rises tall and lovely, opening clusters of dusty rose florets in soft abundance from mid-summer into fall.

Meteorologists have recently discovered a new twist to the weather cycle they call ENSO (El Niño/Southern Oscillation); not only is Pacific Northwestern weather firmly tied in to that complex pattern, but it is affected as well by Eurasian snowfall, unlikely as that may seem. Apparently when the snow blanket is thick, the runoff in the spring is sufficient to slow the annual summer heating-up of the Eurasian land mass, which results in weak monsoons, negatively reinforcing the pressure system that drives our rain elsewhere—maybe to the house that Jack built. Much as we might wish to evoke a weather Monroe Doctrine, we are, after all, part of the world as a whole, bound country to country in unfathomable ways.

Happily, we can do quite a lot in advance to prepare for our dry summers, all of it good garden practice in any year, but especially valuable when chances are good that garden watering will be restricted. Not surprisingly, the place to begin is with the dirt itself. Take time in the gentle, warm days of late winter to evaluate the condition of your soil. If it is less than loose, fluffy, pleasant-smelling, and full of worms, the best gift you can give yourself is a dirt make-over. Putting expensive plants in worn-out soil is like cramming your best clothes in a funky gym locker; it really doesn't give anything a chance to shine, and the results are pretty well guaranteed to be inglorious.

Making beautiful dirt may be a silly theme song, but soil in good heart is pay dirt—it will pay you back over and over again for all the energy, money, and time you put into it. In shrubbery, or in an area without a lot of slumbering perennials to watch out for, you can renovate boldly. Start with bagged manure if you haven't got a source of rotted stable gleanings, and spread it an inch or two thick over the entire bed. You are correct in supposing that that is a lot of manure. If you have adequate compost, add an inch of that as well, and an inch of peat moss or sawdust. Now top it all off with a thick dusting of bone meal, blood meal, cottonseed meal, or soy meal, a scattered handful or two of kelp meal, and we are ready to roll. Dig in deeply, tossing and breaking up any clods, until the mixture is evenly distributed. Rake it all out and you have something fine indeed. In an established perennial bed, short of redigging the entire thing, the best policy is to mulch generously with a blend of the above amendments. Each time you dig a new hole, excavate deeply and fill with fresh topsoil mixed with more of the same (put the tired soil in the compost heap for renewal).

Another good rule of thumb is: when in drought, water deeply but as seldom as possible. This means using soaker hoses, driplines, or having sprinkler hoses running at a bare trickle for at least a couple of hours in each part of the garden. Make sure the soil is wet at least eight or ten inches down before moving the hose to the next spot. After the initial watering, top the soaked soil with several inches of fine mulch (keeping it clear of the crowns of your perennials) to hold that moisture where you want it. Begin this process with recently planted or transplanted shrubs and perennials, and it wouldn't hurt to start watering established plants which looked disconsolate last summer, either. Watering deeply but seldom—perhaps once a month—encourages plants to send their roots down deep in search of moisture, and that is where you want them, away from the desiccating sun. As the summer wears on, cultivate (scuffing the soil between the plants) shallowly, if at all—deeper cultivation increases moisture loss dramatically. A deep mulch blanket keeps the soil from crusting over and makes weeds quite easy to pull as well, eliminating the need to cultivate, so when things heat up, you can take it easy.

Grey and Glorious

he helichrysums are among the most useful plants in the gardener's repertoire, grey-leafed perennials which unify color schemes bright or soft. Their foliage shows a fascinating variety of form; the leaves of some species are round as grey velvet coins, while others look like steel grey needles. Some look like minuscule silver mouse ears, while others are celadon green blotched with cream or gold. In habit they also differ, scrambling through surrounding plants to tame wild color combinations, climbing upright like small trees, making mounds and hummocks or fat, felted cushions which pleasantly punctuate taller perennials. Until recently, the perennial members of this worthy tribe have been scarce locally, but they are beginning to make their way up the coast from California where they have long been popular garden fixtures.

The curry plant, *Helichrysum italicum* (*angustifolium*), forms a rounded bushy shrublet several feet tall and bristling with slender, rather upright stalks. The pins-and-needles foliage has the pungent scent of curry, which on a hot day wanders mysteriously throughout the garden. When the curry plant blooms in midsummer, longer stems shoot up another foot or so, each bearing rounded umbels of tiny flat daisy flowers in soft old gold. This grey-and-gold tapestry looks like sumptuous brocade when viewed against a bank of dark blue agapanthus. In my garden, a large group of the willing *Lysimachia clethroides* is sandwiched between the two, its crooked spires all bending forward at the same angle in a fascinating way. Gold-eyed and creamy, it unites the group's varied tints.

'Nanum', a tiny version of the curry plant, is a spiky little thing in silvery sea green, perhaps a foot all around in maturity. It belongs at the front of the border, particularly when charmingly entwined with sky blue *Commelina coelestis*, the Mexican dayflower with tucked-in cornucopia leaves exactly like those of the *Tradescantias*, common houseplants known collectively as wandering Jew, their close cousins. Thickly planted around roses, 'Nanum' is a wonderful foil for some of the difficult colors of the newer hybrid tea roses. It also makes a pretty, quilted undercover for old-fashioned roses such as 'Alstergruss' with creamy apricot buds, or the fragile, silvered pink cups of 'Dainty Bess', a gem among single roses.

Another small-leafed helichrysum, H. microphyllum, has wiry stems and ruffled little leaves of celadon green edged and lined with softest silver. It will ramble with great goodwill, twining itself intimately into nearby shrubs or perennials, making a silver-white sea beneath the taller plants. All the silvers are good with pale pinks and blues, but they also make a lovely setting for the stronger tones; try rose red godetia, deep blue brodiaeas (the blue dicks of California), and dark pansies. A notable Swiss pansy strain, Roggli Giants, dates back to the thirties, when it was a favorite of Vita Sackville-West's. It has been continuously refined, and outstanding selections from the Roggli mixture are occasionally named. One of these, 'Gemmi', is a knockout with this tiny helichrysum, its huge purple-black petals neatly edged with white, standing out vividly against the cool background.

One of the most pleasing effects in our new border came from a chance association of jetty 'King of the Blacks' pansies with immortelle (Helichrysum petiolare), a middle-size sprawler with rounded grey leaves wrapped around furry white stems. The two together are charming, but what really makes the group go is the addition of an apricot daylily, 'Three Bars'. This is one of the best for Northwestern gardeners, eager to bloom and slow to quit. A four-year-old clump from our town garden was split into nearly 20 good-size divisions, and those which were brought to the island garden bloomed heavily for almost two months the first summer.

A tricolored immortelle, 'Limelight', has taken England by storm; one sees it everywhere. Round, felty petals of chalky yellow, pastel lime, and cream deck the long, lax stems which will flop becomingly (not always the case) through the border, making friends wherever it wanders. With patience and good support, this or any immortelle can be trained as a little treelike standard, making a wonderful tracery against a wall. Perhaps their best use, however, is when unleashed to scramble through those dreary masses of junipers, dwarf rhododendrons, or heathers ubiquitous throughout the Northwest, which they do like lightning.

All of the helichrysums want very good drainage, and, despite chat in print to the contrary, they respond better to good garden soil than to the lean conditions generally prescribed. The grey ones take full sun with aplomb, but 'Limelight' will scorch without partial shade. Morning and evening sun does no harm, but the harsh light of a high summer noon needs tempering if 'Limelight' is to look her best. None of the helichrysums need—or want—any feeding other than what is available in good garden soil, but although the family tolerates drought exceptionally well, new plants will need ordinary amounts of water till settled in. If helichrysums are to do duty on a very dry bank or in poor soil, it is worth amending the site first. The usual additions of bone meal, cottonseed meal, or soy meal, a tad of kelp, some sawdust or peat, aged manure, and/or the indispensable compost will repay any efforts generously. Water will be especially necessary in a sloping site until the plants are showing signs of new, active growth, after which they can be left to their own devices.

All of these plants must be considered borderline in the Northwest, since a really hard frost could carry them away, but they are more likely to succumb to waterlogging. All of those mentioned have successfully wintered over where the drainage was fast, particularly when left unpruned. Those which do come through the winter will not be unscathed, but if they're cut back hard in early spring, a subsequent hearty helping of compost and manure will give them all the bounce they need to put on a good show for another year. Immortal they may not be, but they are certainly both beautiful and invaluable. If they need to be renewed now and then, well, who doesn't?

Butterfly Bushes Bring Wings

One golden August afternoon, the children hustled me out to the garden to see a marvelous sight. We lay on the grass, watching with intense interest as a flock of yellow-and-black swallowtail butterflies—we counted 15, but they moved so much it was hard to be sure—fed from the purple-black blossoms of a butterfly bush. An iridescent green hummingbird was sharing the bounty, muscling the butterflies aside and tipping each dark floret back to let the nectar slip down her slender beak. Buddleias (commonly called "butterfly bush") do indeed attract their namesakes, and nicely grown plants can illuminate the garden from midsummer well into fall.

The bush my boys were so taken with is Buddleia 'Black Knight', a six-foot mound of lustrous green, silver-backed foliage, its blossoms richly dark with a midnight sheen on them like the luster on old pewter. 'White Cloud' and 'Royal Red' are equally good forms which are readily found at local nurseries. For the smallest gardens, two recently developed hybrids, Monrovia's 'Pygmy Purple' and 'Pygmy Indigo' are among the choicest selections. Both have narrow leaves lined with silver, and their yard-long canes are burdened with slim but brilliant blossom spikes. The pygmies bloom from July into October, requiring only a crew cut—hard pruning to within a few inches of the ground—in late winter to keep them in shape. Hardy, healthy, and needing relatively little water, buddleias like these will become increasingly popular, for everybody who sees them in the garden wants one, particularly when they discover how easily these plants are pleased.

The slovenly, unpruned old things one sees in neglected yards and alleys have given buddleias a poor reputation, and indeed, they are apt to look unkempt unless they get proper care. Left to their own devices, the plants become rangy, the gangling canes clothed skimpily in greyish leaves, the slender bloom panicles crowded by dingy hangers-on from years gone by. A bush, old or young, which has received its annual close shave looks entirely different. Dense mounds of flexuous, arching canes, well covered with felted leaves, will be smothered beneath sturdy blossom spikes from midsummer through the fall. Buddleias' demands are few and modest, yet when their minimal wants are met they reward the gardener generously.

Most of the older shrubs are forms of *Buddleia davidii*, a few of which remain outstanding today. Should your yard hold a straggly specimen, try renovation before removal; next February, cut the plant to the ground. Clear away any competing grass or weeds, mulch the root zone with aged manure or compost, and water well during any prolonged dry spells. (Established buddleias are among the most drought-tolerant plants in the garden and do not ordinarily need supplemental water except during the first season after planting.) If that plant has any potential at all, you will soon know it. If it isn't covered with flowers, or if the flowers are a wishy-washy color, root the old thing out and replace it with one of the newer hybrids.

There are other buddleia species which are even handsomer than the newest *davidii* offspring, notably the frosted silver *B. fallowiana* 'Alba'. Often regarded as tender, many plants came through the ugly winter of '88–'89 un-scathed, despite single-digit temperatures. The new growth is almost white, large and thickly felted. Foliage matures to soft sage green with a woolly white lining, lovely when wind-rippled, and each arching stem is tipped with fragrant, icicle white blossoms eyed with golden orange. Slower to fatten up than most buddleias, it can take several years to come to full size and glory—a mature shrub can be as much as six or eight feet wide and high. Knowing this, you might underplant your young shrub with early bulbs and use annuals as placeholders to reserve the space that will presently be occupied by its wide, trailing skirts.

A close cousin of this plant is called 'Lochinch', a probable hybrid between *B. fallowiana* and *B. davidii* which originated in the Scottish garden for which it was named. This midsize shrub carries its periwinkle blue flower spikes against glossy, deeply embossed green leaves. The backsides are palest silver green, like frozen jade, and both foliage and flowers are pleasantly aromatic. *Buddleia nivea* makes a sculptural shrub, its outsize green leaves elegantly curving to show their snowy backs. This, too, requires a fair amount of space, and looks truly magnificent rising from a frothy sea of 'Six Hills Giant' catmint, spiky tussocks of blue oatgrass (*Helictotrichon sempervirens*), and the ruffled silver rosettes of *Lychnis coronaria*, the frankly magenta flowers of which have a Byzantine richness seen against the blue-and-silver background.

Where a large but delicate-looking shrub is wanted, *B. crispa* is just the ticket, for although its canes may reach as much as 10 or 12 feet in all directions, its small silvery leaves have a wavering lettuce-leaf edge that gives the plant a shimmery, ethereal appearance. The scented flowers are lavender with golden throats. By early summer they are so heavy, they tip each twiglet (if the shrub is not pruned, rather later if pruned hard). This buddleia is often allowed to develop into a small tree, getting an annual light trimming to maintain its shapely cascading form.

Another large buddleia, *B. alternifolia*, makes a lovely, weeping little tree if pruned to a single stem. The leader stem will need support until it thickens enough to stand alone, which can take years, so make the stake a generous one. All the lower and side shoots are removed, so growth is concentrated in the leader. Once the desired height is achieved, the top shoots are left to develop into branches which will become blossom falls of rich lilac in early summer. The silver-leafed form, 'Argentea', is spectacular when grown this way, but it will also make a great and splendid silvery mound at the back of a deep border. As a freestanding shrub in meadow or lawn, it rivals the weeping silver pear for beauty. *B. alternifolia* blooms only on old wood, so spring pruning is fatal to the floral cause. After the plants flower, the oldest wands can be removed to renew the shrub, and tree forms may be selectively thinned and shaped without sacrificing next year's display.

Although buddleias grow well in almost any soil, they cannot tolerate wet feet; they perform best in decent garden soil that drains quickly. Once established they need only an annual feeding mulch of compost, applied after you prune. In very dry years the plants will flower more abundantly if watered monthly, but a well-cared-for plant will put on a good show willy-nilly. Buddleias want at least six hours a day of full sun in the Northwest, blooming most luxuriantly when they have plenty of it. Plants in shade will survive and even bloom, but they always look thin and tatty. Young buddleias properly placed will quickly shape into good-looking plants that call to butterflies from afar. The slower-maturing species will take a year or two to settle in, but a little patience earns a disproportionate reward from these long-lived garden treasures that give so much in return for so little.

Too Little, Too Late

STAKING

taking plants is one garden chore that holds no charm for me. I philosophically despise the practice, feeling that our plants should be so well grown that they have no cause to flop. Those which have an incurably flopsy nature should be allotted room to throw themselves about without harming their neighbors. If the gardener is up to snuff, there is no need to stake anything, surely. Besides, it looks ugly early in the season, when the young growth stands up so nicely on its own. The ungainly sticks and heavy twine look like props for a plant bondage movie. No, no, just use your intelligence to place things properly and all will be well.

Sometimes, indeed, careful placement can obviate the need for actual stakes, as when a dithery double peach-leafed campanula is hedged round with a glittering barrier of the low juniper 'Maxistar', which provides just enough support that the loaded stems never actually hit the mud, bob as they may. This can be perfectly practical with small and midsize perennials that are not overly heavy or brittle. However, in a garden surrounded by buildings or trees, a garden necessarily full of long and shifting shadows, it is impossible to find the full, unblocked sun that truly tall plants love.

Torch lilies (*Eremurus*, which you say like a cat mewing: Eh-reh-MEW-rus) and big verbascums will tilt in the best of circumstances, but in partial shade they would as soon topple as look at·you. Worse yet, in the enriched soil of the garden bed, verbascums in particular can take on gargantuan proportions, rising 12 and 15 feet high. This makes a dramatic accent for the garden, especially when those heavy towers tumble, which they do slowly under their own accumulating weight, and rather faster given a bonus of rain and a bit of wind.

This summer I discovered that a *Verbascum chaixii* which had been moved from a hot, dry bed to a rich and partially shaded one was developing excessive tendencies. The stems, once promisingly upright, had taken on drunken, swaybacked postures. Great languid swags lay heavily over every-

177

thing of lesser stature—which was pretty much everything. Here a mangled Russian sage sent out a few tentative spires. Over there a half-strangled clump of the summer wallflower, *Cheiranthus* (*Erysimum*) 'Bowles's Mauve' bloomed bravely through the arms of the oppressor. The verabascum's basal rosette, usually a couple of feet across at the most, was now three times that, flattening everything beneath as effectually as Mike Mulligan's steamroller. Suddenly the scales fell from my eyes; I saw the present harm, envisioned the incipient disaster, and had an original thought: I could stake that plant.

I cast around for a stake, and after a short skirmish, negotiated successfully with my young sons for a hefty pole. The rough brown garden twine had disappeared, used up for pea trellising and bean teepees. It had not yet been replaced, since the next pea season was nearly a year away. I hastily grabbed a ball of soft white kitchen string and headed back to the scene. Slipping silently through the back of the bed, I sunk the stake into the deep soil, a foot or two behind the outermost reaches of the rosette. Approaching the monster from behind, I seized it by the waist and pulled it off its long-suffering companions. Advanced as the season was, the formerly flexible stems had matured into woody stalks that were decidedly set in their ways. Lift as I might, they could not straighten up for me, and no amount of string was going to change their drooping attitude. Not one to be deterred by mere details, I trussed up as many of the lurching turrets as I could, and arranged the smaller one artistically over the strings, which were plentiful. A snow white cat's cradle now stretched from stake to stem, looking like a remnant from a children's treasure hunt by day, a luminescent spider's web by moonlight; a lovely touch I must remember for the white garden.

Naturally, this sorry situation was completely avoidable. Feeling a bit less philosophical and considerably less smug, I went around the garden with my new eyes. A sheaf of 'Regale' lilies were groveling beneath a golden cutleaf elder, to nobody's advantage. This was relatively simple to remedy, and this time the wide, spreading wings of a silvery blue spruce hid the glowing white string more successfully. (I did put garden twine on the shopping list, but the iron was hot, and waiting for trifles like the right twine would all too likely mean that the job would never get done at all.) Farther along, the single slim stalk of a prized plant, the unpronounceable *Michauxia tchihatcheffii* (supposedly you say it like a sneeze, but it must be a Russian sneeze) had been blown into a small cutleaf maple. Though neither plant was in any way harmed, this plainly called for intervention, since the flowers of the michauxia are not something to waste on the desert air or the leafy bosom of an unmoved maple. A bamboo wand—again wrested from my unwilling children—provided all the backbone the plant was lacking, and now its giant, curling white stars shine across the garden, capturing the attention instantly.

Michauxia, a campanula relative native to Turkey, is a biennial that makes a rough, bristly rosette in its first year, from which the second spring brings forth a hairy, skinny stalk four or more feet high. Soon the stiff, prickly side stems are hung with lanternlike buds several inches long that suggest incipient bellflowers. However, they pop open looking more like passion flowers, having slim, reflexed petals centered with a pronounced proboscis laden with pale gold pollen and encircled by tightly coiled twiddly bits that are most decorative, if totally mysterious. Such a plant is not found at most garden centers, and makes a compelling argument for membership in the Hardy Plant Society, whence came its seed, one of over 5,000 kinds available in last year's seed exchange. (For membership information, see Appendix D.) They are also a persuasive reason to set out stakes where wanted before it is too late.

Resolution: buy another huge ball of soft brown garden twine, gather up a decent supply of supports in various sizes, and put them to use before a plant is too woody to work with or the boys find them. It's a simple enough concept, but I am still hampered by that philosophical disinclination to do anything so seemingly unnatural. I sincerely believe that we ought to celebrate the natural tendencies of each plant. I still love the swing and sway of big, sprawly plants, but I need to recognize that I am also an inveterate overplanter, loving most of all the generous look of a plentifully packed border. These two loves are sadly incompatible. The best solution is to move the verbascum yet again, putting it into the rougher, large-scale border that divides the road from the meadow. Here it can wobble and flop to heart's content, for the wicked frosts of February left plenty of room. Its present home still cries out for a bold, emphatic plant, but this time I will choose something that doesn't need staking—perhaps a tall acanthus.

There are still gaps in my new resolve; ranks of Madonna lilies brought low by wind and rain ought each to have a discreet bamboo stake of her own. Some of the leaning lilies make splendid fans, notably the late-blooming *L. speciosum*, while the Aurelians really do need to be propped from behind if they are to reach full beauty. Next year they will be. I swear it.

The
BORDER
in AUTUMN

SEPTEMBER ▪ OCTOBER

AUTUMN

For a while, the hot, sleepy afternoons of fall lull us into a state of lazy acceptance. The border still looks great, it's too early to plant bulbs, the lawn's been mown for (hopefully) the last time—there's nothing to do but share the peaceful garden with the birds. A prolonged streak of mild weather argues persuasively that summer is forever, that winter will never come. The return of the autumn rains breaks the spell, and as the soft warm chinook blows the last of the perennials to tatters, we pull ourselves together and get ready for serious gardenmaking.

Autumn can be the busiest time in the border, where chores abound. Once the rains have softened the earth, taprooted weeds come up sweetly to the hand, running roots are pullable by the yard, and disturbed plants, tucked back into place, settle in without a murmur. All the notes we took through the year come into play now; spring and summer gaps, duly noted, are filled in, and, for a wonder, we have all the right stuff at hand, having ordered replacements not from memory or lust (at least, not exclusively) but from the lists in our garden journal. In March, we noted that a dark blue poppy anemone looked excitingly vivid next to some lamb's ears and accordingly ordered a hundred more bulbs of the silky anemone. Now we can repeat that subtle, singing combination throughout the garden, placing clumps of anemones near other silver-leafed plants for a variation on our theme.

An area marked "short on spring interest" is overcrammed with summer perennials, several in need of division. We'll split those and reset them in renewed earth, putting a few extra pieces aside to create echoes in a corresponding section. Woodland flowers and spring bulbs can be planted beneath more permanent plants, especially deciduous trees and shrubs—a dozen bluebells (*Mertensia virginica*) or a handful of wood anemone (*Anemone nemorosa*, will spread into grand colonies before long, and both will coexist peaceably with summer bloomers.

Combinations which were less than satisfactory may now be dismantled, and the substitutions and rearrangements which you duly noted carried out. If solutions were sketchy or lacking altogether, inspiration may come with a stroll through the nursery area, where unallotted new plants are patiently growing on. If nothing suggests itself, plant what you know you like and leave a few spaces around the incipient group. The new catalogs, already winging toward you, may well hold the perfect answer. It helps to analyze what doesn't work about a recalcitrant grouping. Is it too busy, too static, too sparse, too tasteful? Perhaps your picture just needs time to develop, or an infusion of gaudier color in a related tone to add snap to the composition. Perhaps it lacks contrast. Are all the leaves the same shape and color? Would a big-leafed plant soothe a flurry of bittier ones? Plants of contrasting form might help; hummocks and tussocks need the company of sky rockets, cones, and arching fountain plants to prevent monotony.

Where the plants are more or less in the right neighborhood but their placement seems off a bit, weigh in with a shovel and rearrange everybody to best advantage—this is a splendid time to take care of those niggling little annoyances. Such fine-tuning greatly affects the overall impression one gets from the garden, though the individual changes may seem small. It is amazing how much difference it can make to turn a backward plant face front, to free a crowded clump of grass from pushy neighbors, to divide choked ferns or hostas into single crowns again.

Where large areas are notably unsuccessful, whether from weak design, water stress, or poor soil preparation, we might as well haul in a truckload of stable sweepings or manure and rework the entire section. Wrap the plants in plastic or burlap bags, borrow or rent a tiller, and get to the root of the problem. It is a hard, cold fact that plants grow best in nice dirt. If you haven't got it—and few of us do—then you simply have to make it, or suffer the consequences. The consolation, of course, lies in having healthy, well-grown plants which rarely need feeding or pest intervention. As a final bonus, once the dirt work is done, the fun of replanting is before us again, along with an opportunity to alter the combinations according to our present taste. As we learn about more plants and see more gardens, fresh ideas for all manner of pleasing juxtapositions arise without effort. We may continue to enjoy our earlier plantings, yet refinements or additions may now suggest themselves, involving plants we didn't know about when we began garden-making. We may be braver now, willing to plunge past the strictly tasteful to take visual risks. As experience builds our confidence, we may decide that we like magenta, that too much silver foliage makes for a dull display, that pastels are not, after all, the last word. American gardeners are coming of age, recognizing that our light, our various climates, our native plants, and our architecture are not like their counterparts in England or Japan. As we find our places in the gardening world, our gardens will reflect our increasing self-knowledge, becoming as distinguished and individual as America itself.

Garden Grooming

PULLING OUR SUMMER SOCKS UP

ate summer brings a colorful climax to many American gardens, but here in the Pacific Northwest it is rather a quiet time. The floral fireworks of June and July are past. Behind us lie the lilies, the shrub roses, the peonies, and the delphiniums. Ahead are asters and acidantheras, chrysanthemums and colchicums. Berry and bark have yet to shine. The garden is at a lull, but if we are to fully savor the renewed burst of fall color we must pull our socks up. The fading splendors of high summer linger in our gardens like the aftermath of a particularly good party. A few fine flowers are still to be seen, and many a powerful plant is still burping out the occasional bud, yet if we stand back and view the scene with clear eyes, we must acknowledge that, lovely as it was, the party is over. It is September, time to override sentiment and clear away all the untidy remains of summer exuberance.

Actually, this isn't such a bad chore, once we grab the secateurs and jump into the thick of it. Signs of renewal are everywhere. Remove the lanky, spent shoots of *Geranium psilostemon*, bidding a fond farewell to the last of its magenta-and-black blossoms, and notice the new growth clustered at the plant's base. Shorn of its tatters, its height is reduced from five or six feet to a shapely three or four. Quite often, too, seedlings are revealed, which, potted up, make excellent barter for plants on your lust list. The last of the hydrangea blossoms may be left to fade gently into winter bronze, but not yet, please. Trim off the early dead, and let the plump new flower heads of fall shine undimmed.

All the browning foliage gets stripped off the daylilies and iris, so that the new blades appear clean and fresh. Where these plants are not front liners, you can wait till season's end to do this, getting all the detritus in one swoop. Where these plants take the eye, tidying them now makes a tremendous difference to the overall look of the autumn garden.

Once we start looking around, we'll find plenty of fodder for the compost heap. Those lily stalks whose tips we trimmed in July can be cut back

by half if they are not yet ripe for pulling (only when the stalks have with-
ered to the ground can they be pulled cleanly from the bulbs, but the top
growth can be clipped off as it browns without harming the bulbs). Annual
poppies can be pulled out, their fat seedheads broken and the tiny black seed
scattered or saved for seed exchanges. Foxglove seed has ripened, too, and
may be gathered by clipping the dry stalks into two-foot sections and tossing
them into a shallow box lined with newspaper. Later you can crush the pods
and shake away the chaff to clean the seed. Pull out woody old foxgloves,
resetting a few of the seedlings at their bases. Strains like the chalk pink
'Sutton's Apricot' or soft yellow 'Sutton's Primrose' will breed true if grown
in separate colonies and if the odd rogue seedling is ruthlessly pulled the
minute it reveals its false color. (Unless, of course, its color is something
exceptional; after all, these wonderful strains are simply selections made by
observant gardeners and nurserymen over the years.)

Tall bleeding hearts, *Dicentra spectabilis*, are golden now in leaf and
stem; if unwithered, they can make a lovely splash among the rusts and cop-
pers of fall. If lax and flopsy, though, away with the tatty old things. While
you are carting off browned bloom stalks by the armful, take a look at the
half-spent to evaluate their condition. If a few late blossoms tempt you to
leave anything untouched, remove all the finished stalks, the dead leaves,
and the seedheads, then look again. Some, spruced up a bit, can last out the
fall. A quick trim reveals others to be past their prime, and a second, closer
clipping will bring them a merciful release. Composites of all sorts—helenium, helianthus, heliopsis, and helichrysum—will often rebloom bounti-
fully into fall if their old flowered shoots are cut to the bone in late summer.
Monardas (bee balms) are over and gone, yet where the fading flower stems
were cut clean away, vigorous new growth will often support a second, lesser
blooming in late autumn.

Practitioners of early pinching will see enticing color spreading over
the swelling buds of chrysanthemums, plants that are already flagging in the
gardens of the laissez-faire gardener. Long-season bloomers like *Aster x
frikartii* and *Coreopsis* 'Moonbeams' are well into their stride, but will flower
longer and better if the spent blooms are removed every few weeks. This is
a tedious job to do well, for cutting out only the old without harming the
new requires close observation and plenty of patience. It helps to get comfortable first, plumping yourself down on a thick kneeling pad. Tidy gardeners make it a rule to position such plants close to paths, for unless you can
get at them easily this exercise is as likely to end in disaster as in delight. If

you underplant your beds with colchicums and true autumn crocus, the tedium is relieved by the sight of their long, slim buds emerging.

Remove spent annuals, but save the seed of a chosen few. Among these are the curious, spangled *Bupleurum rotundifolium* 'Gold and Green', which looks like a honeysuckle crossed with a euphorbia. Other keepers include the cheerful, lace-leafed poached-egg flower, *Limnanthes douglasii*; the glowing, green-eyed, rosy cups of *Malope trifida*; and the frowsty little green frizzles of *Reseda odorata*, a plain plant with an evocative, penetrating fragrance that gained it the loving sobriquet, 'mignonette'. When the annuals and the accompanying tangle of dead leaves and weed seedlings that accumulate beneath their canopy have been cleared away, flocks of tiny white flowers are revealed. These are hardy cyclamen, which appreciate the dry conditions that prevail beneath larger, lustier plants, and will proliferate nicely amongst the roots of trees. With their silvery leaves patterned like the swirling Persian endpapers in old books, these *Cyclamen hederifolium* (*neapolitanum*) 'Album' are soon to be joined by pale pink sisters and richer pink cousins in other growing colonies throughout the garden. Natives of Turkey and the southern Mediterranean, hardy cyclamen are now endangered and should only be bought from reputable dealers. Mine come from Montrose Nursery, where Nancy Goodwin has been developing exceptional strains of as many species and variant forms as she can muster without recourse to wild collected plants. She now offers close to 20 kinds, including a 'Super Leaf' series of *C. hederifolium* with especially pretty leaves marked with silver and cream over celadon green, and a pink-flowered strain with pronounced fragrance. *C. coum* 'Silver Leaf' has leaves hazed with a soft sheen of silver, while 'Pewter Leaf' has a delicate matte finish of palest grey. Goodwin is the only source for these treasures, and is furthermore the only (legitimate) source in America for many of the rare cyclamen species. Since cyclamen often thrive in the Pacific Northwest, we can all play a part in the preservation of this threatened plant by growing as many of them as we can, as well as we can.

The blooming of the cyclamen signals the turn of the season, the edge upon which summer slips over into fall. The beauty of these small blossoms reminds us not to mourn for splendors past, but to look ever onward, finding pleasures small and great in the quieter season to come.

Major Impact from Minor Bulbs

ll across the country, autumn brings gardeners to their knees, paying homage not to the splendors of the season, many as they are, but to spring. We crawl about under shrubs and trees, circling the driveway, following each path, planting spring glories by the bagful. Most of those bags hold the magnificent border tulips and daffodils whose portraits are splashed across the covers and front pages of every glossy catalog. The order sheets fill up fast and few of us do justice to the small treasures that huddle, forlorn and neglected, in the catalogs' back pages. Here, for those who dare to venture off the beaten path, are the minor bulbs, a loose-knit and largely unrelated clan that includes crocus and scilla, allium and fritillary. The term "minor bulbs" encompasses a whole host of delightful, if mostly diminutive, spring bloomers, many of which offer years of effortless bloom in return for benign neglect.

Considering the ephemeral nature of big tulips and daffodils in most gardens, it is odd that the long-lived minor bulbs, so rewarding and self-sufficient, should be so little regarded. Perhaps because of their nondescript catch-all name, perhaps because they are seldom used effectively, perhaps because a few are such ardent self-sowers (notably certain muscari and scilla species); whatever the reason, minor bulbs have never managed to capture the attention and respect of American gardeners. This is a shame, for properly handled, minor bulbs can create unmatched displays throughout the spring.

In our old farmhouse garden, the aging apple trees are skirted in February with thousands of soft blue *Crocus tommasinianus* that have colonized over the years in the long orchard grass. March brings the golden bunch, *C. ancyrensis*, in nearly equal numbers, along with quantities of unnameable natural hybrids that have made this garden their home. Snowdrops cover the ground beneath old hedges, while grape hyacinths and scilla haze the shrubbery with blue. When we began renovating the old borders and building new ones, we added some of our favorite minor bulbs—*Anemone blanda*, checker lilies (*Fritillaria meleagris*), and cobalt blue Siberian squills (*Scilla siberica*)—by the hundred. Now sheets of the old blue scillas lighten the woods, echoed in the garden by spreading pools of blue anemone and squills. Tall pink and purple tulips are balanced by low carpets of pink and white anemones, and the burgundy new shoots of the emerging peonies are emphasized with the pink glory-of-the-snow (*Chionodoxa* 'Pink Giant') or the smoky purple and lavender tweed of checkered fritillaries.

To get the most impact from minor bulbs, we use them in bold quantities, often planting 100 or more in each chosen site. We plant them closely, making a few smaller satellite clumps to give the groups a more natural look. Each small tree, each major shrub hosts a young colony of golden winter aconites, white grape hyacinth, and crocus, perhaps 'Cream Beauty' or the purple-striped 'Pickwick'. These early bloomers are interplanted with dogtooth violets (*Erythronium*) and shooting stars (*Dodecatheon*), flowering onions (*Allium*) and fritillaries that bloom in late spring or into early summer. By the time the summer leaf canopy is fully formed and their sunlight is cut off, the minor bulbs are entering dormancy. Under the leafy shrubs and perennials their fading passes unnoticed, and they are largely forgotten until they reappear at the first hint of spring.

Minor bulbs will never replace the border tulips and narcissus altogether, but used in thoughtful combination they can significantly improve the spring show in most of our gardens. Grand clumps of tall tulips, red and purple, yellow and gold, certainly do stand out early in the year, but they often look awkwardly advanced and unconnected with the plants around them. They seem to tower giraffelike amid the emerging crowns of the perennials, and unless they are used in dauntingly generous quantities, can look out of place even among evergreen shrubs. In our small city garden, 100 tulips had tremendous impact, but in the larger setting of the farmyard, it takes 300–400 to achieve the same effect. I now buy them from wholesale suppliers, which makes it quite economical (see supplier note below).

I like the look of soft drifts of one tulip running alongside, then weaving through others in similar or complementary tones. To anchor them firmly to the gardenscape, we group each color boldly, then give every clump an accompanying ruffle of the Grecian windflower, *Anemone blanda*; pink ones around the purple tulips, white ones for the reds, and white or blue for the yellows and golds. We might then pull the clusters together with thick ribbons of inky blue-black grape hyacinths (*Muscari neglectum*) or the porcelain pale stars of *Scilla mischtshenkoana* (*tubergeniana*) to create a satisfying, unified picture.

Even in small gardens minor bulbs should be closely and generously planted. We all swoon over dreamy pictures of English gardens where acres of daffodils fade into rolling woodlands. We may not have the space—or the architecture—to rival those great gardens, but we can profitably take a few tips from them. Even as showy a plant as a border tulip needs company to make the best display; a group of 10, tightly planted and given a supportive underplanting of minor bulbs, will easily outshine 20 or 30 that are dotted about or straggling along a path in single file. No matter how big your garden, tulips and daffodils will look far better if placed among shrubs or perennials that screen the fading foliage as the bulbs go dormant. Bulbs that are allowed to ripen their leaves undisturbed will tend to be longer lived and healthier, so, tempting as it is to cut off the browning foliage, try to resist. If you can't stand the look of dying leaves, you can gently flatten them, or push them under surrounding plants instead.

Here are a few of the most rewarding minor bulbs, with some suggestions for suitable companion plantings:

Alliums (flowering onions)

Although alliums are in the onion family, their flowers often have a pleasant fragrance. Stems and leaves can smell oniony, but only when crushed or bruised. Most of the smallest alliums bloom in late spring, with the taller ones generally trailing along into midsummer. All seed themselves to various degrees—this is more of a problem where summers are warm—unless the plants are deadheaded before the seed ripens. The Italian A. *neapolitanum* is a pretty little thing, with grassy leaves and clusters of white flowers atop 6"–8" stems. Two other common alliums are rather similar, though A. *moly* blooms in lemon yellow and A. *ostrowskianum* is rose pink. All of these can be interplanted with tulips and narcissus, or threaded through beds of perennials. Taller and darker toned is the purple-flowered A. *sphaerocephalum*, the roundheaded drumstick allium, which makes a lovely contrast to peony or sunrose (*Helianthemum*) foliage.

Anemones

Bulbous anemones prefer open, sunny sites, and bloom in early spring. Their dark green foliage is flushed with red, and emerges from the ground in late winter, looking rather like muscular parsley. A. *blanda* comes in a variety of strains, such as 'White Splendor', 'Blue Shades', or 'Pink Star', and all of these make more powerful garden pictures than do the various pastel mixtures on the market. Taller and later, the De Caen anemones are big, silky, poppylike creatures that love sun. These are easier to find in pure color strains from wholesalers, and here, too, the mixtures are fun but better for the cutting garden than the border.

Chionodoxa (Glory-of-the-snow)

These frail-looking creatures burst into bloom before the snow has melted, but for all their apparent delicacy, they take frost and heat alike in stride. They naturalize freely, carpeting the ground between shrubs with their bright, starry little blossoms, most of them blue as a summer sky, lightened with a soft white eye; in the form 'Pink Giant' they are a soft rose color.

Colchicums

The autumn crocuses open glorious giant goblets of color from late summer into fall. They make enormous, cabbagy leaf clumps in early spring that die off dramatically in June. Some gardeners find this distressing sight so offensive that they won't make garden room for these splendid creatures, but everybody who sees them starring the grass wants them at once. Pure, gleaming white, soft lavender or rose pink, plain or checkered (tesselated), the autumn crocuses rise as much as five or six inches above the ground, wobbling on their slender necks. They are all the better for the support of a surrounding ground cover—vinca and creeping veronica work well. Autumn crocuses are only available for fall planting, and sometimes arrive from the supplier blooming in their bags. This won't hurt them a bit; just tuck the big bulbs in place—they will tolerate filtered shade or full sun—and enjoy their bounty.

Crocuses

True crocuses are also planted in the fall. The squirrels love their fat corms, but a handful of mothproofing balls or crystals will generally deter them. The group of species called snow crocus are the first to bloom, often poking through the snow. Quick on their heels come the larger Dutch hybrids in a wonderful range of colors. Crocuses will readily naturalize in sun or shade, provided their foliage (slim, grassy, and rarely unsightly) and their seedpods are allowed to ripen, which can take till the end of May.

Dodecatheons (shooting stars)

Native to both East and West coasts, the various American shooting stars are beloved wild flowers that take quite well to garden life. Easily raised from seed and increasingly available commercially, *D. meadia* may be dark fuchsia pink, pale rose, or pure white. It looks lovely beneath rose bushes, among ferns or trilliums, or planted with dwarf narcissus.

Eranthis (winter aconites)

Many complain that eranthis is hard to transplant, but fresh corms from reliable suppliers should break dormancy without problems. Corms that have been improperly stored may sulk for a year or more before showing their glossy, buttercup-like blossoms wrapped in ruffs of fresh green. If you get very hard, dry corms, soak them in tepid water for an hour or so before planting them; this often helps to wake them up quickly. Once established, eranthis is very long-lived and will slowly colonize if left undisturbed. A large group is a stirring sight on a rainy March morning, like a patch of lost sunshine gleaming through the cold fog.

Erythroniums (dog-tooth violets)

The Dutch are excellent hybridizers and propagators, and are turning this somewhat difficult American native into an easygoing, popular plant. Large mottled leaves in rippling rosettes send up slim stalks topped with slender, tightly furled buds that reflex sharply when they open, giving the flowers a flared, starry look. The golden yellow *E. tuolumnense* 'Pagoda' has proved to be a hardy, adaptable plant in many gardens, and makes a wonderful, dappled ground cover in shady areas among ferns and emerging lilies.

Fritillaries

Checkered lilies (*Fritillaria meleagris*) beguile every visitor to our garden, for the fat little bells of heathery purple, lavender, or rose tweed really are checkered, though the pure cream 'Alba' is the most winning of all. Some half a dozen named forms reputed to be especially purple or big or dark or whatever have proved disappointingly similar, though all are lovely, and this is one case where buying a mixture is more than acceptable. Give them a warm, sheltered spot beneath shrubs, and they will slowly build into enchanting little colonies, each plant perhaps 10" tall. On the opposite side of the scale, the majestic crown imperials (*F. imperialis*) rise a yard above the ground to dazzle all viewers. Lemon yellow, burnt orange, or cinnamon red, all are glorious additions to the spring garden. Although they do well in full sun, they are surprisingly tolerant of shade, building freely by seed and offsets into sizeable groups if left undisturbed. Like any big bulb, they are susceptible to rot, so amend their planting holes well with sand or grit, and tilt each bulb as you set it in the ground; this will prevent water from settling in the necks, and the stems will still come up straight and tall.

Galanthus (snowdrops)

Single or double, snowdrops are among the most beloved of spring bulbs. The initial performance of newly planted bulbs is often disappointing to new gardeners, but snowdrops must be planted in quantity and left undisturbed in order to give of their best. Once settled in, they will seed nicely, never becoming a pest. Best moved in the green (when the leaves are still fresh, but after the flowers have faded), snowdrops can be easily transplanted from older gardens to newer ones in late spring. If you buy dry bulbs—and it is nearly impossible to get them any other way nowadays—soak them for an hour in warm water before planting, and group them very close together.

Iris

Bulbous iris are among the first flowers of spring, often appearing in late winter where the climate is mild. The yellow I. danfordiae tends to break up into small bulblets after blooming; these don't achieve blooming size for several years, by which time they have generally been killed or dispersed all over the garden by the busy trowel of the impatient gardener. Most of the blue-flowered forms are more perennial, and come in a lovely range of colors, from teal to cobalt. The reticulated iris, I. reticulata, is a rich, dark blue, only 3"–4" tall, and makes a wonderful companion for the snow crocuses.

Muscari (Grape hyacinth)

Beautiful but incorrigible, the eager spikes of M. armeniacum have given the whole tribe a bad name. Where other bulbs may seed freely, this one seeds ceaselessly and with profligate abandon. Far less rowdy is its cousin, 'Blue Spike', a fluffy-looking double form with much better manners. The clean white form, 'Alba', is equally domesticated, and may be introduced even into small gardens without a qualm. A rather bizarre form called 'Plumosum' sports fuzzy blue spikes that look coated with floral cotton candy; this one blooms later and increases very slowly, if at all. Dark and mysterious-looking, M. neglectum looks especially pretty among the vivid leaves of the golden Creeping Jenny, Lysimachia nummularia aurea.

Scillas and squills

Nothing is bluer than the small, glowing bells of the Siberian squill (*Scilla siberica*) when it carpets the garden in earliest spring. Not a rampant pest, it increases readily, filling the beds with ineffable color long before most plants have even considered rousing themselves for the new year. The same pallid blue as freshly skimmed milk, *S. mischtshenkoana* (*tubergeniana*) blooms over several months, uniting the earliest crocuses with the midspring tulips, and is tolerant of a wide range of conditions. The wood hyacinth, *S. campanulata*, is a charming plant often found in abundance in older gardens. Too coarse and invasive for the garden proper, it is a lovely plant for rough places, lining woodland paths or edging the hedge around the garage or compost heap.

Caveat: buyer be wary. Many minor bulbs are now endangered in their native habitats, and concerned gardeners will buy only from firms that supply only field-grown species bulbs. If a catalog does not specifically state that the bulbs are field-grown, examine what you receive carefully. If the bulbs are unevenly graded, with many small bulblets included, show a striking diversity of form, or have smooth dents (from growing between rocks) they may well be wildlings. If you suspect this to be the case, you can do several things. First, write to the supplier and state your disapproval of such practices, adding that you will no longer patronize that company. Second, you can forward a copy of your letter to the Garden Club of America. This group has an active conservation committee that is interested in knowing both about reputable and suspect suppliers. The following companies have a firm policy to sell only field-grown species bulbs and plants: Van Bourgondien Brothers, Dutch Gardens, and Hylseeds of Holland.

Kirengeshoma

A WOODLANDER FROM JAPAN

 hady Northwestern gardens can be cool, leafy havens on hot summer days, but greenery alone rarely makes a garden. Gardeners are always on the lookout for fascinating plants that bloom well in shade, and the appearance of a new one is greeted with glad cries. One of the handsomest has only recently made its way to our shores, a striking little woodlander from Japan called *Kirengeshoma palmata* (accent on "sho"). This herbaceous perennial has no common name, for it is not yet a common plant, but it could and should be more frequently planted in Northwest gardens. Well suited both to acid soil and to the dappled semishade so prevalent in our region, kirengeshoma takes to Northwest gardens readily, where it quickly looks at home, quietly stunning both in and out of flower.

Even if it never bloomed, kirengeshoma would be highly valued for its bold, effective foliage. The lower leaves are rich, deep green, and crinkly, lobed much as a poinsettia's are, and looking quite similar. As the bronzy purple branches lengthen, big pairs of toothed leaves spout long clusters of lax stems, each carrying several fat buds. These swell enticingly, and in time the waxy yellow flowers open, though never very far. Generously planted, kirengeshoma makes a refreshing companion among rhododendrons and azaleas, a stimulating counterpoint to smaller broadleafed evergreens like leucothoes, laurels, pieris, or photinias. For a lasting effect, plant a number of them in a wandering band, the crowns perhaps four feet apart, among spring-blooming shrubs. The new shoots are exciting-looking, vigorous and dusky in spring. Early summer sees the large leaves develop, till by midsummer, the buds are thick, and the flowers come heavily for several months at summer's end.

Each blossom is perhaps 1½ inches long, soft banana yellow with a subtle, leathery gloss like the lightly glazed kid of French gloves. The five petals are very thick, almost puffy, each folded centrally like a taco shell. They are arranged in a tight, overlapping whorl filled with fat golden stamens. Once half open, the flowers hang poised, tantalizing, as if about to expand fully. They stay like that right up until they drop, leaving the green calyx and the swelling ivory ovary behind, both mildly ornamental in their own right. Flowers begin to open in late summer and in a mild, damp year may continue through the fall till frost puts an end to them.

This is a plant for moist shade, not the dry, matted root zones of large trees, though high, dappled shade (from branches far above the ground, as on tall trees) seems to please it better than dense, low shade (from directly overhanging branches or large shrubs). Kirengeshoma can take a fair amount of cool Northwest sun, and although it needs some room to grow well and look its best, it takes nicely to life in the mixed border. Given deep, rich soil, it can withstand some root competition, and would thrive on the north or east side of an evergreen hedge, tucked among other small shrubs and perennials. It is of course a choice plant for a woodsy garden, if not too dry, and is very much at home among our native salal, mahonias, and small ferns. In a moist site, plant it in the company of masterworts (astrantias), the variegated Siberian dogwood, and American viburnums.

Always a fairly small plant, kirengeshoma may reach three or four feet in a wet year, rather less in a hot, dry one. The fat storage roots (rhizomes) increase each year, making a spreading clump over time. If you like, you can split up your plant in early spring, much as you divide dahlias. Allow each division a couple of eyes or shots; this gives you several fair-sized plants which will probably not bloom that year. Container-grown kirengeshoma can be transplanted almost anytime, but it would be best to wait till the cooler days of fall, after the rains have softened the earth a bit. You can find kirengeshoma at the Wells Medina Nursery, and it is starting to show up with regularity at the plant sales of the Washington Park Arboretum, the Northwest Perennial Alliance, and the Hardy Plant Society. Wherever you find it, grab it, take it home, and make it welcome. Take the time to give it good soil, well prepared, and this remarkable woodlander will settle in with great goodwill, effortlessly gracing your garden with its elegant good looks.

Bulbs for Children

arents often puzzle over getting their children actively—yet benignly—involved in gardenmaking. Anybody who spent childhood hours weeding somebody else's garden will acknowledge that there are better ways to inspire a lifelong love of plants. One of these ways is to offer the children a bit of earth where they may do whatever they like. This area might become a truck garden, with real trucks and a few stunted strawberry plants, or a wilderness of jumbled sunflowers and pumpkins, morning glories and zinnias. It is important to recognize right from the start that this space belongs to the child and may never resemble the charming little haven which we romantically envision for our children. In fact, nontraditional options are most likely to delight the kids, and any of them, however unlikely, can eventually lead to the love of gardening as we know it. The hardest part for adults is keeping our hands off and our mouths shut, for all of us, however new to the art of gardening, are old hands at the art of telling our children how to do things the *right* way. A personal garden can be a fine place to let kids learn for themselves. Whatever happens, they can take all the credit and enjoy the multiple pleasures of discovery as well.

We generally think of the children's garden in terms of food plants and bright annuals, but spring-flowering bulbs are both exciting and satisfying things to plant. Fat, rounded, and heavy in the hand, bulbs are interesting both to look at and to feel, with their odd, varied shapes and rough, papery little jackets. Best of all, bulbs are almost infallible; unless exposed to excessive heat or planted in a soggy puddle, come spring they are bound to bloom beautifully. This is one of their most valuable qualities, since part of the hook for any kid is success. Who could fail to be proud of her very own crown imperial (*Fritillaria imperialis*), dangling great stinky bells of chrome yellow, tawny copper, or rusty red from stout stalks that reach some four feet toward the sky?

Nearly all bulbs are easy to handle, and you can help by providing a range of sizes. Give the smallest children miniature daffodils, or species tulips like the handsome *greigii* hybrids with their showy, dappled leaves and bright flowers, short-stemmed but brilliant. Older kids with bigger hands might get giant hybrid daffodils and a selection of gaudy border tulips—try the outrageous flamed parrot tulips, or the fringed ones with lace-edged petals. Add a few slim, swaying lily-flowered tulips and some fat, blowsy peony tulips for contrast and to introduce the idea of plant varieties. Even very young children can participate; we recall one memorable occasion when our then 4-year-old solemnly told his brother, aged 18 months, "Now remember, Andrew, pointy part up," as the two of them carefully—and successfully —installed several dozen daffodils in their part of the garden. (They had first prepped the ground with peat, bone meal, and gritty sand, with admirable single-mindedness, using a toy earth mover to excellent effect.)

To ensure success in your own yard, choose the sunniest space available for the children's garden. Have the kids dig and chop the dirt up at least a few weeks before they are ready to plant. If the soil is heavy or soggy, have some coarse sand or grit at hand for them to add, for bulbs and quite a few other plants will rot without good drainage. Digging in compost and/or peat moss improves the quality and texture of common dirt, making for soil with a nice texture; it should look, feel, and smell inviting. Well-nourished soil supports good root growth, among other things, and it will soon be observed that well-rooted plants are less apt to blow down and usually bloom more generously than less endowed ones.

It generally takes very little urging to get children interested in mixing and stirring soil, particularly if they have appropriately sized tools. This doesn't necessarily mean laying out large chunks of cash, though the cheap sets do tend to break in a disheartening way just when the action heats up. We finally invested in a very well constructed set of four small tools, including a hoe, rake, border fork, and shovel, which have all been in constant use this summer. They are super tools for grown-ups working in tight places, and for those who like to garden while sitting or kneeling. The kids use them too, given half a chance. (An excellent set is available from the Kinsman Company; another from Walt Nicke.) Soil prep is tremendously exciting work even without proper implements—big clumps of dirt unearthed by an adult can be broken up by bashing them with sticks, lacking anything better. Once the mayhem is over, the final raking should leave a slightly mounded bed of smooth soil.

One caveat to keep in mind is that bulbs do need reasonably deep planting in order to bloom well. If very young children can't make adequate holes easily, perhaps you, an older friend, or sibling could dig, and the youngest child could place the bulbs and cover them up. I have learned not to straighten crooked rows or tidy up "imperfect" planting designs, but where such a laissez-faire policy means death to the plant, it may be time for some tactful advice: "That bulb looks as if it might get pretty cold in the winter. What about a big scoop of dirt for a warm blanket?" Even if the planting ends up lumpy or looking like Mighty Mole passed through, it will probably work out just fine.

One of the intriguing things about bulbs is that they do so much of their growing in the winter, when most plants seem to be asleep. If you like, a bulb or two can be planted in a big pot, then sunk into the ground to be dug up at some point in midwinter. Have the kids tip out the contents and check on the bulbs' progress. This will graphically illustrate how much root growth takes place underground, even during the coldest times. Young scientists may enjoy slicing the burgeoning bulb in half—easiest if done from top to bottom straight through the neck—an operation which displays the developing flower and leaves tucked amid the surrounding tissue. Bulbs left in the ground undisturbed may show emerging foliage shoots as early as December, and eager watchers will soon detect swelling buds among them. Don't worry about such early-bird greenery; it is quite frost-resistant, and the flowers too will come to no harm. A mulch of shredded bark or chopped straw can be heaped over the bulbs when the first shoots are noticed; this will keep spring mud from splashing on the flowers when they arrive.

Tulips and daffodils are great favorites, but the so-called minor bulbs are wonderful discovery plants for children. All of the following are relatively inexpensive experimentation materials (most under two dollars a dozen). Sweetly perfumed hyacinths, puffy as cotton candy, are impressive to kids and adults alike. Small checkered fritillaries (*Fritillaria meleagris*) never fail to fascinate; the dangling bells are patterned like tiny checkerboards in tweedy blends of pink and lavender and cream. Tiny iris, easy and delightful, often bloom as early as January. The blue flowers of *Iris reticulata* last better than the yellow *I. danfordiæ*, which seem to get snapped up by birds and slugs as quickly as they open. For the quickest results, splurge on some autumn crocus or colchicums, relatively expensive bulbs which will often be found blooming leafless in their bags if not planted quickly enough in the fall. If they like, the children can bring a couple of colchicum bulbs into the house to flower unplanted, relegating them to the garden once their bloom is spent. They look a bit uncomfortable when treated this way, blooming naked and lonesome with no comforting soil blanket, but it amuses the children and doesn't harm the bulbs a bit.

Although cheap enough to be treated as a single-season experience without a twinge, many bulbs will persist in good soil for years. If longevity is a goal, an annual fall feeding mulch of raw (unsteamed) bone meal—a teaspoon per bulb, a tablespoon per clump—well blended with a handful of compost and some peat moss or aged manure, will go far toward promoting permanence. Our youngest son was given a pot of the miniature narcissus 'Tête-à-tête' when he was born. Planted out after the flowers faded (the first plant in his garden), the bulbs were carefully fed and mulched. They return and multiply each year, blooming shortly after his January birthday. So often gardening begins in May and ends in September, but bulbs make a pleasant bridge across winter, giving child and parent alike an excuse to get out in the garden early and late.

Dear Allen

September 29, 1988

Dear Allen,

I've thought so many times of your visit—too short, and I hope to be many times repeated—to my shambles of a garden. Of all the Great and Famous who trailed through here this summer, I felt you two, perhaps alone, really understand what it means to write and have a garden, to struggle, often lose, yet find so much pleasure in the process. I almost felt I needn't apologize.

Almost.

Now the main meadow border has fallen into ashes, but some are still glowing. Mounds of *Euphorbia amygdaloides* 'Rubara' carry lovely, sullen bloom stalks tinted ashy purple, ember red, and lime green. Behind it, a shrub of Cape fuchsia, *Phygelius capensis*, blows red trumpets on dark red stems, and a great fan of New Zealand flax, *Phormium tenax*, stands bronzed and glittering in the autumn sunshine. A similar plant on a much smaller scale, *Libertia peregrina*, spreads vivid little fans of burnt sienna, bright orange, copper, and gold, in front of all this warmth, and lowest of all, the flat rosettes of *Geranium sessiflorum* 'Nigricans' are turning pumpkin color and tobacco brown.

At the end near the old cherry tree, huge feathery bushes of *Boltonia asteroides* 'Snowbank' are so laden with their whiskery white daisies that they slump over a drift of 'Lemore', a compact, greeny-yellow goldenrod. Nearby, the great brazen leaves of *Macleaya cordata* show their silvery undersides with every breeze, and the fading coral plumes, beaded and heavy, droop in autumnal melancholy. A gilded, shooting spray of that handsomest of grasses, *Miscanthus sinensis* 'Silver Feather', rises just beyond that, the stalks and leaves toning splendidly with the dark gold of Parker's achillea and the paler turning leaves of *Abutilon x suntense*. One of the shrub roses, 'Nastarana', is laden with late flowers, small, round, and white, and very pink in the bud. This has *Gaura lindheimeri* for a neighbor, which is now an airy confection spewing endless red wands, each tipped with a fluttering white butterfly and yet more pale pink buds. Between and beneath them run thickets of the lacy filigree of *Artemisia* 'Lambrook Silver', a Margery Fish plant par excellence, and behind are some bushes of *Senecio greyi*, their ever-grey leaves sage grey edged in silver fur.

My friend Daphne gave me a whole flat full of lavender, semidouble colchicums that she had thinned out of an overgrown bed in her old garden —we trade our garden weeds, for one person's bane may be another's treasure. We have swapped great bundles of her blue aconites for my white gooseneck loosestrife, Canterbury bells for pink oenotheras, raspberries for rhubarb. These colchicums were especially welcome, for I want to put them beneath a small, elderly plum tree which carpets the grass with its fruit. The plums are rather wormy, but they look absolutely gorgeous when spangled with dew, their rich, plummy skin softened with a silvery bloom and faintly freckled with purple. I heaped straw mulch all around the tree, and when we till up the ground late in October, the colchicums will get tucked in to emerge next autumn amid the fruit fall. Won't that look striking? It might get a bit dubious as the fruit goes off, but we can pretty well rely on our out-sized Northwestern slugs to keep them cleaned up.

As for what's still in bloom, it might almost be easier to list what isn't. Even though this garden is quite new, there are masses of things in flower, and plentiful color from foliage and berries. Partly this is due to the previous owners, three generations of ferryboat captains, all of whom gardened to some extent or other. Aging *Viburnum opulus* and pyracanthas are full of birds, the hollies (which are a perfect weed around here) are studded with ripening berries, and a huge, ancient forsythia (the excellent, soft yellow *F. suspensa*) is turning lurid shades of red and bronze. I have added half a dozen kinds of callicarpas, the beautyberries, with small, round fruits of intense purple and leaves that turn dusky, wonderful shades of mauve and lavender, purple and slate. Some I put near a queenly old *Pernettya mucronata*, a tiny-leafed evergreen with fat, fuchsia pink berries the size of marbles. Gaudy, yes, but eminently satisfying. I am adding several dozen bulbs of *Nerine undulata* and a few *N. bowdenii*, both South Africans with astonishing ribbon-petaled flowers in shocking pink. They have a luster on them, a gloss like that nasty ribbon candy old ladies have in a bowl in the hall at Christmas time. These bulbs bloom late, often through November, and are one of fall's most memorable sights when found, dripping with dew, early on a foggy morning.

Already the toad lilies (*Tricyrtis* species) are establishing themselves, making running colonies through several beds. They do no harm to anything, and now their tall, whorled stems all end in sprays of delicate, weird little flowers. Most are purple or lavender, spotted and speckled with black or darker purple, but some are white or yellow, pale shadows of summer flowers, yet very welcome as the year closes in. Tricyrtis need to be set at the edges of paths or borders, because they don't make much show from a distance; you have to get right up close to appreciate the detail work on these finely crafted little treasures.

Some of the catmints are still going strong, especially the form called 'Six Hills Giant'—I got mine from Canyon Creek Nursery, and the three tiny starts I tucked in this spring are now a yard across (each of them) and nearly as tall. All summer they have been abuzz with bees, and they still are, even in the waning of the year. Each leaf node puts up successive sprays of those dusty blue flowers, and the bushes—they deserve the name—are still loaded with bloom. Half lost in them, a great mat of *Diascia rigescens* is also carrying on bravely, having bloomed nonstop since May. The flowers are small but profuse, and of a peculiar shade of pink, pink with some copper in it, not brash, yet strong enough to carry well amid bolder colors. This one must contend with a great neighboring wash of *Alonsoa warscewiczii* (say that fast, three times), which it does handily. The alonsoa has a very similar flower, lipped and flared, but this time in flaming red, a vivid red infused with orange. It can be a difficult color, but this big patch is threaded with long strands of velvet grey *Helichrysum petiolare*, a favorite cooler of hot colors. Both have looked terrific since early June, and still look as fresh as paint (I did deadhead the alonsoa heavily in late July).

This same border—my hot border—is centered with a big shrub rose, a lovely unknown that blooms hard and heavy from late April through the first frosts, and is now bearing nearly 60 blossoms and buds. They are very double, of a concentrated warm pink, and the bush has an underplanting of a native, *Artemisia purshiana*, a splendid sage from the Great Basin area that starts off the year in timid silvery sprouts and ends, as now, in great languid swags of tinsel, marvelous with the rose. I will cut this back hard when frost turns it all to mush, but revel in it to the last possible minute. The artemisia in turn has an underplanting of a quick little ajuga, 'Burgundy Glow', that holds its lovely soft colors nearly all year. Right now the rosettes are purple, pink, cream, and green, big flat mats of them running between clumps of *Knautia rumelica* that look as fresh and full as they did in June. Once a scabious, knautia has the familial pincushion look; the flowers are tight bouquets of amethyst purple florets that fade to oxblood, each centered with an elegant, pinheaded white pistil, showy but well bred. For you, it would probably be an annual, but it comes very easily from seed, which I am sending you.

A big *Viburnum tinus* at the end of this border is full of fragrant white flowers, though still packed with dense, dark red buds for the winter, which is its proper season. Threaded through its limbs are trailing runners of *Eccremocarpus scaber*, the 'Rubra' form which carries tubular red flowers lipped in soft coral; they look exactly like fat red goldfish, mouths agape. This too is generally considered an annual, and makes quick work of covering a wall in a warm climate. The finely dissected leaves look frilly and soft against the leathery viburnum, a host it shares with a fascinating species clematis, C. *calycina*. Generally considered a variant of C. *balearica*, it too blooms during the winter, opening greenish yellow bells whenever the weather is mild—around here, it often is as warm in January as in May—though hard frost is also very likely during both months.

In the long border, dedicated to spring bulbs and fall foliage, there are scads of asters (mainly species), late phlox, and of course chrysanthemums —I don't scorn them, but do try to label them for best placement in the spring, when they get divided. I found one especially lovely bronzy red that is a perfect counterfoil for the clear, brilliant red of the oxydendron, another coppery-bronzy-greenish one that offers just the right sort of verdigris effect beneath the *Parrotia persica*. Several kinds of fothergillas are tucked into the little bays formed by the big native rhododendrons, salal, and evergreen huckleberry that are the backbone of this area. A neglected native plant, Indian plum, makes a shower of old-gold confetti, dangling ripe reddish plums from every twig, till the birds strip them. Tall, nodding wands of *Smilacina racemosa*, another ignored native, look very like Solomon's seal, except that they bloom in plumes, rather than nodding bells, and carry quantities of red berries. They, too, go quite golden in old age, and look dramatic when backlit by slanting late-season light. *Euonymous europaeus* is decorated with bobbing pinky-red seedpods, while E. *alatus* is taking on its late-season coat of screaming scarlet. These and a good many others are all threaded round with various running grasses, wide-leafed bergenias, and all sorts of clematis, some of which are still going strong. C. 'Lady Betty Balfour' is a late, great plant, with big, ruffled flowers between cobalt and periwinkle, the fluff of stamens at their throats of softest lemon-juice yellow. 'Will Goodwin' is sky blue now, but by late November the flowers will be ice blue with cold. The sweet autumn clematis is heavy with scent and bloom, and 'Bill McKenzie', a selected form of C. *orientalis*, has a good crop of drooping bells, the petals the color and texture of orange peel.

This could go on—I haven't told the half of it—but there is the dinner to get and the children to tend to...still, I must mention two truly spectacular performers, sibling dogwoods, that are hands down the prettiest things in the yard. One, 'Cherokee Daybreak', has white flowers and handsome variegated leaves of cream, celadon, and sage green, but now is going deeper and deeper pink, verging on raspberry. It's a C. *florida* hybrid, very resistant to the usual dogwood ills, and it performed like a trouper in a bad, dry year. This one has a tall variegated physostegia next to it, which has leaves striped in white and green for the summer, but puts on tints of pink and violet for autumn wear. It blooms quite late, September into October, and the flowers are also of a clear, pale violet with white throats. Behind both is an oddity, *Leycesteria formosa*, rather a flopsy thing, but burdened with wonderful, dangling bracts like Chinese pagodas, each hanging from the other, successively smaller, ending in a clasped pair of red leaflets like a little chime. The reddish-black berries are beloved by birds, and taste exactly—but exactly—of butterscotch, the homemade kind, just slightly scorched. It's uncanny.

The sister dogwood, 'Cherokee Sunset', belongs in the gold garden, for its leaves are variegated in butter yellow, cream, and green. The flowers are deep, soft red, very handsome, and unusual in a variegated form. Now it is turning sunset colors indeed, all sorts of oranges with tan, buff, copper, and bronze. I'm not wild about hybrid teas, but exceptions must be made for exceptional plants. The English rose, 'Just Joey', is one such, and when it opens its flagrant, fragrant orange-sherbet blossoms nearby, the two together are showstoppers. In between are lots of silver things—more *Senecio greyi*, artemisias, sages, and wide sheaves of crocosmia hybrids, many of which are late, 'Lady Emily McKenzie' being the best just now, a golden girl of breeding and distinction. Enough?

Are you ready to receive packets of plants? I have *Hypericum x moserianum* 'Tricolor', the double blue lobelia, and quite a few other things you indicated an interest in. I will ship bare root, but am doing some things in P4 (hydrophilic polymer) to keep them nice during the trip. All the best, and do come again as soon as you can—there's lots more to see up here!

Divide and Conquer

he garden takes on a new character as the days draw in. Autumn backlighting turns crocosmias into translucent fans of green glass. The late roses glow from within, candled by the soft, oblique sunlight. The garden remains enticing throughout the mild, open days of fall, which are optimal for reorganizing, dividing spring-blooming perennials, splitting up overgrown clumps of bulbs, and rearranging plant relationships that irked us through the summer. Before grabbing fork and shovel, consider well where you intend to put the divisions. If their future home is ready for them, bed neatly made and invitingly turned down, they will make the move without turning a hair. Too often, our newly divided convalescents get dragged all over the garden while we seek a haven for them, deciding at last in frustration that any old hole will do. If their hastily chosen new home is neither commodious nor well prepared, the poor, parched plants will droop disconsolate, needing several seasons to recover.

When working up a small stock of some treasured plant to fill a generous area, tuck the mother clump in the shelter of a tarpaulin or a big basket of soil while you amend the old planting site. Many nonwoody perennials can be divided by hand, the multiple crowns gently pulled or teased apart. Prizes like the glossy little *Haquetia* (*Dondia*) *epipactis*, with golden, green-ruffed April flowers, are too rare to risk under the knife, and respond best to the fingers of the solicitous gardener. Tough-rooted plants such as geums—perhaps the creamy apricot-yellow G. 'Lionel Cox'—and hardy geraniums such as 'Kashmire White' may be cut if need be, each new division tucked into damp peat while you complete the operation on the mother plant. Where you want a settled, natural effect, divide Mom into one or two larger clumps, then surround these with smaller offsets spaced to look like seedlings. A series of equal-sized divisions will be most useful for formal planting or for edging beds and paths.

With long-established perennials, division often yields more new plants than one actually wants or needs. It saves trouble if you have pots and soil ready to receive any overflow, which you can then trade among your friends or keep as door prizes for garden visitors. Remember, too, that many plant societies appreciate named divisions of good perennials for their fundraising sales. It is always recommended that old pots be well washed and bleached to avoid passing plant pathogens around, but all I ever do is knock out old soil before reusing them. So far this has not led to trouble—but then, I also hold all suspicious acquisitions (those which come from unfamiliar nurseries or other sources) in quarantine until it is clear that all is well. (Usually this means holding plants in pots for a full season.) Any that appear diseased get unceremoniously tossed, pot and all.

The rule of thumb for fall division is that anything which blooms in spring or early summer is fair game. If in your renovations you uncover thick clumps of spring bulbs, they too should be split up and reset in refreshed soil (add bone meal and blood meal, compost, and some coarse sand or grit to each new site). Running ground covers that have grown overcrowded or ceased to bloom can be renewed by pulling out chunks at regular intervals, removing perhaps one plant in six. Pot these up for use elsewhere and fill the gaps with compost fortified with cottonseed meal and manure. This mixture can also be scattered among the crowns of the remaining plants, if you can get at them. Where the carpet is truly congested and past its prime, it is worth having the whole business up and replenishing the exhausted soil. You will find that the effort—which is not inconsiderable—is amply repaid in handsome, lush new growth. Sometimes when plants no longer please us, a second chance of this sort works wonders, reminding us of what drew us to them in the first place. If it simply confirms the fact that you have outgrown that plant, pass it on and replace it with a new love that brings you joy.

Clumpy plants like astilbe and rodgersia can be divided now, as may tired, tatty-looking bergenias. Loosen the soil around a big mamma with a garden fork, then uproot the whole thing. Shake off any soil that clings to the roots, then pull or tease the crowns apart. When you reset them, spread their long roots out. Give them plenty of room; if you are just going to jam them into a tiny hole, you might as well cut them off and be done with it. Primroses—particularly the wonderful old hose-in-hose and Jack-in-the-green forms—can get woody and lose vigor in just a few seasons. They grow best when divided every other year, and you may do this any time between now and the New Year, weather permitting.

Dividing daylilies can be a daunting job if delayed too long. It is well worth the bother to split up fast-growers every third year, as long as they are also heavy bloomers. If not, replace them with something more satisfying.

Plants that fatten up slowly and continue to bloom well can be let go for five or six years, or until crowding reduces the show. When coping with significant clumps, get help; this job requires two backs and two sturdy forks—lesser forks (and backs) are sometimes destroyed in the process. If you don't really love the plant, compost it instead.

Siberian iris can also be intractable, but a sharp hatchet will reduce a stubborn old clump to nice little divisions quite quickly. Discard the woody central portion, which will never recover, and chunk the outer fans into 2"–3" pieces. Reset them six or eight inches apart, and unless you adore chopping wood, don't let them get so big again. Bearded iris of any size can also be split now; many experts feel that these must be divided and reset in August, but in practice you can get away with it successfully through October at least. If the old clumps are rotting and slimy, cut off all of the soft old rhizome (burn it rather than risk spreading trouble through the compost heap) and set the divisions in an airy place out of the sun. Let them dry off for a day or two, then replant them in new soil with rather better drainage this time (add grit or coarse sand to clay or dense loam).

Pacific Coast iris may be split up or moved about in late summer, though this isn't a job to be undertaken lightly, for there is greater risk of failure than with the relatively insensitive bearded ones. Over time, most PCs build into grassy, round tussocks that bloom less than generously. Dig up the whole mass with a fork, gently shake off the dirt, then pull the plants apart, tossing any bits that look spent. Plants handled as quickly and gently as possible have the best recovery rate and will often bloom strongly the following spring. Winter-blooming *Iris unguicularis* should also be left alone unless they are overgrown or languishing. If they need to be moved, this is the time, and a suffering plant often comes round quickly if given better conditions—any well-drained soil in full or nearly full sun. You probably won't get blooms this winter, but you may well keep your plant. Although it may be tempting to put off moving a plant for the sake of one more season of bloom, one of gardening's important lessons is to learn how to sacrifice a short-term pleasure for the long-term good of both plants and garden.

Gardening for the Birds

n October, the garden is alive with birds. Dozens, even hundreds of them are busily foraging through the toppling garden borders. Since we put off the main garden cleanup till spring, many perennials are heavy with seed. Though some plants are usually shy about setting seed in the mild Northwest, unusually hot summers give them the message to self-propagate or die. After such summers, we may reap a moderately abundant seed supply from *Crepis incana*, a hawkweed that looks much like a pink dandelion, as well as from both the white agapanthus and several fussy southern-bred daylilies which usually produce small seeds that never mature.

The shrubs and small trees of the mixed border provide welcome cover for small birds, though they must share these splendid headquarters with our two small boys, who also think them swell. Flocks of waxwings and kinglets rub wings with finches, chickadees, and redpolls, all bickering away fiercely over the garden's seedy treasure. When Davy Crockett and his sidekick Georgie Russell make their way toward the river pirate's base, clouds of little birds rise squawking from the bushes only to flump indignantly down a few yards farther away. Cross but undeterred, they quickly resume their gleaning, muttering angrily under their breath. Kids!

Huge robins compete fiercely with other thrushes, several sorts of flickers, and starlings. They all come to feast on the berries which linger in leafless swags on vines and trees throughout the older part of this crowded garden. Cotoneaster and pyracantha, viburnum and barberry are represented by several species each, all visited with regularity by the hungry birds. Most popular of all are the windfall pears and apples which lie in gloppy drifts beneath the aging fruit trees. At first we composted these drops (as apple pickers call them), but when we saw how the birds relished them, we decided we'd rather share. It certainly isn't the most hygienic practice, but it has clearly been going on for years; the grass grows most thickly beneath these neglected old trees, which are surprisingly prolific for their age and condition. The woodpeckers ignore the apples but find the old trees a rich source of insects; each broad, gnarled old trunk is neatly drilled in wandering rows from the base to the highest branches. The oversized pileated woodpeckers are so tame that we can walk—slowly—to within a yard of them as they make their bobbing way up and around the tree trunks. They cock their heads and eye us, shifting their territory a bit, but seem unimpressed by our propinquity.

Quail love the apples, and graze avidly for berries as well, especially relishing the red and the black of holly and ivy. Several resident families have merged from peeping flocks of babies into a single clutch of plump dowagers, usually accompanied by a lone triumphant male. From the time they were tiny, the entire group would chat for hours in a certain weeping willow by the kitchen garden. Now when they swarm the willow, its flexible golden twigs bend nearly to the ground under their combined weight, for these gals are no longer downy balls of fluff.

Gardeners who enjoy the company of birds during the winter and would like to encourage more of them to frequent the garden would do well to grow many such berrying plants. Even in small gardens, berrying vines and creepers can be unobtrusively tucked into odd corners where they won't spoil the overall design or color scheme. Come fall and winter, the unexpected flashes of color will brighten the fading scene. Many good berriers are climbers that can easily be induced to clamber up an existing tree or scramble through a mature hedge. Fences can serve the purpose as well, though you may need to attach some wire netting or plant hooks before vines can successfully scale them.

Should you wish to cover house walls with berrying plants, it is a good idea to build a very solid framework, with or without trellis panels, to support the plants. Set the feet of the structure in cement at least a foot out from the house walls—two feet away is better still. Make the framework sturdy, for mature vines can weigh a surprising amount; you don't want to discover the truth of this the hard way. The point of all this effort is twofold. First of all, the plants will be healthier, stronger, and more productive if grown well away from the dry walls—even two feet out from the wall, the soil will be appreciably better than the stuff smack against the wall. Second, a frame keeps the plants off the house wall, where they really don't belong at all unless the house is of stone or brick. This breathing space also comes in handy should you ever want to paint the walls or perform other such practical chores. (Actually, once you let the plantstuff rip, nobody will be able to tell whether you have painted or not, another big point in favor of this technique.) Watching the birds from the comfort of an armchair as they feed on the berries which now frame your windows is yet another benefit when the wet winds blow.

Cotoneasters, especially C. *dammeri*, C. *adpressus*, and C. *horizontalis*, will make their lacy patterns against low walls (up) or steep banks (down), to the delectation of birds and humans alike. The blueberry creeper, *Ampelopsis brevipedunculata*, sports sprays of berries in ocean shades, and both Boston ivy and Virginia creeper (once considered *Ampelopsis*, but now called *Parthenocissus*) carry bird berries, and should you prefer to see vines tumbling out of trees, all are attractive when grown that way. Rose hips and honeysuckle berries will draw a good crowd as well, and the plants themselves are pleasing through several seasons. All of these are good candidates for bringing birds to the garden, and all are tough enough to take it in the city. Next time you think about adding a little green to the urban jungle, plant one for the birds.

Purple Haze

hen we have a lovely, lingering Indian summer, many gardens show great beauty well into October. Where foliage plants are a major feature of border or bed, the last flowers of fall are seen in the solidly supportive setting they need, and the blossoms gleam out bravely against the strong greens and dappled golds.

Usually such late bloomers appear in bits and pieces, scattered through the garden in patternless patches. Here a lingering rose reblooms unaccompanied, there a forlorn snapdragon puts on a last flush of bloom. Without worthy companions, their beauties are diminished or lost outright. Frame these latelings in a sea of leaves, whether green or gold, silver or blue, and however sparse, their blossoms will gain firepower from the firm setting. Late performers like asters and goldenrods, chrysanthemums and dahlias look spectacular, rather than slightly melancholy, given the right company. Small but nicely arranged groups can easily outshine large and expensive mass plantings that are dead weight all spring and summer.

In our garden, one incendiary grouping is still blazing away, breathtaking in the golden autumn light. The flagrant rose, 'Just Joey', is still opening an enormous candelabra of buds, its impossibly huge cups of gingery peach strongly scented on the sharp, crisp air. Behind it sparkles *Fothergilla gardenii*, a small shrub that took a bow in spring, then sat in a back seat all summer. Now its big, pleated leaves are scarlet and crimson, gold and bronze, in a lively and resplendent mixture. Great fans of *Crocosmia* 'Emily McKenzie' in burnt orange and coffee, each floret the size of a silver dollar, teeter like 'Just Joey' on the very knife edge of tastelessness. Tall, lemony pokers of *Kniphofia* 'Vanilla', the third set to bloom this year, add an exclamatory note. Behind them, a gold-and-green variegated dogwood, 'Cherokee Sunset', colors more warmly than ever, orange and copper and gold lightening its tapered leaves before they finally tumble. This cultivar holds its leaves rather longer than most dogwoods do, and begins to color earlier as well. At its feet, a pale pumpkin-colored chrysanthemum, the perennial, single-petaled

'Mary Stoker', gleams softly like a small patch of lost sunshine beside the brighter orange cups of the ever-blooming *Meconopsis cambrica*, the indefatigable Welsh poppy. This last seeds itself exuberantly, as does the sunny, clear yellow kind which is equally willing (a recently introduced crimson form is somewhat less so). However, where the colors are grown together, the orange generally predominates and soon crowds the others out altogether. The solution is segregation, allotting each its own portion of the garden where it may mingle with other plants unoppressed.

This gilded, glowing scene does not please everybody; there are gardeners who would rather suffer an invasion of hungry cows than see an orange flower in their totally tasteful border. All is not glitter and gold, however, and a short way down the border, a less clarion combination that has been satisfying for several months is still in excellent form. A huge shrub of purple-leafed hazel came with the garden, and has become the centerpiece to many a seasonal color scheme. Just now it plays background to a vivid tumble of purple and lavender from both flowers and berries. There are no fewer than three different beautyberries (*Callicarpa* species) planted in the small shrubbery hedge behind it—I am a great believer in excess—all similarly burdened with thick clusters of purple berries the size of a pinhead, not showy in themselves but definitely striking en masse.

The berries' color is picked up by the glossy red stems of *Fuchsia riccartonii*, a clump of which had been growing by the house for years. Fuchsia cuttings root with great ease, and soon a yearling was placed here, to fan out behind the dusky hazel. Each stem now ends in a thick fringe of drooping, narrow-skirted flowers, for, like most fuchsias, this one really hits its stride in fall. These flowers are shocking pink and dusky purple, finely textured and extremely generous of bloom, though the bush itself is far from shapely and benefits from regular pruning to keep it open and graceful.

A wide carpet of lavender colchicum, often called autumn crocus, spreads at ground level. These are children of another old garden near my own, in which an original few bulbs had multiplied into incredible colonies over 50 years. (This gives one hope when shelling out the two or three dollars a bulb colchicum command in today's market; each will speedily proliferate, and a dozen planted today will make a creditable host in 10 years.) They glow softly, full of a weird, sad light all their own, and often appear uneasy or irrelevant in border plantings. Here, they are firmly anchored by low, glittering blue 'Maxi Star' junipers, which so far seem impervious to the viruses that are decimating junipers throughout the Northwest (to the delight of many, and the consternation of those like myself, who can genuinely see beauty in the ubiquitous).

Further softness comes from a species gladiola, a far, far different creature than the bold, upright border hybrids. This one, *Gladiolus papilio*, blooms on sinuous, lanky stems that get wound (by me) through the stiff branches of the beautyberry bushes to keep their faces off the ground. The flowers are fat and hooded, cream tinged with purple, and each is marked with two grimy green teardrops on its pallid cheeks. They begin in late August, and often go on through October. The bulbs emerge through a thicket of purple-leafed culinary sage, which nicely masks their bare knees.

All this hazy lavender and purple is lovely, if a bit morose, but perky sprays of lively pink and purple pea flowers from a small shrub, *Lespedeza bicolor*, add a dash of more cheerful color. I once saw this shrub standing against a dark purple smoke bush, *Cotinus coggygria*, in an accidental juxtaposition of pots, an effect well worth duplicating at home. The *Lespedeza* also associates gaily with a pink, rose, and cream variegated barberry, 'Rose Glow', a hot crowd of Schiaparelli pink nerine lilies at its feet. It is too much to ask a small garden to be at full steam at this time of year, but even tiny ones can have a corner or two devoted to such multiseasonal glories, thereby extending the garden year well beyond the presumed boundaries.

An Excess of Zeal

As encroaching autumn gradually thins the proud ranks in bed and border, the gardener may begin to feel an odd restlessness, an itch that can't be stilled. Though similar in quality to the wanderlust that courses through younger veins in this season of change, it is decidedly different in effect. In the early stages, one suddenly discovers that catalogs unexamined since June have mysteriously returned to circulation. One begins flicking through them idly, circling a few things —not many; after all, the garden is still going strong—then sets them aside for a rainy day. As foggy mornings become the norm, pens somehow leap to hand and order forms magically fill themselves. Diagnosis: gardener in urgent need of a plant fix. It is curious that, while gardening is on the one hand among the most satisfying of life's experiences, it has this dark side too, the incurable, wracking pain of plant lust. The delights of spring, the satisfactions of summer, many as they are, are simply not enough. Intelligent nursery owners issue fall catalogs with precisely this phenomenon in mind.

The beginning of the long garden sleep can be even more disastrous than spring for plant lovers. Perhaps we feel more vulnerable, sensing our mortality most when the year is sliding into the downward portion of its cycle. Perhaps we want to make up for the disappointments of a summer that didn't achieve its promise. Perhaps we are simply greedy, wanting a season which exceeded all expectation never to end. In any case, the plant lust of fall burns deep, and we are apt to wake up one day to discover, say, 1,300 bulbs on the front porch (a totally hypothetical situation, of course). We may suddenly realize that this is a *large* quantity, a fact obscured by the catalog-generated enthusiasm which made us think in terms like "generous" or "ample." Worse yet, we may now remember that this shipment represents only a portion of our total commitment to the floral new year, a commitment with immediate consequences that drive us to our knees. Trowel in hand, we look hopelessly for 1,300 empty spaces.

Well, if one has been profligate with bulbs, at least some circumspection has been preserved in regard to plants. I am proud of myself this year, for after suffering through several seasons without proper gardens or nursery beds, I managed to remember how overwhelming it feels to over-order plants. I was stern with myself, recalling that however *de luxe* it seems to order everything that appeals from every conceivable source, the picture is less pretty when the boxes begin to arrive. All too soon there's no room, no time, no attention. Nothing is savored, nothing is treasured; it all melds into a muchness that is simply too much. Naturally I pored over the catalog pages —no harm in that. I even circled dozens of likely sounding candidates—just a thought. I then set the catalogs aside for a few days (to bring the fever down) before actually ordering the few—relatively speaking—which still called my name. I am proud of myself this year, for this was the year of control. This year we only added one new bed—well, one and a half—and it barely doubled the size of the garden. This year every inch of garden ground was improved, and almost all of it got mulched—really a significant achievement. This year weeding was a pleasurable indulgence rather than a dire necessity, an excuse to get in and see what was up. This year nobody had to ask where the garden was; the beds were full to overflowing and everything that wasn't winter-damaged was well grown.

This was the year of restraint, a year of ordering only what we could plant. The pot-plant ghetto was reduced almost to zero. Every new acquisition was in the ground within two days. So maybe the kids and I got a little carried away with the bulbs (my patient husband took one look, got out the Rototiller, and headed out to break new ground). A few plants will be coming too, so actually, a new bed might be a good idea.

As we slip out to mail off the restrained fall order (just a modest one), a small stack of boxes—new boxes—block our path. "Look, Mom, presents!" shout the unsuspecting children. Boxes already? I suddenly realize that this is the second, or perhaps the third, attack of plant frenzy this season. I mail the last order anyway—mustn't waste stamps—and together we open the first box, a full one from Forestfarm. I ordered this? Three *Cotinus coggygria*? Now I recall a summer vision of a small grove of smoke bushes, not the highly colored purple kind, but the subtler species form that smokes more sumptuously and colors even better in fall. Well, that sounds pretty. Besides, these plants represent a terrific bargain, for they are fully as large as costlier ones from fancier nurseries. Here are several ribes, not the native flowering currant that fills the woods in spring, but a California cousin with fat red fuchsia flowers and red-hot fall color (*Ribes roezlii*) and the piercingly fragrant buffalo currant (*R. odoratum*), both destined for the spring/fall borders. Buffalo currant sells for four times as much in a certain trendy East Coast catalog, and the plant my neighbor got from that not-to-be-named source was distinctly less prepossessing than this one; one should always take advantage of a true bargain. Here, too, are young fringe trees, both Chinese and American—the ingredients for making detente right in one's own back yard. Both are highly rated small shrubs, shapely and precocious bloomers which ought to grace more gardens than they do.

Fortunately, a large nursery bed, deep dug and rich with manure and compost, has just become available, emptied of a wedding's worth of flowers this very morning. As I begin to row out these first few—relatively few—plants, I decide that even though there are other boxes yet to come, and even though I just mailed a probably unnecessary further order—one really mustn't waste stamps—it is not wrong to amass plants. After all, these are excellent specimens, in splendid condition and bought at excellent prices. So there is no immediate home for them; if we have no holding beds, how can we fill unexpected gaps, make fortuitous combinations, find soulmates for plants we don't yet know? Do artists wait until they have a use for rose madder before springing for a tube? Should we not keep flour on hand except when actually engaged in breadmaking? Plants are the ingredients of a garden, and if plant frenzy has its purpose (as I suspect it does), it must be to take our gardens beyond the conventional, the easy, and the readily accessible. After all, one of the crucial elements in any garden is that of surprise, and, if nothing else, acute plant frenzy ensures plenty of surprises.

The BORDER in EARLY WINTER

NOVEMBER ▪ DECEMBER

EARLY WINTER

There is so much that needs doing in the garden just now—here some glaring horticultural horror that pleads for correction, there yet another bag of unplanted bulbs or hopelessly crowded clump of seedlings that simply cannot be put off till spring. Time is in short supply, however, and I had taken to trotting through the garden with averted eyes, muttering: "Later, later, I promise."

The other morning, a long shaft of diffuse November light pierced the clouds and spilled over the table where I was working. I took it as a sign, pushed aside all my papers, and ran out into the garden. The day looked very nasty, dripping and foggy, yet the air was mild, and before long, gloves on and shovel in hand, I was hard at work. It didn't last, of course—some pressing duty or other arose almost at once—but it was an instructive incident, for it proved yet again that a lot can be accomplished in short bursts of energy and time. When the children were toddlers, 20 free minutes was a luxury. Now that both are schoolboys, we are getting spoiled and consider less than a few hours worthless. That industrious morning has started a new habit: every day I do at least one thing in the garden. It's amazing how many niggling little chores have gotten themselves done this way— even the plant-holding ghetto by the kitchen door is looking tidy. Tidier.

Late-season dabblers are rewarded in many ways—not only do their chores get done, but all the small details of the autumn garden that are so easily overlooked by the hasty can be savored one by one. A last ivory green spray of lockets hang from a splendid native bleeding heart, *Dicentra oregana*, with steel blue, much-dissected leaves. Those in rich, loamy soil and half shade seem in their first youth still, while others in drier ground and more sun have turned appealing pumpkin shades of orange and muted yellow. Dusky leaves of black labs, *Viola labradorica*, run around and through the blue dicentra, and just a handspan away, the first fat buds of *Iris unguicularis* are unrolling, silvery-pink in the soft autumn light. They open quickly when the sun warms them, releasing their peculiar, pungent perfume on the crisp air. In the summer these flimsy flowers would not be rated highly, yet now they seem porcelain pure, their white throats netted with violet, licked with gold, standing out sharply against falls of deep river blue, the ivory styles fluffy with pale gold dust. They are often imperfect, gnawed by slugs or blotched by weather, yet they have the distinct air of a thing in its proper season—not a lost bloom of summer, but a true winter flower, sturdy and impervious to cold.

When we moved I brought every scrap of hardy cyclamen with me, and now a brief weeding tour reveals small pools of the round green and silver leaves spreading beneath each of the old fruit trees that line the incipient peony walk. *C. neapolitanum* 'Album' is my favorite, the tight, pointed buds rising on slim swans' necks amid tarnished pewter pear leaves. Creeping mats of tiny *Alchemilla ellenbeckii* tie the pools together; this minute relative of the drooping, popular lady's mantle has tiny leaves shaped exactly like their garden border counterparts, yet the biggest is the size of my little fingernail, edged with glimmering dewdrops. Big lady's mantles can get aggressive, swamping anything of lesser stature, but this prostrate form makes a good neighbor for the cyclamen. It also provides excellent low cover for the small bulbs that huddle below the surface here: *Narcissus bulbocodium* in several forms, which multiply readily in the deep, well-drained soil; purple-black *Muscari neglectum*, each floret rimmed with a pencil-thin line of white, which mingle with every named form of the checker lily (*Fritillaria meleagris*) that the catalogs afford. Dim purple 'Charon', lilac-and-green tweed 'Artemis', 'Saturnus' in red-violet, and pale 'Alba' get tucked in among the cyclamen this year, for the bulbs set here two years ago have already built into budding colonies. Behind the sleeping bulbs, bold *Helleborus foetidus*, dark and slim-fingered, are tipped with a froth of icy green buds and pleated new growth.

There is never an end to the garden year, for even as we bid good-bye to the last of the summer flowers, the autumn- and winter-blooming things appear, fitfully at first, then thick and fast. *Prunus subhirtella* 'Autumnalis' is a light mist of pink just now—how I long for the clean white form, the one the English scorn so, since they have it in abundance. We have nothing but this washy pink, which the Brits prize simply because it is unobtainable across the water. I suppose we would feel the same, were the situation reversed. Most camellias are frumpy plants in or out of flower, but the fall-blooming *C. sasanqua* polishes its leaves to a lacquered gloss, and its dainty blossoms are apt to shatter cleanly. Double or single, these are invariably more delicate and less blowsy than their spring-blooming relatives, and far less likely to look like wads of wet tissue. Some years each flush of flower will be spoilt by rain and wind and frost—most frustrating—but in a mild, open year the semidouble flowers of the princely 'Hana Jiman' open well, clean white streaked with blushing pink. Even better is 'Setsugekka', bearing loads of ruffled white blossoms with the texture of heavy silk amid glittering, bronzy olive leaves.

The usual autumn campaign to plant far too many bulbs continues to present the gardener with fascinating little puzzles—where do you place a tulip like 'Wallflower', purple, green, and chestnut brown? It sounds awful, but is absolutely stunning, a flower arranger's dream. In the border it associates splendidly with old-fashioned perennial wallflowers which bloom in root beer, mahogany, faded purples, and mauves. Big and bunch-flowering, 'Wallflower' also displays to advantage in large terra-cotta pots, mingling with the sinuous, sinister 'Black Parrot', the deep violet 'Max Durand' with its thickly fringed petals, and the rosy, plump

‘Queen of Bartigons’, all similarly late-bloomers that complement the curious, rather Victorian coloring of ‘Wallflower’.

Pots and border positions suit most tall tulips, but the majority of the species tulips look most comfortable in more naturalistic settings, and we must look further afield for places to set off their small charms. When placing treasures like the softly fragrant lemony balloon flowers of *Tulipa sylvestris*, we look to the woods edge, to the rhododendron ghetto, or to the mixed shrubbery for inspiration. Here, beneath this wonderful *Kalmia latifolia*, tucked amid a carpet of creeping veronica, perhaps? Emerging from the skirts of a spreading skimmia? Among the sarcoccocas?

> *The Night is mother of the Day,*
> *The Winter of the Spring,*
> *And ever upon old Decay*
> *The greenest mosses cling*

(says Whittier), which anybody can see is perfectly true, both on our rooftop and in the woods behind the house. As we paw through the woodsy litter beneath the old trees and shrubs, looking for likely spots to tuck just one more bag of bulbs, we find the freshest banks of thick moss or selaginellas rising up along the "nurse logs," ancient trees long fallen, that are also host to native rhododendrons, acteas, salal, and hundreds of little ferns. When this wilder part of the garden is brought into cultivation, these nurse logs and their small charges will be kept on in positions of honor, though joined by foreign imports. This won't happen soon, but fall and winter are dreamtimes for the gardener, times to renew both plans and vision, even in those few stolen moments among the quiescent plants.

A Tumble of Late Roses

he year is closing in; we have had frosts, though only light ones, and there is definitely less color—or less brilliant color —in the borders. Nonetheless, December opens mild and fair, if a trifle wet, and like all addicted gardeners who know no season, we try to weed, transplant, or generally meddle for an hour or two every day. Certain pictures continue powerful even into winter; a smoke bush, *Cotinus coggygria* 'Velvet Cloak', takes on rather deeper tones than the usual tawny oranges of 'Royal Purple', though with lots of high red tints. This curvaceous shrub abuts a mature blue spruce, up which a climbing hybrid tea rose called 'Butterscotch' is being coaxed to marvelously subtle effect. 'Butterscotch' isn't the flat, harsh color of children's candy, but the soft, buff-brown-gold of the homemade stuff, just the color of linen dyed with China tea (as when one spills it all over the tablecloth). The faded native bracken ferns that mask the rose's long legs are the same color, if a few shades deeper.

Next to the cotinus, a sturdy little mountain ash is still showering gold confetti on everything. It is flanked by a rising shrub of *Berberis thunbergii* 'Rose Glow' on its other side, which associates well with the smoke bush for most of the year. Ruffled mats of a creeping polygonum called 'Dimity' spread below both to tie the scene together; 'Dimity' has pink candlestick blossoms from early spring on, but now the last few late ones are bright red, above warm golden-red leaves.

Some of the best fall backbone things for any mixed border are culinary herbs. Sages, for instance—the muted, frosty purple kind looks nice all winter if it has been cut back quite hard in August. This is also true for the cream-green-and-pink tricolor form. Both the lemon-lime variegated sage and broadleaf forms of grey cooking sage make neat subshrubs all year, needing only occasional shaping in late summer to keep trim. Rosemary is invaluable in the winter garden, not only for basting chickens with lemon and white wine, or for threading through lamb with lots of garlic, but for its solidly evergreen quality. 'Tuscan Blue' is especially handsome in autumn and winter; columnar to five or six feet, with Italian-sky blue flowers—even now a few are left. Lavender comes in many forms, some, like the Mediterranean *Lavandula stœchas*, pleasantly architectural in winter, when the measured, whorling patterns of its grey needles stand out amid the muted mush of the perennials. Blue rues (*Ruta*) are splendid just now; nothing contrasts better with the lacquer reds, high oranges, and imperial yellows of autumn leaves than the silvery blue of lacy, droplike rue foliage. When a cut-and-scalloped maple leaf of Chinese red meets the tapered coppery leaves of *Prunus serrulata* 'Ukon' against a bushy mound of ice blue Jackman's rue, a visual magic occurs.

There are still a few things in their first freshness. The saffron crocus, *C. sativus*, is opening purple cups for the last late bees on warm days, and the rather smaller white ones of *C. ochroleucus* look tender and frail in the thin autumn sunshine. Nearby, a super form of *Saxifraga fortunei*, 'Wada's Variety', is holding sprays of white, fluffy bellflowers above lustrous, waxen leaves that turn blood red in cool weather (all summer the undersides are silvery red and veined darkly, like rabbits' ears). Nerine lilies rise ghostlike in the early morning mist, their glossy ribbon-candy stripes shining shocking pink against the wisps of grey fog. Schizostylus is a trouper for us, with two cultivars outstanding at the year's end; 'Sunrise', a form selected by Eric Smith and introduced by The Plantsmen some years ago, is big, wide, and satin pink, looking like an overblown gladiola. The long, braided bloom wands twist sinuously, and the flowers blow in odd tufts, a few at a time, for months on end. ' Vicountess Byng' is much the same, though rather smaller in all parts, and may appear more or less constantly from October through March. Both have flopsy, grassy foliage that is best hidden between shrubs— they do remarkably remedial things to those everlasting banks of junipers in city gardens.

A shapely nasturtium relative, *Tropæolum tuberosum*, has circular, scalloped foliage and blooms with a great goodwill late in the year—sometimes too late, and its orange, tubular trumpets are lost to frost. A form that kicks in earlier looks delightfully gaudy winding through the ridiculous, wonderful orange-sherbet rose 'Just Joey'; called 'Ken Aslet' after a superintendent at Wisley, it begins to bloom in August and hasn't quit yet. The old-fashioned canary creeper *T. peregrinum* is another nasturtium, an annual that often self-sows. It blooms and reblooms endlessly, often into the new year. In fact, it performs most strongly early and late, skipping the driest parts of the summer altogether but coming back into its own with the fall rains. Some is twining through a huge clump of masterwort (*Astrantia maxima*) now in full rebloom, its pink and green pincushions starry and shrunken with cold. The canary vine has looped around the masterwort and neatly tied in the long, bobbling stems of the bluest of salvias, *S. guaranitica.* Lots of the tall blue-flowered salvias do well here, carrying on till hard frost. They are only borderline hardy, but cuttings can be potted up and bits can be stuck in a sunny window and carried over very easily.

Certain of the roses are still in fine fettle; 'Nearly Wild', a blushing pink single with a white eye, has remarkably fresh foliage even now, and is still in heavy bloom. Our bush of 'Betty Prior' is nearly 10 feet tall (that isn't supposed to happen, but goat pruning affects some plants strangely) and it is still pouring a tumble of silvery, rosy blossoms through the arms of a neighboring beauty bush, *Kolkwitzia amabilis*, spangled with fizzy, rusty little seedheads that contrast delightfully with the roses. 'Old Blush' will bear till the hardest frost and recommence at the first thaw—it never really stops, though the icy little ivory-pink buds get a sort of glaze on them and can't open properly in the coldest weather. 'Golden Showers', that redoubtable old climber, makes a lush, stocky bush if carefully pruned, and is scarcely ever without a flower from May through December. The tiny frizzled florets of the green rose open late in the year, perhaps to avoid cruel comparisons with more glamorous cousins. Not everybody likes this rose, and indeed, when the cool green blossoms turn rusty orange, they lose their eldritch appeal. In the bud, however, and as it first opens, there is nothing more weirdly wonderful than *Rosa viridis*, the rose of winter.

Never Too Late

t is always a delight to stroll through the late autumn garden, savoring each bit of color, marveling over every stalwart bloom. Even at this late date, and after a summer of stress, there is a remarkable amount of beauty in the yard. The huge old bridal wreath, *Spiraea prunifolia*, is still sending up showers of bright sparks after nearly two months of brilliance. This old-fashioned shrub is too often scornfully banned from modern gardens; it is dependable, lovely in several seasons, and very graceful when well grown, with its trim waist emphasizing the billowing fountain spray of its wide arms. Perhaps that is the key, for generally these older shrubs are neglected, poorly pruned or not pruned at all, and the resulting tangle gets them the cold shoulder. If you have such a plant, wait till the flames die down, then put it on your winter pruning list. Just now it would take a heartless gardener to cut into it, for it is glowing with ever-increasing intensity, the outer leaves rosy, the inner ones clear yellow and old gold, so each bush smolders, lit from within.

There are still some delightful combinations going, as where the soft blue flowers of the prostrate rosemary, a frequent repeat-bloomer, are echoed by the clear blue daisies of *Felicia amelloides*, the blue marguerite which is mostly hardy here. A bit of sawdust around Felicia's feet would be a wise precaution and will keep her blooming straight through a mild winter. Long trails of a nasturtium relative, the sunny little canary vine, brings fluttering flowers of clear lemon to the scene, always a good complement to clean blues. It finds its echo in the central boss of the ubiquitous daisy-flowered feverfew, *Matricaria parthenium*, a willing and incredibly prolific member of the chrysanthemum family.

Nearby, a smudgy purple-leafed sage is backed by tall, translucent red sheaves of Japanese blood grass, *Imperata cylindrica* 'Rubra'. It takes some skill and experience to use this stunning plant effectively. Curiously enough, more is frequently less with this one; a really big patch can look sullen and a bit dim, while several smaller clumps planted within a few feet of each other set up recurring shock waves, the bright blades insistently blazing.

Both the blood grass and the purple sage are dramatically underplant-ed with wandering ribbons of wild red wood sorrel. This familiar cloverlike plant is a persistent native that I welcome into the border, to the horror of some visitors who insist it is a pernicious weed. It does get around, I agree, but is easy to root out, unlike certain of its relatives, and to its credit it often puts itself in marvelous juxtapositions—in front of Japanese blood grass, for instance, and beneath several hydrangeas, dark red, purple, and soft pink, or nuzzled up to a group of the larger iron-cross oxalis, *O. tetraphylla* (*deppei*). In this form, each broad leaf is boldly marked with the reddish purple of the wood sorrel, which in turn echoes the leaf shape on a miniature scale.

In another area, the little red sorrel has cozied up to a young beauty-berry, *Callicarpa bodinieri giraldii*. The shrublet is covered with tight clusters of shiny berries, deep lavender over a white base. The berries are tiny, but generously clustered, and even as a youngster a beautyberry will put on a good show. Where several are planted together, the berry crop is heavier still, attracting flocks of flower arrangers who beg for twigs. Both this and its plumper cousin, 'Profusion'—which bears larger berries in deeper, glossier purple—deserve wider planting. Even small gardens could afford room for a plant or two, for they are slight and airy in structure, with slender, swoop-ing branches that trail nicely through more solid stuff, whether plant or fence or arbor. Although callicarpas may reach five or six feet over time, a harsh winter will kill them to the ground. Spring will bring them bouncing back from the roots, and they take even hard pruning without a whimper. The wispy little flowers are deep purple and slightly fragrant, and the long, handsome leaves take on mysterious shades of pink and purple before falling, setting off the berries enchantingly. Beautyberries like plenty of sun, good drainage, and ordinary soil, and appear to advantage among silvery sub-shrubs like Russian sage (*Perovskia atriplicifolia*) with ferny little leaves of sea green, and the broader, fuzzy-leafed Jerusalem sage, *Phlomis fruticosa*.

Of bright berrying things, there are plenty still pouring out their riches: berberis and holly, pernettya and sorbus. Great swags of pyracantha tumble out of spruce trees, heavily beaded with berries of orange, crimson, or dark, lustrous red. Those of a particularly pretty cultivar, 'Gold Rush', of which the birds are very fond, are warm yellow. With such abundance, we shouldn't grudge the birds their mite, and indeed the garden is livelier for their presence. I feel much the same about the little red wood sorrel, plebian interloper that it is. It is a bad thing to be above common plants simply because they are common, to ignore their very real graces in favor of something that has only its rarity or difficulty or great price to recommend it. The same might be said of accidentals, plants introduced by birds, or charmingly self-sown where we had never thought to put them. The very best plans may be improved upon by such fortuitous intrusions, if only we have the grace to accept them.

Swaddled and Slipcovered

hen the weather bureau gives us clear warning that winter —real winter—is on the way, then a bit of foresight will save endless moaning later. The wise will take their lead from the heavy morning frosts and prepare for invasion despite deceptively mild afternoon temperatures. The time to act is not yet upon us, but if we are ready to respond, 24 hours' notice of a significant freeze will be ample.

The first step in preparing for a winter freeze is simple: make a thorough garden inventory. Stroll through your beds, noting the weak, the vulnerable, the new and the tender. Write down your observations as you ramble, so that nothing is forgotten. Once back inside, make a simple map, marking the locations of every plant that might need protection, and indicating how many plants are in each spot. As you do this, assess the needs of each. Many shrubs are wounded as much by wind or sudden sun on frozen leaves as they are from the frost, especially broadleafed shrubs. New mountain laurels, rhododendrons and leucothoes, young plants of grey-leafed *Senecio greyi* or *Melianthus major* (the South African honey flower, silver blue and smelling of peanut butter), ceanothus, even the native ones—all should be marked for covering, top and bottom. This means heavy mulching with chipped bark or wood shavings, and covering the upper growth with sheets or old blankets. Roses, of course, suffer dreadfully, especially those which have been brutally pruned—so if you haven't got around to that chore yet, don't. Roses and other tender deciduous shrubs should get a deep mulch of compost and/or shredded bark.

Questionably hardy perennials, too, need adequate coverage. Mark down any promising clumps of *Euphorbia wulfenii*, *E. martinii*, or *E. amygdaloides*, as well as New Zealand flax (*Phormium* species), Dierama (the wand flower called angel's fishing rod), or any *Libertia*. All such tender perennials with evergreen tops want loose insulation—sawdust, leaves, straw—dumped generously over their root zones, plus a top covering of bag, box, or sheet. Think back to previous years, and make a star on your map beside anything which showed signs of stress after a great frost.

Now that you have the vulnerable plants identified, you can see how the patterns lie. Where practical, you can group several plants, treating them as a unit to be covered by a single cloth or tarp. Evaluate each cluster of plants as to the kind of protection required. Most will need an insulating blanket of dry material; some will need a covering, while others need only screening from excess sun and wind. Singletons in exposed sites may need to be given a windbreak of hay bales or cardboard boxes. Winter-blooming plants which are not dormant are particularly at risk, yet they can't be given prophylactic treatment; bundling them up too well too early might do more harm than the weather would. Evergreens in particular must be protected loosely in order not to smother.

Mark the results of your analysis on the map, too: "New rose—large sheet, sawdust. Tender azalea—dry leaves, medium bag. Euphorbia—tall box, leaves." Small and medium-size plants can be quickly covered; slip plastic garbage bags—opaque ones are preferable, as they block the light—loosely filled with one of the above-mentioned horticultural insulators over shrubs and evergreen perennials. Secure them gently around trunk or main stem, and heap additional insulation around root zone as needed. Larger shrubs get heaped with shredded bark or whatever, then cloth or plastic is draped over their extremities and fastened in place with twine or bungee cords, rocks or bricks.

Now you have a master plan, ready to be enacted at a moment's notice. The next step is to organize your supplies. If these are on hand well in advance of the frightful event, all you will need to do when the time comes is to methodically follow the steps of your plan, and disaster will be diverted. There will be no need to wander mournfully through the yard with a bucket of sawdust wondering what to save first, as I did in January of '89. The materials will be bulky, but it will certainly be worth taking time to clear out some storage space in garage or shed for a bale of straw, a huge sack of leaves, or boxes of sawdust. Stacks of old blankets, sheets, shower curtains, and plastic drop cloths won't take up much room, nor do their fasteners. Paper cartons and shopping bags, paper grocery sacks and plastic garbage bags in several sizes, as well as old newspaper, which when crumpled up makes fine short-term insulation—all can be stored flat.

A brief practice run—sort of a horticultural fire drill—will reveal any inadequacies in your preparations. Don't get carried away, however, for taking these precautions too early could prove fatal. At present, both ground and plants are wet and warm. Cutting off the air supply with insulation will set up splendid conditions for breeding mold, rot, and various unpleasant diseases that are the horticultural equivalent of iatrogenic illness.

Objects need care as well as plants; that same January, innumerable terra-cotta containers were cracked or broken in the freeze. A friend lost a huge, ancient Chinese vase that originally held carp; it simply exploded into potsherds when the water inside froze. Take heed and bring that birdbath in now. Put those hoses and hand tools away. Bee skeps and hanging baskets, plaster *putti* and clay fountain bubblers, all must be gathered in. While you're at it, you may as well clean your gloves; leather gloves of kid, goat, or sheepskin can be rinsed well in warm water. When they're clean, blow into them to restore shape to the fingers, and let them dry flat. When they are half-dry, rub them all over with neatsfoot oil. I like to coat my hands with Eucerin (a wax-based skin cream) and pull the oiled gloves on—this puts a film of waxy cream on the insides, keeping the gloves soft and flexible and my hands unchapped. Rubber gloves may be washed inside and out, blown into, and hung to dry. Before you put them away for the winter, powder the insides with cornstarch and the fingertips won't stick shut.

There. Now you are well armed against the worst that winter can do. When disaster looms you can respond, not with the traditional hysteria, but with calm certainty. When those first fell flakes appear, ominous and grey, you will be out there within minutes, executing your precisely orchestrated master plan with smug confidence. The garden lies swaddled in its manger of hay, awaiting the epiphany of spring. Each tender shrub is slipcovered. Let it snow!

Winter Twigs

O n Christmas day I wandered through our island garden searching for signs of life. In the town garden, I knew, there would be stalks of schizostylus yet in bloom, fat trumpets of winter jasmine blowing silent against the east wall, blue-eyed periwinkles and soft drifts of sweet alyssum still in flower. Swelling buds still decked the China rose there, and pushing, eager snouts of crocus and snowdrops would be appearing on the south bank. Here on the island, however, there was little to be seen—this is essentially a brand-new garden, though fitted within the shell of a very old one. Gardens at both extremes of age are likely to be less productive in every way than an established garden in its first flush of strength, or even one in comfortable middle age. Feeling a bit forlorn, I cut a handful of twigs from the sagging old forsythia and brought them into the house.

On New Year's Day the first flowers opened. Placed in a sunny window just over the sink, the flowers dangled down at eye level. Each sun-colored bud unfurled, splaying four pudgy fingers wide to display a throat touched with lime green and penciled with radiating red lines. I don't believe that I had ever actually looked at a forsythia flower before. Within days each branch was liberally decked with gold, and the first tender leaves were unfolding. This was so heartening that I unearthed the garden trug and sallied out again, clippers in hand, eager for more plunder. Birch twigs, willow wands, strands of kerria and fat branchlets of sanguisorba, bits of flowering quince and big branches of glossy camellia studded with heavy buds—all found their way into the basket. As I snipped I was dismayed to notice that each plant I raided was in progressively worse condition. This is an old, old garden, and everything in it stands in dire need of pruning, shaping, or cutting back. Moreover, it is a very big place and there are many, many such bushes. What can any one person hope to accomplish where so much needs doing?

I felt terribly discouraged at having left a garden in town that was at long last approaching maturity and showing definite signs of fulfilling our intentions (always a doubtful point until a garden is truly established).

Moreover, though certainly too small, the town garden was finally under control, so that one person could keep it in trim with just an hour or two of work each week. In horrific contrast, this island garden looked as if it would be a lifetime of labor, and possibly labor lost. Nettles and brambles abounded, the woods were closing in, and it all suddenly seemed an endless, impossible task. Disgruntled, I lugged the burdened trug back to the house.

My spirits lightened as every vase and jar in the house came into play, for there were a great many sticks to be housed, and every room wanted freshening with greenstuff. It's amazing how resilient the spirit can be, given a glimpse of something to look forward to quite soon. Hmm. Perhaps this was a hint to make some achievable short-term goals for the garden as well.

Most gardeners are aware that a great number of spring-blooming shrubs and trees can be forced indoors—not only forsythia, but flowering plums, crabapples, redbud, and all sorts of things. Our native flowering currant, *Ribes sanguineum*, is outstanding in this respect, and stems cut now will quite soon come into flower. Vita Sackville-West writes of sticking buckets full of ribes into a dark, warm closet, where they will proceed to open as they would in the kitchen, but bleached by lack of light, they will be a clean white rather than red. Since all our closets are in frequent and vigorous use, I poked a few stems into a vase and left it in the basement near the furnace. Sure enough, the resulting blossoms are a gentle pink—perhaps the often-entered basement doesn't stay dark enough to bleach them completely.

Set in a large south-facing window, the great curved camellia leaves become translucent and surpassingly beautiful, though the buds don't look a bit interested in opening. They give definition to the wispy bits of less solid stuff which are unfurling delicately beside them. Leaves of hazel and kerria open sharp knife-pleats in an acid shade of lime—the sun turns them to curling leaves of green glass. The sanguisorba releases puffs of feathery fans, each plumy little leaf wrapped in celadon tissue paper. Out of doors these plants seem unchanged from week to week; inside we are all newly smitten with the forms and variety of their emerging leaves. I had never seen the faint down on baby kerria leaves, or noticed how charmingly alder catkins soften and droop as they swell. These proved to shed a fair amount of pollen as they swelled, and had to be banished, but not before we all admired their Victorian grace—they reminded us of those melancholy maidens swooning over fresh graves on old cross-stitch samplers.

In the front garden a native willow, as yet unidentified, showed felted, silvery undersides to its tapered leaves. The twigs I'd brought in gave me great pleasure, because the rooting hormone which all willows exude in quantity encouraged a hitherto recalcitrant arboreal or mature ivy from the front garden to root. I deliberately mingled shoots of the willow and ivy in a dark vase, for although young ivy roots quite readily, when it matures to its shrubby, non-clinging state, it roots less willingly. The willow twigs have coaxed it to reconsider and have put out copious roots themselves. Come spring we will reward the willow's willingness by planting these rooted twigs along the small stream that divides the house and garden from the rough meadows and woods beyond. Besides carrying leaves lined in silver fur, this willow has huge long pussies which begin to expand in late January, in early intimation of spring. Since it also boasts a handsome winter silhouette, more will be very welcome.

Not surprisingly, these forced flowers and leaves are short-lived and need frequent replenishing. A day or two ago I went out to restock and found that a huge main branch of an old Santa Rosa plum tree had blown to the ground in the night. Bending near, I saw that the entire tree was so rotten that daylight showed plainly through the trunk. An old climbing rose which had been twining through the plum tree for many years was lying in pieces nearby, shattered by the wind. Sadly, I looked up at the maimed tree-top and saw that one remaining cane bore a fat spray of pink roses, tossing in the winter breeze. Looking down again, I noticed new shoots were already growing strongly from the old rose which I had hastily pruned last summer. What clearer message could any garden give than that?

APPENDIX A

NORTHWESTERN NURSERIES WITH MAIL-ORDER CATALOGS OR LISTS

Only a few regional nurseries are listed here; all are places that I have actually visited and/or ordered from. I included only places that seemed of general interest, or that are mentioned in the text of this book. The Pacific Northwest is full of fine nurseries, with new ones appearing all the time, so lack of mention here does not mean that a nursery isn't wonderful. If I have skipped any that you think ought to be better known, please write to Ann Lovejoy c/o Sasquatch Publishing, 1931 Second Avenue, Seattle, Washington 98101.

BRITISH COLUMBIA

Alpenflora Gardens
17985 40th Avenue
Surrey, B.C. Canada V3S 4N8

Alpines, dwarf, and miniature plants. Good selection, some unusual. Catalog free.

Alpenglow Gardens
13328 King George Highway
Surrey, B.C. Canada V3T 2T6

Another good source of alpines, dwarf and miniature plants, good stuff. Catalog, $1.

Clay's Nursery
3666 224th Street
P.O. Box 3040
Langley, B.C. Canada V3A 4R3

Specialties are rhododendrons, kalmias, azaleas, junipers, cedars. Catalog free—wholesale to trade only. Nursery open to all.

CALIFORNIA

Alpine Valley Gardens
2627 Calistoga Road
Santa Rosa, California 95404

Splendid collection of modern daylilies, good size and quality, reasonable prices. Catalog free.

Barbara's World of Flowers
3774 Vineyard Avenue
Oxnard, California 93030

Fuchsias upon fuchsias, best selection around. Catalog $4, credited to first order.

Bio-Quest International
P.O. Box 5752
Santa Barbara, California 93150

Bulbs and seeds of South African natives. Nerines, homeria, lots more. Catalog $1.

Canyon Creek Nursery
3527 Dry Creek Road
Oroville, California 95965

Exceptional collection of border perennials, many unavailable elsewhere. Catalog $1—excellent quality.

Cordon Bleu Farms
P.O. Box 2033
San Marcos, California 92069

Daylilies galore—great selection. Iris too. Catalog $1.

Las Pilitas Nursery
Las Pilitas Road
Star Route, Box 23X
Santa Margarita, California 93453

California native plants; wide and great selection. Price list free; catalog $4.

Maple Leaf Nursery
423 Greenstone Road
Placerville, California 95667

Bonsai and plants for small gardens. Catalog $1.

Roses of Yesterday & Today
802 Brown's Valley Road
Watsonville, California 95076

A splendid collection of roses, old and new. A must. Catalog $2.

Yerba Buena Nursery
  19500 Skyline Boulevard
  Woodside, California 94062

  California native plants, good selection and quality. Catalog $1.

OREGON

Angelwood Nursery
  12839 McKee School Road
  Woodburn, Oregon 97072

  Ivy by the score, many fine types unavailable elsewhere. Catalog free.

Bateman's Dahlias
  6911 SE Drew Street
  Portland, Oregon 97222

  Good selection. Send SASE for catalog.

The Bovees Nursery
  1737 SW Coronado
  Portland, Oregon 97219

  A Pacific NW heaven of a nursery; shrubs, shade plants, natives, everything.... Catalog $2, credited to first order.

Caprice Farms
  15425 SW Pleasant Hill Road
  Sherwood, Oregon 97140

  Daylilies galore, lots of iris and hostas also, tree peonies, other perennials. Catalog $1, credited to first order.

Chehalem Gardens
  Chehalem Drive
  P.O. Box 693
  Newberg, Oregon 97132

  Iris, Siberian tetraploids, and newer hybrids. Spurias and others of interest. Catalog free.

Forestfarm
  990 Tetherow Road
  Williams, Oregon 97544

  NW natives, many perennials and shrubs. Excellent quality and selection. Catalog $2.

Russell Graham, Purveyor of Plants
  4030 Eagle Crest Road NW
  Salem, Oregon 97304

  Most unusual selection, some wonderful bulbs, great quality. Catalog $2, credited to first order.

Grant Mitsch Daffodils
  P.O. Box 218
  Hubbard, Oregon 97032

  Top American hybridizer offers exceptional bulbs, very different! Catalog $3, credited to first order.

Oregon Bulb Farms
  14071 NE Arndt Road–M.O.
  Aurora, Oregon 97002

  Jan DeGraff hybrid lilies, many newer varieties as well. Catalog $2, credited to first order.

Schreiner's Gardens
  3625 Quinaby Road NE
  Salem, Oregon 97303

  Iris, tall and dwarf. Visit if you can. Wonderful color. Catalog $2, credited to first order.

Siskiyou Rare Plant Nursery
  Dept. 72
  2825 Cummings Road
  Medford, Oregon 97501

  Extensive selection of alpines and dwarf plants; shrubs, trees, perennials. Catalog $2.

WASHINGTON

A & D Peony Nursery
  6808 180th SE
  Snohomish, Washington 98290

  Many modern hybrids, some Saunders seedlings. Fine plants, good prices. Send SASE for catalog.

Aitken's Salmon Creek Garden
  608 NW 119th Street
  Vancouver, Washington 98685

  All sorts of iris, NW natives, hybrids. Send stamp (first-class) for catalog.

B & D Lilies
330 P Street
Port Townsend, Washington 98368

Good selection of lilies, also alstroemeria; helpful staff. Catalog $1, credited to first order.

Bailey's
P.O. Box 654
Edmonds, Washington 98020

Primroses of various unusual sorts. Plants of top quality. Catalog free.

Barfods Nursery
23622 Bothell Way SE
Bothell, Washington 98021

Ferns and ferns allies—wonderful stuff. Call first (206) 483-0205. For mail order, see Fancy Fronds.

Connell's Dahlias
10216 40th Avenue East
Tacoma, Washington 98446

Great selection, display garden. Catalog $1, credited to first order.

Dahlias by Phil Traff
1316 132nd Avenue East
Sumner, Washington 98390

Great selection, nice display garden. Size of tubers and prices both right. Catalog free.

Donna's Lilies of the Valley
1221 Highway 7 North
Tonasket, Washington 98855

Wonderful list of modern daylilies, some iris. Quality and prices tops. Catalog free.

Dunford Farms
P.O. Box 238
Sumner, Washington 98390

Agapanthus and alstroemerias. Excellent quality. Catalog free.

Fancy Fronds
1911 Fourth Avenue W
Seattle, Washington 98119

Many, many ferns; wonderful selection, excellent quality and prices. Catalog $1.

Foliage Gardens
2003 128th Avenue SE
Bellevue, Washington 98005

Ferns for the gardener and the connoisseur— many unusual things. Prices very fair.

Heaths & Heathers
62 Elma–Monte Road
P.O. Box 850
Elma, Washington 98541

Large selection, great plants. Selections to bloom in all seasons. Send long SASE for catalog.

Heronswood Nursery
7530 288th Street NE
Kingston, Washington 98346

Uncommon woody plants, lots from Chile and Japan. List $1.

Lamb Nursery
East 101 Sharp Avenue
Spokane, Washington 99202

Excellent selection of border perennials, shrubs, unusual stuff. Catalog free—quality exceptional.

Pacific Berry Works
963 Thomas Road
P.O. Box 54
Bow, Washington 98232

Specializes in varieties of berries for the Pacific NW. Catalog free.

Pacific Wetland Nursery
7035 Crawford Drive
Kingston, Washington 98346

Natives and perennials for damp spots. Free list for SASE.

Puget Garden Nursery
10322 SW 165th Street
Vashon Island, Washington 98070

Excellent source for unusual plants of all
categories. Catalog $1.

Raintree Nursery
391 Butts Road
Morton, Washington 98356

Trees, shrubs, vines, all with edible fruit. Great
selection for the NW. Catalog free.

Rex Bulb Farms
2568 Washington Street
P.O. Box 774 S
Port Townsend, Washington 98368

Lilies of all sorts. Species and hybrids, good
stuff. Catalog $1, credited to first order.

Sea-Tac Gardens
20020 Des Moines Memorial Drive
Seattle, Washington 98198

Dahlias and fuchsias, display garden, cut flowers,
helpful staff. Send long SASE for price list.

Skyline Nursery
264B Heath Road
Sequim, Washington 98382

List $1.

West Shore Acres
956 Downey Road
Mount Vernon, Washington 98273

Good selection of bulbs, top quality, nice
display garden. Catalog free.

OTHER NURSERIES OF INTEREST

Applesource
Route 1
Chapin, Illinois 62628

Bluestone Perennials
7211 Middle Ridge Road
Madison, Ohio 44057

Wonderful selection, great prices. Rooted
cuttings only. Catalog free—excellent.

Busse Gardens
635 East Seventh Street
Route 2, Box 13
Cokato, Minnesota 55321

Fine perennial collection; lots of daylilies, iris,
and hostas, species and hybrids. Catalog $1,
credited to first order.

Carroll Gardens
444 East Main
P.O. Box 310

Westminster, Maryland 21157
Best collection of perennials in the country.
Catalog $2.

The Daffodil Mart
Route 3, Box 794
Gloucester, Virginia 23061

Family-run daffodil farm, wide selection, many
unusual, good stuff. Catalog $1.

Dutch Gardens
P.O. Box 200
Adelphia, New Jersey 07710

Exceptional stock of bulbs from Holland.
Minimum order of $2. Catalog free.

Gurney's Seed & Nursery Co.
Yankton, South Dakota 57079

Perennials, shrubs, roses, trees. Catalog
free—fun, too.

Hylseeds
P.O. Box 157
2180 AD
Hillegom, Holland

Bulbs galore. Excellent quality at wholesale
prices. List free.

McClure & Zimmerman
1422 West Thorndale
Chicago, Illinois 60660

Bulbs of all sorts, many unusual. Pricey but
quality is good. Catalog free.

Montrose Nursery
P.O. Box 957
Hillsborough, North Carolina 27278

Catalog $2.

Van Bourgondien Brothers
P.O. Box A
245 Farmingdale Road, Route 109
Babylon, New York 11702

Solid selections of bulbs and perennials. Quality is tops, very consistent. Some true bargains. Catalog free.

Wayside Gardens
Hodges, South Carolina 29695

Splendid selections, many rare and unavailable elsewhere. Color. Catalog $1.50, credited to first order.

White Flower Farm
Litchfield, Connecticut 06759

Some choice plants, unavailable elsewhere. Lovely catalog, $5, credited to first order over $25.

Gilbert Wild & Son
Sarcoxie, Missouri 64862

Daylilies in full and accurate color—excellent quality, true bargains. Catalog $2, credited to first order.

APPENDIX B

SEED COMPANIES

Some catalogs cost a bit initially, but once you get on mailing lists, the succeeding catalogs are free.

Abundant Life Seed Foundation
P.O. Box 772
Port Townsend, Washington 98368

NW natives, flowers, herbs, vegetables. Catalog $1.

Butchart Gardens
Box 4010, Station A
Victoria, B.C. Canada V8X 3X4

Flowers; collections from the Gardens. Old-fashioned favorites, herbs. Catalog $1, credited to first order.

Canadian Garden Products
160 117 King Edward
Winnipeg, MB Canada R3H 0Y3

Canadian source for Thompson & Morgan seeds; hundreds of flowers and vegetables. Catalog free.

Chehalis Rare Plant Nursery
2568 Jackson Highway
Chehalis, Washington 98532

Seeds of many small plants, alpines, daylilies, hostas, primroses. Long SASE for catalog.

Chiltern Seeds
Bortree Stile, Ulverston
Cumbria LA12 7PB
England

Stellar list of border plants from seed. Takes Visa. Catalog $2 (American).

The Cook's Garden
P.O. Box 65
Moffitt's Bridge
Londonderry, Vermont 05148

Ornamental vegetables and select greens. Catalog $1.

Gardenimport
P.O. Box 760
Thornhill, Ontario Canada L3T 4A5

Canadian source for Sutton's Seeds. Many flowers, excellent vegetables. Catalog $1, credited to first order.

Good Seed Company
P.O. Box 702
Tonasket, Washington 98855

Interesting collection of unusual and old-fashioned vegetables. Catalog $1.

Gurney's Seed & Nursery Co.
Yankton, South Dakota 57079

Flowers and vegetables, some unusual. Catalog free—a classic.

Ed Hume Seeds
P.O. Box 1450
Kent, Washington 98035

Flowers, vegetables for the NW. Catalog free.

Nichols Garden Nursery
1190 N. Pacific Highway
Albany, Oregon 97321

Many herbs, also vegetables and flowers. Catalog free—a classic.

Park Seed Company
Cokesbury Road
Greenwood, South Carolina 29647-0001

Flowers, herbs, and vegetables, some unusual. Catalog free.

Peace Seeds
1130 Tetherow Road
Williams, Oregon 97544

Herbs and vegetables, many rare. Long SASE for catalog.

Sanctuary Seeds/Folklore Herbs
2388 West Fourth Avenue
Vancouver, B.C. Canada V6K 1P1

Herbs, vegetables, and flowers, some unusual.
Catalog $1.

Shepherd's Garden Seeds
7389 West Zayante Road
Felton, California 95018

Marvelous vegetables, many collections.
European varieties. Catalog $1.

Stokes Seeds, Inc.
Box 548
Buffalo, New York 14240

Best range of annuals and flowers for the cutting garden. Catalog free.

Suttons Seeds Ltd
Hele Road
Torquay, Devon, England TQ2 7QJ

Territorial Seed Company
P.O. Box 27
Lorane, Oregon 97451

Vegetables, herbs, and flowers. A Pacific NW
classic. Catalog free.

Thompson & Morgan
P.O. Box 1308
Jackson, New Jersey 08527

Possibly the largest seedhouse in the world;
flowers, herbs and vegetables, shrubs, trees....
Catalog free.

APPENDIX C

TOOL AND SUPPLY SOURCES

Throughout this book, the importance of improving and maintaining garden soil is stressed repeatedly. Where local outlets for suggested materials are scarce, here are some reputable and efficient suppliers of soil amendments, garden tools, and other supplies, sources for those gardeners who must buy through the mail. Many of these items are very heavy and costly to ship, especially the soil amendments, so it is worth a few trips—or telephone calls —to local feed stores, co-ops, and rural hardware stores to try to locate sources for some of these things closer to home. Certain items, like Bulldog tools, are simply not available except by mail. If you know of good regional sources which are not included below, please write about them to Ann Lovejoy, c/o Sasquatch Books, 1931 Second Avenue, Seattle, Washington 98101.

Ernst Home Centers
Throughout our region.

Sale prices on manure excellent. Many soil amendments in spring.

Green Earth Organics
9422 144th Street E
Puyallup, Washington 98373

Numerous amendments and fertilizers. Some safe pesticides, more. Catalog free.

Kinsman Company
River Road
Point Pleasant, Pennsylvania 18950

A. M. Leonard, Inc.
6665 Spiker Road
Piqua, Ohio 45356

Catalog free.

Walter Nicke Company
P.O. Box 433
Topsfield, Massachusetts 01983

Puget Consumers' Co-op
Ravenna & Kirkland stores
(in Seattle area)

Has bulk soil amendments in 5-, 10-, or 25-lb. bags. Discount for co-op members. Good selection. No mail order.

Raintree Nursery
391 Butts Road
Morton, Washington 98356

Some soil amendments in bulk, good tools, netting, woven mulches, "ecological" pesticides. Catalog free.

Smith & Hawken
25 Corte Madera
Mill Valley, California 94941

For excellent garden tools, there is no finer source than this. The quality and service are exceptional. Catalog free.

Territorial Seed Company
P.O. Box 27
80030 Territorial Road
Lorane, Oregon 97451

Offers row covers, knives and tools, heavy-duty sprinklers, books, more. Catalog free.

APPENDIX D

One of the greater pleasures of gardening is the company of other gardeners. Sooner or later, most of us meet up with like-minded friends, but joining a garden club or plant society can hasten the process and increase the pleasure enormously. Most of these groups meet monthly, and hold plant sales, lectures, slide talks, garden tours, plant-seeking hikes, and similar activities throughout the year. Many have newsletters or magazines as well, and welcome articles from gardeners at every level. You don't have to go to any meetings at all; some people join plant societies just to get in on the seed exchanges. Attending even an occasional meeting can be refreshing, and you are certain to go home with new ideas, and possibly new plants.

For local garden clubs, check the yellow pages of your phone directory. Regional addresses are given below; a letter of inquiry will put you in touch with any local activity in your area.

BRITISH COLUMBIA

Alpine Garden Club of British Columbia
Erika Hobeck
13751 56A Avenue
Surrey, B.C. Canada V3W 1J4

Monthly meetings, plant sales, talks. Has monthly newsletter. Friendly with several NW (U.S.A.) groups. Dues $13/year (Canadian).

Canadian Rose Society
Dianne Lask
686 Pharmacy
Scarborough, Ontario
Canada M1L 3H8

Chapters throughout Canada. Some newsletters, meetings. Dues $15/year (Canadian).

The Canadian Wildflower Society
James A. French
35 Bauer Crescent
Unionville, Ontario
Canada L3R 4H3

Groups forming throughout Canada. Seed exchange, meetings. Dues $15/year, U.S. funds for U.S. dwellers. $15/year Canadian for Canadians.

Vancouver Island Rock and Alpine Garden Society
P.O. Box 6507, Station C
Victoria, B.C. Canada V8P 5M4

Active group. Some co-meetings with U.S. groups. Monthly newsletters, plant sales, trips. Dues $8/year (Canadian).

PACIFIC NW–USA

American Fuchsia Society
Dept. P—County Fair Building
Ninth Avenue & Lincoln Way
San Francisco, California 94122

Very active group in the Pacific NW. Monthly meetings, talks, plant sales. Most local units have newsletters, plus national monthly bulletin. Dues $12.50/year.

American Hemerocallis Society
Elly Launius
1454 Rebel Drive
Jackson, Mississippi 39211

Daylily fans are few but avid in the NW, with frequent round-robin letter flights and annual meetings. Great group. Journal, newsletters. Dues $12.50/year.

American Horticultural Society
P.O. Box 0105
Mount Vernon, Virginia 22121

Bimonthly magazine with newsletters in alternate months. Dues $35/year.

American Iris Society
Jeane Stayer
7414 E 60th Street
Tulsa, Oklahoma 74145

Active NW chapters abound. Special group for NW native iris fans. Meetings, seed exchange. Quarterly bulletin. Dues $9.50/year.

American Primrose Society
Jay G. Lunn
Route 5, Box 93
Hillsboro, Oregon 97124

Local interest runs high, thanks to natural affinity of these plants to NW conditions. Quarterly journal. Dues $10/year.

American Rhododendron Society
Executive Secretary
P.O. Box 1380
Gloucester, Virginia 23061

Again, local conditions make this one a natural. Much local activity. Quarterly journal. Dues $25/year.

American Rock Garden Society
Buffy Parker
15 Fairmead Road
Darien, Connecticut 06820

Splendid source of information, attracts the best gardeners in any area. Meetings, sales, seed exchange, tours, trips, more. Quarterly bulletin excellent. Dues $15/year.

American Rose Society
Harold Goldstein
P.O. Box 30,000
Shreveport, Louisiana 71130

Active NW chapters. Seattle group hosted National Rose Show in 1986. Monthly magazine, meetings. Dues $18/year.

Bellevue Botanical Garden Society
P.O. Box 7081
Bellevue, Washington 98008

Recently formed support group for the development of a botanical garden near downtown Bellevue. A great group, and a rare chance to participate in such a major project. Monthly newsletters, meetings, talks. Dues $10/year.

Garden Club of America
598 Madison Avenue
New York, NY 10022

Hardy Plant Society
Connie Hanni
33530 SE Bluff Road
Boring, Oregon 97009

First U.S. chapter was in Washington, the second in Oregon. Regional interest and activity high. Annual study weekends exceptional. Same seed exchange and biannual journal as English HPS. Dues $12/year.

Heritage Rose Group
Miriam Wilkins
925 Galvin Drive
El Cerrito, California 94530

Local interest considerable. Meetings, plant sales. Quarterly newsletter. Dues $5/year.

Native Plant Society of Oregon
1920 Engel Avenue NW
Salem, Oregon 97304

Just like it sounds. Dues $10/year.

Northwest Horticultural Society
Center for Urban Horticulture
University of Washington
Seattle, Washington 98195

An estimable lecture series, unmatched in the region, makes this group stand out. Meetings, plant sales, and quarterly magazine. Dues $20/year.

Pacific Northwest Lily Society
19766 S Impala Lane
Oregon City, Oregon 97045

Another natural for our region. Seed exchange, bulb sales. Dues $5/year.

Perennial Seed Exchange
Michael Pilarski
P.O. Box 2466
Chelan, Washington 98816

All gardeners welcome to participate. Many fine plants otherwise hard to obtain may be easily raised from seed. Seed lists $3.

Puget Sound Dahlia Association
Roger Walker
544 129th Avenue SE
Bellevue, Washington 98005

Strong local group, new members welcome.
Annual Dahlia Show in Seattle a classic.
Meetings, shows, monthly newsletter, annual
bulletin. Dues $10/year.

Rhododendron Species Foundation
P.O. Box 3798
Federal Way, Washington 98063

Excellent display garden (Federal Way). Talks,
walks (for spring flowers and fall foliage), slide
shows, seed exchange. Quarterly newsletters,
annual bulletin. Dues $30/year.

Tilth Association
4649 Sunnyside N
Seattle, Washington 98103

City group interested in composting, soil building, urban gardening, and more. Monthly
newsletter. Dues $15/year.

Washington Native Plant Society
Department of Botany
University of Washington
Seattle, Washington 98195

Field trips and lectures are a draw for this local
group. Great speakers. Quarterly magazine.
Dues $12/year.

Washington Park Arboretum
Arboretum Foundation
University of Washington XD-10
Seattle, Washington 98195

A group dedicated to the support and development of the Washington Park Arboretum. Has
fine quarterly bulletin, monthly newsletter,
many lectures, sales and activities. Publishes
Cuttings Throughout the Year, $3 at Visitors
Center, $4 mail order. Dues $15/year.

APPENDIX E

MAGAZINES, BOOKS, AND GARDEN WRITERS

Public libraries in the Pacific Northwest tend to have very good collections of older gardening books. This reflects the historically strong local interest that, sadly, waned after the war. As gardening regains popularity, public collections are becoming stronger, with recent works better represented. Libraries will often track down requested books through the inter-library loan system. Some bookstores will seek books for you as well, both currently listed and out-of-print. With any expensive books (and garden books can be very expensive indeed without being correspondingly useful), it is a good idea to borrow a copy from the library before making a major investment. Exploring the garden books section (appropriately placed within the arts) is a fine way to discover unfamiliar garden writers. As you develop favorites, it becomes a pleasant game to track down ALL their books. British Columbia has been a hot-bed of gardeners for many years, and used bookstores in that area are particularly rich in garden treasures. Plant society book sales nearly always yield gold.

The GARDEN BOOK CLUB is an excellent source of books that may be hard to find elsewhere. The selections are varied and reasonably priced, often listing at substantial discounts. Some very attractive bonuses are offered to new members; currently either a set of four Gertrude Jekyll books or a copy of HORTUS THIRD for $19.95 (HORTUS in a bookstore will run you $125). The initial obligation is to buy three more books during the first year; this is not a chore. Each fourth book bought thereafter brings a choice of free bonus books as well. Many imported books and gardening classics are offered.

MAGAZINES

Harrowsmith
Ferry Road
Charlotte, Vermont 05445
Bimonthly issues
$24/year

Celebrates country life, regular garden articles (this is the U.S. version of the well-known Canadian magazine of the same name).

Horticulture, The Magazine of American Gardening
P.O. Box 53879
Boulder, Colorado 80321-1455
Monthly issues
$24/year, $42/2 years, $56/3 years

The best general gardening magazine around.

Pacific Horticulture
P.O. Box 22609
San Francisco, California 94122
Quarterly issues
$15/year

Joint publication of four horticultural or arboretum societies. Has a California bias, yet most articles are of value for the entire maritime Northwest. This magazine has improved markedly over the past years; now is of consistently excellent quality.

Rodale's Organic Gardening
33 E. Minor Street
Emmaus, Pennsylvania 18098
Monthly issues
$25/year

Originally an organic farming journal; gardening has taken over. Recent years have seen many changes, and in its present form, OG will be of interest to many gardeners who do not necessarily embrace the entire organic doctrine. This newest version has lightened up considerably; there are practical garden tips, a new section on perennials, and a monthly chore calendar for each climate zone. If you were turned off in the past, take another look.

Sunset Magazine
Lane Publishing Co.
P.O. Box 3051
Menlo Park, California 94025
Monthly issues
$16/year for Western states, $20/year for other states

Needs no introduction; has regular garden section, monthly activity calendar.

BOOKS AND WRITERS

A few books stand out as indispensable; Sunset's NEW WESTERN GARDEN BOOK, for instance, belongs on every Northwestern gardener's shelf. The carefully charted zone maps make this book unique and exceptionally useful for experimental gardeners as well as beginners. For the most part, however, maritime gardeners will find that English garden books better serve their needs than those written for the eastern U.S.A. Since our climates are so similar, English cultural and hardiness tips are far more valuable than any from Massachusetts or Ohio.

It used to be a common complaint that English books were frustratingly full of wonderful plants unavailable locally. Thanks to the efforts of keen regional gardeners and far-sighted nurseries, this is no longer the case. Perhaps the bulk of English imports are still found chiefly in mail-order catalogs, but we are fortunate in having innumerable and reputable small nurseries throughout the Northwest. The majority sell plants of top quality, ship with care, and stand behind their offerings. Barbara Barton's splendid compendium, GARDENING BY MAIL, will give you hundreds of addresses for regional nurseries.

It is dull to read long lists of any kind, so the following will be a short sampler of recommended books and writers. Further pursuit, and the joys of discovery, are left up to you.

The Garden Book Club
250 West 57th Street
New York, New York 10107

An excellent source for garden books; good selections, great prices.

Gardening by Mail
Barbara J. Barton
Houghton Mifflin

A remarkable, fascinating reference book for everything and anything a gardener might want. Highly recommended.

Sunset New Western Garden Book
Lane Publishing Co.

Arguably the single most important book for Northwest gardeners.

Right Plant, Right Place
Nicola Ferguson
Summit Books

One of the most useful books for the home library. Plants are listed and described according to the conditions they tolerate: urban pollution, boggy ground, etc.; to appearance: variegated leaves, silver or grey, winter beauty; or to the use they serve: ground cover, shrub, etc. A must.

Complete Shade Gardener
George Schenk
Houghton Mifflin Co.

Mr. Schenk is an experienced Northwest gardener who presents a lot of material in a most readable form. A useful and delightful book.

Color in Your Garden
Penelope Hobhouse
Little, Brown and Co., Inc.

One of the few oversized, beautiful coffee-table garden books worth its price—or its weight in gold. An excellent resource.

Making a Cottage Garden
Faith & Geoff Whiten
Salem House

A practical handbook. Strong on design, rather basic as to plants, but an excellent and accurate guide and a lovely book.

Hillier's Colour Dictionary of Trees and Shrubs
H.G. Hillier
David & Charles
The Complete Handbook of Garden Plants
Michael Wright
Facts on File
The Color Dictionary of Flowers and Plants for Home and Garden
Roy Hay & Patrick Synge
Crown Publishers, Inc.

Pretty picture books abound, but few are of much use. These three heavily illustrated plant dictionaries are all very useful.

Principles of Gardening
  Hugh Johnson
  Simon & Schuster

  Practical and fascinating overview, recommended.

Dictionary of Plant Names
  Allen J. Coombes
  Timber Press

  Another dictionary that is accurate and thorough, yet small enough to be in constant use.

Any discussion of garden writers must include Vita Sackville-West, who for many years wrote a weekly newspaper column beloved throughout England. Some of her columns are reprinted in her GARDEN BOOK, still widely available. The late Margery Fish wrote a number of fascinating gardening books; she grew thousands of plants, and passes on invaluable experience to her readers in a pleasantly informal style. At least five of these have been recently reprinted; all are well worth reading and re-reading. Christopher Lloyd is a contemporary writer with enormous experience and a playful, relaxed style; all of his many books are both useful and delightful. Graham Stuart Thomas is a much-respected horticulturist and writer of great depth; try his THREE GARDENS for a start.

On this side of the Atlantic, we should all be thankful to several university presses for reprinting the wonderful garden books by Elizabeth Lawrence. Although some of her titles might suggest that the books are strictly for Southern gardeners, Mrs. Lawrence had numerous correspondents throughout the Pacific Northwest. She refers often to the similarity of climate in the Southeast and the Northwest, and notes the many plants that do well in either area. Both Henry Mitchell and Allen Lacy have books of gardening essays in print, and both are frequent contributors to national magazines.

Nearly all of the above writers focus on ornamental plants. Those interested in raising food as well will enjoy THE COMPLETE BOOK OF EDIBLE LANDSCAPING by Rosalind Creasy (Sierra Club), as well as Ms. Creasy's other books. Steve Solomon's GROWING VEGETABLES WEST OF THE CASCADES (Sasquatch Books) is unmatched for solid cultural advice for the maritime Northwest.

Pacific Northwest native plants are many and varied, and there are quite a few guides to their identification. Some of the very nicest come from the British Columbia Provincial Museum, and the booklets are well represented at bookstores and museum shops all over the province. The series is underwritten by the province's Department of Recreation and Conservation, and numbers in the dozens. All are amply and clearly illustrated, and all are intelligently presented.

INDEX

About the Author

Ann Lovejoy is a contributing editor for *Horticulture* magazine and gardening columnist at the *Seattle Weekly*. Her gardening pieces also appear in *House & Garden*, *Harrowsmith*, various plant society bulletins, and other national publications. She is a recipient of a Garden Writers Association award for excellence and the Washington State Governor's Writers Award for *The Year in Bloom*. Ann lives with her family on Bainbridge Island, Washington.

Lawn fert.   bone meal + kelp meal
              1 cup + 1 T   or soy meal
              or cotton seed meal.

A.M. Leonard.   air & water lawn aerator